KAHLIL GIBRAN:

WINGS OF THOUGHT

The People's Philosopher

Young Kahlil Gibran in his studio in 1898 in Beirut.

KAHLIL GIBRAN:
WINGS OF THOUGHT

by JOSEPH P. GHOUGASSIAN, Ph.D.

Assistant Professor in
Comparative and Arabic Philosophy
University of San Diego

THE CITADEL PRESS · SECAUCUS, NEW JERSEY

First paperbound printing, 1973
Copyright © 1973 by Philosophical Library, Inc.
All rights reserved
Published by Citadel Press
A division of Lyle Stuart Inc.
120 Enterprise Avenue, Secaucus, N.J. 07094
In Canada: George J. McLeod Limited
73 Bathurst St., Toronto 2B, Ontario
Manufactured in the United States of America
ISBN 0-8065-0387-4

DEDICATED TO my wife Zena and my daughter Yasmine.

Your . . . real work is beyond what in this generation or perhaps for many generations even you can realize. Only the future can show its scope. And in that day when man is calling the twentieth century an embryonic stage of himself, he will call you *like* himself. But you when that day comes will still be creating tomorrows. . . . To you now, what you write and paint expresses mere fragments of your vision. But in time the whole vision will appear in it. For man will learn to see and hear and read. And your *work* is not only books and pictures. They are but bits of it. Your work is you, not less than you, not parts of you. . . .
Your silence will be read with your writings some day, your darkness will be part of the LIGHT.

(Miss M. Haskell's prophecy of Gibran's fame. Private Letter, Sunday, November 16, 1913).

CONTENTS

CHAPTER SEVEN

Gibran's Philosophy of Religion

CHAPTER EIGHT

Evaluation of Gibranism

PREFACE

We find in many countries philosophy and the philosophers divorced from the local culture, customs, ethics and the simple *Weltanschauung* of the inhabitants. Yet, we also find in many civilizations a complete marriage between the intellectuals and the traditions of the country. One thinks, in this way, for instance, of Indian philosophy, or Mexican philosophy, or African philosophy. Gibran's trend of thoughts, also, has undergone the process of *"acculturation,"* meaning that his philosophy has assimilated the culture and beliefs of both the Western and Eastern hemispheres.

The distinction I am getting at, differentiates between a people's philosopher and a philosopher's philosophy. The latter is academic, incomprehensible to the average citizen of the world, and quite abstract. The former is simple, unsystematic, yet deep in meanings which can be grasped by the reader. It is my firm conviction that Gibran is a people's philosopher as my present book will confirm till the last page.

Now it was not easy for me to expound Gibran's philosophy because he never wrote academically or logically; I had to resort to the science of *hermeneutics* in order to dig up his ideas which are scattered unsystematically in his books, and put them together following a logic that he himself expressed, but which is encumbered with emotions. Moreover, I have relied on the method of *comparative* philosophy, with the view of bringing to light the significance of Gibranism as it stands in the light of the history of philosophy. My discovery reveals that Gibran is an *existentialist of the right wing,* though he was influenced by other mainstreams of thoughts.

Also to render Gibran relevant, I have endeavored to inform the reader about the historical events that surrounded the life and pen-ink of our author, notwithstanding the fact that I have attempted to interrelate his art, literature and philosophy with his biography.

Finally, I am greatly indebted to my wife and daughter for having had the patience to tolerate the strain of the long hours involved in the preparation which kept me away from their presence. A last expression of thanks goes to Mrs. Renate Streiter Smith for her generous help in typing the manuscript.

JOSEPH PETER GHOUGASSIAN
Assistant Professor in
Comparative and Arabic Philosophy.

University of San Diego
San Diego, California
December 21, 1972

TABLE OF ABBREVIATIONS OF TITLES

P.   *The Prophet.*
PR.   *The Procession.*
T.L.   *Tears and Laughter.*
Th.M.   *Thoughts and Meditations.*
T.S.   *Tear and Smile.*
T.D.   *Twenty Drawings.*
M.S.   *Mirrors of the Soul.*
MM.   *The Madman.*
S.P.   *A Self Portrait.*
S.S.   *Spiritual Sayings.*
S.F.   *Sand and Foam.*
S.H.   *Secrets of the Heart.*
B.W.   *The Broken Wings.*
W.G.   *The Wisdom of Gibran.*
V.M.   *The Voice of the Master.*
N.V.   *Nymphs of the Valleys.*
E.G.   *The Earth Gods.*
FR.   *Forerunner.*
G.P.   *Garden of the Prophet.*
W.   *The Wanderer.*
J.S.M.   *Jesus the Son of Man.*
P.P.   *Prose Poem.*
S.R.   *Spirits Rebellious.*
B.P.   *Beloved Prophet. The Love Letters of Kahlil Gibran and Mary Haskell. And Her Private Journal.*

CHAPTER ONE

SHORT HISTORY OF LEBANON

HUMAN "EXISTENCE" is an unending "drama" so long as the individual's heart beats. It unfolds in the historical context of the person. Yet, the person's historicity is to a large extent determined, as would say Karl Marx, by the historical processes conditioned by the laws of social development. In each period these laws change, due to the fact that the social relations between individuals and countries through the intermediary of productivity constantly mutate. Human existence reflects the impact of history; and in its behaviors as well as thinking it is heavily impregnated by the Zeitgeist of the history it shares.

It is my firm belief that it is utterly impossible to understand Kahlil Gibran's philosophy and see his relevance, for instance in the fields of religion, law, and marriage, unless it be born in mind that he lived intensely the entanglements of the historical events, that have set him on his way to become the philosopher he is. Therefore, a brief survey of the history of Lebanon will shed some light on the themes that Gibran tackled and explain the "whys" of his thoughts.

History of Lebanon under the Ottoman Conquest

All historians remind us that Lebanon was originally Phoenicia, and had Tammuz and Ishtar for a religious cult. The Tammuz myth corresponds to the Greeks' Adonis and is identified with the Egyptians' god Osiris. According to the Phoenician legendry, one day while Tammuz was hunting the wild boar, he was attacked by the beast and fell dead in the river of Afqah, today named Nahr Ibrahim. Following his death, life on earth began decrepiting. Then Ishtar "penetrated into the nether world" and revived him.[1] This commemorated the marriage between Tammuz and Ishtar, the goddess of love and fertility. Till the present days, poets, philosophers and painters of Lebanon like to refer to their mythological heritage. Gibran too made of Ishtar and Tammuz his muses of inspiration.

Lebanon, which means "white" in ancient Semitic language because of the eternal flakes of snow on the peaks of its mountains, has been invaded by more than ten civilizations of the world, from the Assyrian to Ottoman and Westerners, all of which brought along their culture. This explains why Lebanese immigrants feel almost at home in any foreign country and have no psychological stress in finding normal adjustments in their new environments. At any rate, everytime that a new era of dominion took place, new geographical frontiers were established. Amazingly, however, Lebanon was always annexed to Syria. Either under the Assyro-Babylonian influence or the Ottoman Empire. It is only under the French Mandate after the first world war, beginning on September 1, 1920, with General Gouraud, that present day Lebanon with its geographical boundaries was proclaimed "independent."[2] And on May 23, 1926, The Greater Lebanon was made a republic. However, not until November 26, 1941, was Lebanon declared completely autonomous from the mandate and free to decide for its own course of destiny. Gibran (d. 1931) did not live to see his beloved country become sovereign master of its actions. Nevertheless, what he lived to witness was the hope of such full realization.

From 1516 until 1918 Lebanon remained under Ottoman rule, and became part of an Empire that stretched from Hungary to the Arabian Peninsula and up to North Africa. The illustrious conqueror of these lands was Sulayman I (1520-1566) who became known to his subjects in as much across the European continents as Sulayman the Magnificent. In the words of the famous Arabian historian, Philip K. Hitti,

> No such state was constructed by Moslems in modern history. Nor did any other Moslem state prove to be more enduring. To his people Sulayman was known as Al-Qanuni (the lawgiver). . . . To outsiders he was known as the Magnificent, and magnificent indeed he was, with a court exercising patronage over art, literature, public works and inspiring awe in European hearts.[3]

Because of lack of space in this book we are not permitted to delve into the detailed history of Gibran's homeland. Still, to quench our intellectual curiosity, I will briefly mention a few historical data under the Ottoman Empire, since this was the main foreign oppression Gibran lived under.

When the Sultan Selim I defeated in 1516 the Mamluks and established a Turkish dynasty, Lebanon was then mostly inhabited by peasants and farmers. In the northern part, Kisrawan, the Maronite Christians were predominant while in the southern districts of Shuf, the Druze constituted the majority. The Ottoman conquest did not affect deeply the political structure, the language and the way of life of the people of Lebanon. In practice customary law was supreme, and social power was in the hands of the feudal lords, on whom the Ottoman governors, like their predecessors the Mamluks, mainly relied for the security of local order and the collection of taxes.

Such being the flexibility of Ottoman politics, it was possible for the feudal dynasties of the country to pursue their factions and virtually one to vanquish the other. Thus, the greatest figure at that time was the Druze Amir Fakhr al-Din II, the head of the Ma'anids dynasty of the Shuf, who governed Lebanon throughout the sixteenth and seventeenth centuries. During his reign (1586-1635), he extended the geographical boundaries far beyond Lebanon, sometimes reaching up to the portico of Damascus and down to the Pilgrimage route that leads to the Hijaz. He was open minded toward foreign religious creeds and on several occasions encouraged European missionaries to build Christian churches. In matters of internal affairs, he cared for the prosperity, the warfare and the welfare of his country. With the aid of European architects and advisors he erected castles, developed agriculture and traded with Europe.

Captured in 1635 after a defeat by the governor of Damascus, Kuchuk Ahmad Pasha, he was sent prisoner to Istanbul where he was sentenced to death for wanting to overthrow the Ottoman Sultan. With his death followed the decline of the Ma'anids, who were succeeded in 1697 by the Chihab hegemony. This new Amirate ruled throughout the 18th century; flocks of mountaineers of the Maronite Kisrawan then migrated to the southern Shuf and mingled with the local Druzes, working unanimously for the betterment of the unified Lebanon. Of course, life was not so peaceful; from time to time there were misunderstandings between families and factions of the two traditional descendants of the Ancient Arabians of Qays and Yaman. The former were settlers of North Arabia, the latter of South Arabia. However, when Haydar Chihab won victory against Mahmud Pasha, head of the Yaman faction, many of the Yamani Druzes emigrated from the metropolis of Lebanon to the hilly district of Mountain Hawran in Syria now called *Jabal-al Druz*. For conclusion to this period the historian Hourani writes,

> In the remainder of Syria no less than in Lebanon the eighteenth century was marked by conflict and unrest. Finally a great part of the country fell into the hands of Bosnian Jazzar, Pasha of Acre, who ruled it ruthlessly and cruelly from 1775 until 1804.

Generally speaking, the history of Lebanon during the Ottoman Turks was principally the story of the Maronites and

16

the Druzes. Both of these religions have shaped the political fate of Lebanon. I may even say, religion or "confessionalism" was the whole politics in this part of the world. Nowadays also the political institution of Lebanon is still deeply determined by the partitions of the various religious confessions.

The Maronites are followers of the hermit St. Maron (d. 410), an ascetic monk who lived on a mountain in the region of Apamea, in Syria secunda. Being persecuted by the caliphates of Damascus and Baghdad, the Maronites escaped the Northern Syria and began some time during the 8th century to seek refuge from the harassments by the Melchites, Monophysites and Muslims in the impenetrable mountains of Lebanon.[5] The Maronite Church, to which Gibran belonged, still uses Syriac language in the liturgy and adheres to Catholicism. Their first temple erected in the mountains of Lebanon was established around 749. Ever since their settlement in Lebanon the faithful organized a feudal system of government in the northern parts under the combined leadership of clergy and nobility, delegating the patriarch as their feudal in religious affairs and civil matters. At the time of the Ottomans the clergy feudalism exerted a fearful and ferocious influence over the poor peasants. Often, the clergy would practice "simony" and play the role of a corrupt politics. Most of Gibran's criticisms aimed at religion stem from and are directed against the feudalism of the Maronite institution.

As for the Druze religion, it entered southern Lebanon in about 1020. Such creed owes its name to Muhammad ibn-Ismail Al-Darazi (tailor in Turkish). It began in Egypt when a missionary of the Egyptian Fatimid, Al-Hakim (996-1021), while following the Ismaili doctrine of the Imam as the supreme authority and protector of Islam, proclaimed himself the incarnation of the Deity, in the same manner that Jesus Christ was for the Christians.[6] The peculiarities of the Druze religion is to be utterly secret. Their holy book is called Al-Hikma (wisdom), and is quite different from the

17

Koran. The Syrian mountain Hawran, *Jabal Al-Druz,* bears their name because of the influx of refugee that took place at the end of the eighteenth century as a result of the victory of the Druze Qaysites, most of whom were converted to Christianity, over the Druze Yamanites.

In the nineteenth century, the Druze-Maronite relation caused two major events in Lebanon that proved to be detrimental to the security of the nation. The first important date prolongates from 1830 to 1860. In 1830, Syria and Lebanon fell under the occupation of the Egyptian armies of Ibrahim Pasha, the son of Muhammad Ali. The Egyptians were helped by Bechir Chehab II, Emir of Mount Lebanon (1789-1840), who wanted to drive outside of his territories the jurisdiction of the Sublime Porte, i.e. Turkish dominion. He consented to the invasion of Lebanon provided he was given help by the Egyptians to strengthen his power meantime. After the conquest, Bechir II was offered by Ibrahim Pasha to rule over the entire Syria, but he declined the offer in order to care for the Lebanese alone.

The most interesting happening during the occupation is that the Maronite peasants who had travelled from the northern to southern districts of Lebanon, thus outnumbering the Druzes in their own regions, were all in favor of Ibrahim Pasha's invasion. Many times they joined the Egyptian armies to fight back the Turkish Sultan, despite the fact that the Druzes preferred the Turks. However, around 1840 the Maronites joined forces with the Druzes to expel the oppression of the Egyptians that was becoming burdensome, even to them.

Following the downfall of Ibrahim Pasha's reign, Lebanon came to be divided into two governorates. The northern mountainous areas were put under the supervision of a Maronite *qaim maqam,* or governor; while the southern was governed by a Druze *qaim maqam.* And both of them were controlled by the direct representative of the Ottoman Sultan, who presided in Beirut and Sidon. The politics of the Sublime Porte during the following fourtieth and fiftieth was the application of the old military principle of *divide et impera,* the

18

divide and rule policy; thus the Porte would irritate the two classes against each other so that he remained powerful over the weakened governors. Moreover, Turkish authorities never really intervened whenever internal upheaval and civil wars broke out between Maronites and Druzes. For instance, in 1858 the Christian farmers of Kisrawan revolted against their feudal lord, the Khazim family. The Khazim family was a system of primogeniture; they owned the lands of Kisrawan, made the peasants pay exorbitant taxes, and refused to the peasants the right to elect their own *wakils,* or representatives, as it was the case in southern districts. In their insurrection against the Khazim, the peasants received moral encouragement from the Maronite clergy, and on many occasions asked assistance from the Druzes of the south.

At first, the south had decided to lend support to the beleaguered Christians. Yet, at the advice of Kourshid Pasha, the Turkish governor of Beirut, they retracted their forces and thought to protect themselves from possible peasants' revolt on their own lands. Kourshid Pasha's prediction was accurate. For around 1860, the Maronite peasants of the south, inspired by their brethren of the north, arose against their Druze overlords. Immediately, news spread that the intention of the Maronites of the south was not only meant to eliminate the feudal Druzes but also was directed against the Druze as a people. The lady historian Leila Meo writes about this incident:

> This class struggle soon turned into a religious war when the rank and file of the Druze, seeing the uprising as a direct threat to the continued existence of their own people, came to the assistance of their feudal chiefs. The Druze was well organized. The Maronites, although more numerous, lacked both organization and adequate arms. And so a general massacre of Maronite and other Christian villages ensued, while the local Turkish authorities made no immediate attempt to put an end to the bloodshed.[7]

19

Europe was not happy with the 1860's massacre, although I have to admit she was not so innocent in the whole affair. Ever since the Crusaders landed in the Levant, and due especially to the existence of the Maronite Catholics and other Eastern Christian rites, five European countries have incessantly muddled in the Levant politics sometimes wisely, sometimes unwisely. France called itself the *protégé* of the Maronites; Russia made itself a duty to look over the interests of the Greek Orthodox; England took sides with the Druzes of Lebanon; Austria-Hungary played the mitigated role of the Catholic sects of the Eastern churches; and Prussia more for political jealousy than other reasons, interfered in the politics of the Sublime Porte.

The immediate historical consequence following the 1860 event was the establishment on June 9, 1861, of the *Mutasarrifyya* of Mount Lebanon. This happened with the intervention of the Concert of the five European powers and the Sublime Porte. The pact concluded between these six countries, stated clearly that *Mutasarrifyya* signifies that the two governorates would unify into a single governorate, presided by a Christian non-Lebanese Governor General, whose duty would be to report to the Sultan in Constantinople and not any more to the Turkish Pasha of Sidon as it was before. Furthermore, the Governor General was to be elected by the Porte and confirmed by the Concert of Europe.

The first Governor General to be appointed over the new autonomous Lebanese province, was Daoud Pasha, "an Armenian by birth, Roman Catholic by persuasion, director of the telegraph at Constantinople and author of a French work on Anglo-Saxon laws."[8] After him seven other Mutasarrifs followed until the outbreak of the first world War. From 1861-1914, Lebanon had calm political conditions as well as prospered economically and culturally particularly with the introduction of the Jesuit College (1875) and the presently called American University of Beirut (1866). Also, this is the period of dense immigration of Lebanese youths to the new continent of North and South America.

All of the Governor Generals ruled over a Lebanon which was geographically much smaller in superficies than the one of the Ma'anids and Chihabites Emirates. For instance, Beirut, Tripoli, Sidon, the Biqa valleys, and many more provinces were not annexed to the Mount Lebanon, but were parts of the Ottoman.

Such was the geography and history of Lebanon at the time Kahlil Gibran was born in 1883. His native village Bsherri was then located in the *Mutasarrifyya*. In over-all the Ottoman rule in Lebanon was in many respects corrupted; the rich enjoyed privileges either from the clergy or the feudal government while the poor were exploited.

FOOTNOTES

[1] Hitti, P.K., *Lebanon in History*, New York: Macmillan Co., Ltd., 1957, p. 130. According to some texts of mythology, the marriage of Tammuz (or Dumuzi) was rather with Inanna, the fertility of nature. Also, Tammuz (or Dumuzi) was a shepherd-god appointed by Enki who in his turn was asked by Anu and Enlil to organize the economic life of Mesopotamia, by instituting different social functions in the different parts of the country. Now, the yearly marriage of the goddess Inanna to the god Tammuz (or Dumuzi) commemorates the revival of "the creative powers of spring." (H. and H.A. Frankfort, and J. Wilson, and Th. Jacobsen, *Before Philosophy: Adventure of Ancient Man*, Baltimore, Maryland: Penguin Books, 1971, p. 175; pp. 214 - 215).

[2] Meo, Leila, M.T., *Lebanon: Improbable Nation. A Study in Political Development*, Indiana University Press, 1965, pp. 40 - 64.

[3] Hitti, P.K., *op. cit.* p. 364.

[4] Hourani, A.H., *Syria and Lebanon*, London: Oxford University Press, 1946, p. 25. *See also* P.M. Holt, *Egypt and the Fertile Crescent 1516-1922*, Cornell University Press, 1966, pp. 112-123.

[5] Hitti, P.K., *op. cit.*, pp. 247-252.

[6] *ibidem*, pp. 257-265.

[7] Meo, Leila, M.T., *op. cit.*, p. 30.

[8] Hitti, P.K., *op. cit.*, 443.

Chapter Two

LIFE OF KAHLIL GIBRAN

R ARE ARE the writers who receive world recognition during their life. The factors causing the oblivion of a literator while still existing are many; the most important ones are: the life span, the economic situation, the geographical location, the educational and political activities' backgrounds of the family of the writer as well as the friends of the writer.

Did Gibran enjoy an international reputation while among men? Of course, he did not personally witness the translation in twenty languages of his masterpiece *The Prophet,* but still he did reach the Arabic readers and some American literati.[1] His fame really grew after his death, especially with the blow of his posthumous works.[2]

Gibran came from a modest socio-economic class and his presence on earth was quite brief, forty-eight years only. He was born on January 6, 1883 in the small village of Bsherri. Bsherri is geographically located in the Northern part of Lebanon, and not far from the famous Cedar forests of Biblical times, at an altitude of over 5,000 feet; it is embedded in the blue sky and pure air with the far sight of the Mediterranean Sea. The town has not much changed since the birth of Gibran, except that the population has grown in number and it has became an international spot of tourism and pilgrimage. Presently, Bsherri counts 4,000 people; it is situated as always among beatiful vineyards, apple and mulberry orchards, waterfalls and deep gorges of the Kadisha valley so much spoken of by our author. In the middle of the village is the tomb of

Gibran buried in the Chapel of the Monastery of Mar-Sarkis,[3] and a little museum dedicated to him on the third floor of Mr. Gibran Tok's building. The museum contains some of Gibran's water colors and canvases as well as several belongings of the poet.

The Gibrans belonged to the Maronite Catholic Church.[4] The father, Khalil ben Gibran, was a shepherd with no ambition to alter his peasant's fate. All he cared for was playing *Taoula* (trick-trak), smoking the *Narjjile* (water pipe), visiting friends for chit-chats, drinking occasionally a sip of native *Arrak* and strolling in the vast field of Mount Lebanon. The father had hardly any psychological impact on his son Gibran. Yet, mother Kamila played an important role in the intellectual maturation of her son. She was the last child of a Maronite priest, Estephanos Rahmi and was born when her mother attained the age of fifty-six. At the time Kamila met Gibran's father, she was the widow of Hanna Abdel Salam with whom she had emigrated to Brazil and from whom she had a boy, Peter.

The romance between Kamila and Khalil ben Gibran occured after a sudden encounter when one day he heard her singing in her father's garden. "He did not rest until he had met her, and was immediately impressed with her beauty and charm. And there was no peace for him or anyone else until he had won her hand."[5]

Kamila conceived three children from her marriage with Khalil ben Gibran. Besides our author who was named after his father, she bore two younger daughters, Mariana and Sultana.

Gibran received his first education at home. His mother, a polyglot, (she spoke Arabic, French and English), and endowed with artistic talents for music, was his first tutor. We are told that she acquainted her son with the famous Arabian old tales of Haroun-al-Rashid, *The Arabian Nights* and the Hunting Songs of Abu N'Was.[6] She was also the key person who prompted him to develop his artistic sense for painting, not that she taught him to handle brushes and mix the colors, but in that she knew the rules of the game of the psychology of Behaviorism. That is, the environment in which a child comes in contact with, tends to mold somehow deterministically the capacities of the child's future personality. The situational event that caused Gibran to develop an interest for writing and drawing and to declare that "every person is potentially an artist. A child may be taught to draw a bird as easily as to write the word"[7]—goes back when at six years old he was offered a volume of Leonardo reproductions by his mother. His biographer, Barbara Young, writes:

> After turning the pages for a few moments, he burst into wild weeping and ran from the room to be alone. His passion for Leonardo possessed him from that hour, so much so indeed, that when his father rebuked him for some childish misdemeanour the boy flew into a rage and shouted, 'What have you to do with me? I am an Italian!'[8]

In 1894, Peter, the half-brother, then 18, wanting to alleviate the financial burden of his step-father and to break through the apathetic poverty of the family, decided to follow the path of many of his country friends. It came to his mind to sail to America, land of opportunity, adventure and the dollar. First the mother objected but later hearing the good news that several youth villagers had prospered in the Promised Land beyond their fathers' dreams, Kamila consented to the project of Peter with the condition that the family accompany Peter to the New World. The father refused to travel on the grounds that somebody had to take care of the small property they owned.

In the same year, Kamila, Gibran, Mariana and Sultana under the leadership of Peter, set foot in the United States and went directly to Boston where other natives of Bsherri along with other Syrians had comprised a colony in Chinatown.

While the mother, Peter and the two sisters worked to bring

25

money home, Gibran was forced benevolently to go to school to get the education his parents were not granted. During the two years of learning he spent in the public school of the district, Gibran recorded the highest scores from among his U.S. classmates. His teachers saw in him the precocity of his genius. Also, it was at their suggestion that he abbreviated his initial name Gibran K*h*alil Gibran into Kahlil Gibran by rotating the letter *"h"* of his first name.[9]

After two successful years of intense studies in American curriculum, Gibran asked permission from Peter and Kamila to return to Lebanon in order to cultivate his native language and become acquainted with Arabian erudition. His wish was met and from 1896-1901 he studied a great deal of subjects at the eminent *Madrasat Al-Hikmat* (School of Wisdom), today located in Ashrafiet, Beirut. Among the courses he enrolled in were international law, medicine, music and the history of religion. Also, during the period of 1898 he edited the literary and philosophical magazine *Al Hakikat* (The Truth). Finally, in 1900, motivated by admiration for the great Arabian thinkers he had studied in classes, he undertook to make drawings of these personages though no portraits of them existed. He made sketches of the early Islamic poets Al Farid, Abu N'Was, and Al Mutanabbi; of the philosophers Ibn Sina and Ibn Khaldun; and of Khansa, the great Arabic woman poet.[10] But most particularly Gibran had one love experience which marked his life deeply. It was his first romance with Miss Hala Daher whom he immortalized in his novel *The Broken Wings* (1912) under the name of *Selma*. He wished to marry her but was refused because she issued from a wealthy family, and was promised already as a child by her parents to the hands of someone else. This first contact with the aristocratic Lebanese family made him resent all his life the oriental tradition of marriages that were prearranged on the grounds of social classes.

At eighteen, Gibran graduated from *Al-Hikmat* with high honors. But, still eager to acquire knowledge, he decided this time to go to Paris to learn painting. On his way from

Beirut to Paris, in 1901, he visited Greece, Italy, and Spain. Gibran stayed two years in Paris, during which he wrote *Spirits Rebellious,* his famous criticism of Lebanese high official society, religious ministers, and corrupted marriage love. For this book, Gibran was excommunicated from the Maronite Church and exiled by Lebanon's Turkish Government; also both of them burned his work in the market place in Beirut.

In 1903, Gibran received a grim letter from Peter requesting him that he get back to Boston because his sister Sultana had just died from tuberculosis and his mother Kamila was seriously sick in bed. Shortly after his arrival Gibran had to take his mother, who was suffering from tuberculosis, to a hospital where she laid bedridden for many long months. The miseries of Gibran increased when in March of the same year Peter, the beloved half-brother who paid for his entire education, succumbed under the yoke of the same plague; three months later his mother remitted her soul into the hands of the Good Lord. The loss of Kamila was depressing on his morale for he loved her immensely. In my opinion she was his first female poetic "muse." The lines that he dedicated to motherhood in *The Broken Wings* were inspired by his mother love.

The most beautiful word on the lips of mankind is the word "Mother," and the most beautiful call is the call of "My mother." It is a word full of hope and love, a sweet and kind word coming from the depths of the heart. The mother is everything—she is our consolation in sorrow, our hope in misery, and our strength in weakness. She is the source of love, mercy, sympathy, and forgiveness. He who loses his mother loses a pure soul who blesses and guards him constantly.

Everything in nature bespeaks the mother. The sun is mother of earth and gives it its nourishment of heat, it never leaves the universe at night until it has put the earth to sleep to the song of the sea and the hymn of birds and brooks. And this earth is the mother of trees and flowers. It produces them, nurses them, and weans them. The trees and flowers become kind mothers of their great fruits and seeds. And the mother, the prototype of all existence, is the eternal spirit, full of beauty and love.[11]

Death's wretchedness left him alone with Mariana, his other sister. It goes without saying that the misfortunes of 1903 engraved deep traces of sadness on the poet's soul. Historically, I believe that if Gibran has become a philosopher of human sorrows, and a great psychologist of the finitude of human nature, it is because he immensely experienced the existential anxiety of suffering, and the facticities of human predicaments.

During the following years Gibran painted, designed book covers and wrote in Arabic many short essays as well as he revised for the second time *The Prophet* written in Arabic. By early 1904, he held an exhibition of his paintings in the studio of Fred Holland Day, a friend photographer. When the studio was opened, only a few visitors showed up. To his embarrassment no one asked the price; the audience rather criticized and laughed at his work. However, among the spectators, came one woman named Miss Mary Haskell, a principal of school, to whom Gibran's work appealed so much to her sense of beauty and mysticism that she offered him the opportunity to display his paintings in her institution: Cambridge School for Girls. From such a miraculous encounter, an everlasting tie of friendship formed between Gibran and Miss Haskell. She became his first patron and benefactress.[12] Thus, it was she who advised him to go for a second time to Paris in 1908, and financed his studies at the *Academie Julien* and at the *Ecole des Beaux Arts*. In a letter he wrote to a friend he personified Miss Haskell as heaven and a she-angel: "who is ushering me towards a splendid future and paving me the path of intellectual and financial success."[13]

It is worthwhile to pause for a moment at this point and

ponder on the relationships Gibran nurtured with two women of this epoch. For one he had a Platonic love while for the other it was a Freudian love. The first was Miss Haskell, toward whom he had a spiritual and intellectual love. The second was Emile Michel, a young, beautiful and self-confident French woman, nicknamed Micheline who taught French in Miss Haskell's school where Gibran met her. The two loves had a great effect upon him, to the point that he always spoke of women in his writings, and like John Stuart Mill he made himself a duty to promulgate the Women's Liberation from the males' deceitful customs.[14]

The departure of Gibran for Paris in 1908 was not merely undertaken for the sake of learning painting, but also Gibran as an Arab who feels grateful to those who bestow gifts upon him, wanted to forget Micheline, for he knew that this love was contrary to his sense of gratefulness toward Miss Haskell. Yet, to his surprise Micheline came unexpectedly to him in Paris. "Gibran forgot the world and he forgot Mary with the world. He opened his arms to Micheline and offered to live with her,"[15] not, however, as his wife. He asked her to be his mistress; Micheline refused because she wanted to be married to him. This was the end of a second frustrated love, the first being Hala Daher.

While in the "City of Arts" and "the Heart of the World" as he used to refer to Paris,[16] he met and made portraits of many illustrious artists, poets and writers from all over the world. Above all he tied a strong friendship with the distinguished sculptor Auguste Rodin, under whom he studied and who one day said of him that he was the Willian Blake of the Twentieth Century,[17] signifying by this the great resemblance in writing, painting and biography between Gibran and Blake. Also, it was in 1908, that Gibran received news from a friend in Lebanon announcing that with the replacement of the old despotic Turkish government by the Young Turks, his exile was revoked. The news made him happy but did not instigate him to sail to his homeland.

Back to Boston in 1910, Gibran began to suffer from

29

remorses. The favors Miss Haskell poured on him had become a burden of responsibility on his shoulders. In the midst of indecision, confusion and guilt, Gibran not knowing how to repay back in gratitude to Miss Haskell, he offered to marry her, though the idea in his mind was despicable. But Miss Haskell, guessing the struggle into which his soul was plunged, made clear to him that she preferred his friendship to any burdensome tie of marriage. Gibran felt relieved.

In exchange for the moral and pecuniary support he obtained from Miss Haskell,[18] Gibran immortalized her by dedicating to her memory many of his writings, such as *The Broken Wings,* the poem "The Beauty of Death" in *Tears and Laughter,* etc.

Around 1912, Gibran moved to New York where he took residence till the end of his life, at 51 West Tenth Street, on the third floor of the famous "Studio Building" exclusively built for painters and writers. Before and after the World War, Gibran's fame began to grow steadily ever more. He held numerous exhibitions in various galleries of the east coast. On the other hand he produced a vast literature of short essays, novels, poems, stories, aphorisms etc. . . . . all of which dealt with the existential themes of the concrete life. Finally, with the publication of *The Prophet* in 1923, Gibran's reputation spread both in the Middle East and in the United States.

If today's Arabic literature feels at ease with the rules of rhyme and rhythm, it is because Gibran along with some other literary friends, broke away from the stagnant traditional prerequisites of the Arabic verse by proposing as early as 1920 a new poetic form called "prose poem." This new idea came about, when on April 20, 1920, a new literary circle was formed after a meeting held in Gibran's studio. This was called *Arrabitah,* the Pen-Bond. Gibran was elected president among several other poets, all of them Arab immigrants in the U.S. The purpose of *Arrabitah* was to modernize Arabic literature and to promote this newly conceived idea among the Middle Eastern writers. *Arrabitah* made the name of Gibran a daily topic of discussion either among the intellectuals in the Arab countries or in the newspapers published in the Middle East.

Before concluding his biography, let me report two important incidents that occured with two other women. One took place in 1912 with the female writer May Ziadeh, a Lebanese of origin whose family had moved to Egypt, while still young of age. May's home was a gathering place of the Egyptian intelligentsia where often Gibran's publications were matters of philosophical conversation. We are told that it is May who first introduced herself to Gibran, writting him a letter of admiration. Touched by her candid thoughts, it seems that Gibran fell in love at first sight with his correspondent even though he never met her in flesh and blood. In *A Self-Portrait,* which is a collection of his letters, we read that Gibran had asked May, when his book *The Broken Wings* first appeared in Arabic, to send him her impressions about his thoughts expressed on marriage and love. Her reply on May 12, 1912, did not totally approve of Gibran's philosophy of love. Rather she remained in all her correspondence quite critical of a few of Gibran's Westernized ideas. Still he had a strong emotional attachment to Miss Ziadeh till his death. He dreamt a lot of her and wished very much to end his moments of life close to May. A few years before his death he wrote her:

> I wish I were sick in Egypt or in my country so I might be close to the ones I love. Do you know, May, that every morning and every evening I find myself in a home in Cairo with you sitting before me reading the last article I wrote or the one you wrote which has not yet been published.[19]

The second of these important happenings is the meeting with his one day biographer, Miss Barbara Young. Of her known, she tells us that it was in 1923, after listening to the reading of an exerpt of *The Prophet* in the Church St. Mark's In-the-Bowrie in New York, that she decided to let Gibran know about her admiration for him. Cordially in his reply he invited her to come visiting him in his studio and "to talk about poetry and to see the pictures" he had drawn.[20] From there on Barbara kept on going regularly to the studio that was located on 51 West 10th Street. Gibran employed her sometimes as his secretary. No remuneration was paid; she was simply fascinated by this slender, mustachioed Lebanese immigrant, five feet four inches tall, with brown eyes fringed by long lashes. While Gibran was still alive, she would go to some distant city, lecturing on our author's thoughts and paintings. In her biography of Gibran she repeatedly defined her relation as "friendship," meaning probably Platonic. After Gibran's death she spread widely his fame, and even wrote a small brochure about him. Yet, in 1944, she published the now famous biography *This Man From Lebanon,* in which she recorded the personality of the Gibran she knew during his last seven years. Miss Barbara Young traveled on October 1939, to Beirut and visited the various places where Gibran lived, long before she undertook the composition of her book.

Kahlil Gibran closed his eyes peacefully on April 10, 1931, at the age of fourty-eight, in St. Vincent's hospital in New York. Gibran was not buried in America but his remains were taken, to meet his wish, to Lebanon and laid down in the old deserted monastary of Mar-Sarkis in Wadi Kadisha.

The Lebanese of today, not to exempt the Arabs of the other countries, feel proud of Gibran, because with a sole hand he has elevated the dignity of the immigrants and proved to foreigners the erudition and wisdom of the Middle-East mystics. His fame can best be tested by the reader, if the latter consents to take a short trip to his nearest bookstore and witness the sale of the works of our author.

FOOTNOTES

1 Naimy, Mikhail, "A Strange Little Book", *Aramco World,* XV, 6, 1964, p. 12.

2 In reading some of Gibran's commentators we get the impression that Gibran attained the peak of his fame while alive. Unfortunately, these historians wrapped in the emotion of pride, fail to stress bluntly the distinction between the "before" and "after". (See for instance: Andrew Dib Sherfan, *Kahlil Gibran: The Nature of Love,* New York: Philosophical Library, 1970, pp. 29-31; and Habib Massoud, *Joubran Hayyan wa Mayyitan,* Beirut: The Rihani House, 1966, p. 21 sq.). Yet, in the opinion of others, such as Suheil Bushrui and John Munro, Gibran hardly received recognition from academic modern American literature; and when his books were printed none of the leading Journals in the West ever reviewed his books. (*Kahlil Gibran: Essays and Introduction,* eds., by Suheil Bushrui and John Munro, Beirut: The Rihani House, 1970, p. 1 sq.). This amounts to saying that he truely became world famous after his death only.

3 The Monastery of Mar-Sarkis was the playground of Gibran and his refuge for meditation whenever things did not work out at his home. The young Gibran always had hoped to buy someday the deserted cloister. Incidentally, we are told by his best friend Mikhail Naimy, that "he had begun negotiations to buy the monastery" prior to 1923. But really, he did not succeed paying the full amount requested by the real estate because he became bankrupt after trying unsuccessfully to collect his due from some old lady to whom he had rented a building he had bought in Boston during the depression time." (Mikhail Naimy, "A Strange Little Book," *Aramco World,* XV, 6, 1964, p. 15; *see also* by the same author, *Kahlil Gibran, His Life and His Work,* Beirut: Khayats, 1964, p. 197).

4 The Maronites accept the infallibility of the Pope. And in contrast to the Latin priests, the Maronite priests may contract marriage legally. However, today more and more the idea of marriage among the clergy is fading away. Historically, it was in 1736 that the Maronite Church joined affiliation with the Roman Church. The precursor is Mar-Maron. *See below* p. 17.

5 Young, Barbara, *This Man From Lebanon,* New York: A. Knopf, 1970, p. 144.

6 Otto, Annie Salem, *The Parables of Kahlil Gibran,* New York: The Citadel Press, 1963, p. 16.

7 Young, Barbara, *op. cit.,* p. 10.

8 *ibid,* p. 7.

[9] *PR.*, p. 13. It is unfortunate that some writers keep on spelling Gibran's family name differently from the way he himself used to sign in Roman alphabets. For example, to name only two, the French orientalist, Jean Lecerf, spells our author's name as "Djbran Khalil Djbran", (*Orient*, magazine, 3, 1957, pp. 7-14); and the illustrious Harvard professor, Sir Hamilton Gibb refers to him as "Jibran Khalil Jibran," (*Studies on the Civilization of Islam*, Boston: Beacon Press, 1968, p. 272). In my opinion these false ortographies are due to the fact that some of his commentators still prefer to write foreign nouns as they sound to their ears, even though their correspondent Roman inscriptions already exist.

[10] Miss Young (*op. cit.*, p. 184) and Miss Otto (*op. cit.*, p. 20), commit a grotesque historical error when they call Avicinna, a pre-islamic poet and Ibn-Sinna, a philosopher. Actually, those two names, are of the same person. The former is spelled (improperly) in Latin (it should be Avicenna) and the latter in Arabic. Furthermore, Ibn-Sina (980-1037) lived after Mohammed. He is considered as one of the greatest Moslem philosophers of the medieval eastern group. For a good presentation of his philosophy consult Majid Fakhry, *A History of Islamic Philosophy*, Columbia University Press, 1970, pp. 147-183.

[11] *BW.*, pp. 82-83.

[12] Young, Barbara, *op. cit.*, p. 185.

[13] *SP.*, p. 8.

[14] "The Bride's Bed" essay condemns the rotten customs of marriage, in favor of women's freedom. (*TL.*, pp. 87-94). I believe that if Gibran had lived to witness the new movement called "Women's Liberation Front," he would have lent them full support with his sharp pen. He had a profound understanding of the psychology of women. He also avowed that he was indebted for everything that he possessed to the intervention of the women in his life: "I am indebted for all that I call 'I' to women, ever since I was an infant. Women opened the windows of my eyes and the doors of my spirit. Had it not been for the woman-mother, the woman-sister, and the woman-friend, I would have been sleeping among those who seek the tranquility of the world with their snoring." (*SP.*, p. 96). Indeed, his "philosophy of woman" finds some similarities with Simone de Beauvoir's book: *The Second Sex*, and with the Dutch psychologist F. Buytendijk's book: *Woman. A Contemporary View.* His sharp critic is advanced unconditionally against anybody who degrades the function of the female in society. Definitely the nowadays abundantly printed pornography finds no room for justification in his ethics. Finally, he writes: "Writers and poets try to understand the truth about woman. But until this day they have never understood her heart because, looking upon her through the veil of desire, they see nothing except the shape of her body. Or they look upon her through a magnifying glass of spite and find nothing in her but weakness and submission." (*WG.*, 81).

[15] *The Prophet*, translated by Sarwat Okasha, Cairo: Dar al Maarf, 1959, "Introduction", p. 14.

[16] *SP.*, p. 4.

[17] Massoud, Habib, *Joubran, Hayyan wa Mayyatan*, Beirut: The Rihani House, 1966, p. 20.

[18] According to Joseph Sheban, there is rumor that the true benefactress of Gibran was a wealthy Lebanese lady named Mary Khoury. Up to date, however, there is no evidence that shows whether Mary Khoury did really give financial aid to our author. Nevertheless, it seems that a lady by such a name did exist. As to what was her genuine relation with Gibran, it is unknown yet. (*MS.*, pp. 88-89).

[19] *SP.*, p. 97.

[20] Young, Barbara, *op. cit.*, IX.

CHAPTER THREE

THE CONTRIBUTIONS OF THE WRITER

ONE WAY of understanding an author consists in deciphering his thoughts through his works. After all a book is a perfect self-projection of the personality, desires, ambitions and frustrations of the writer. In good philosophical language we say that there is a relation of proportionality if not identity between the "cause," the producer, and "effect," the product. Now, it is true that Gibran would sometimes refuse to be confused with his heroes, as he said, for instance, in a letter to Miss May Ziadeh concerning the personage The Madman.[1] Still, I hold the theory that the motives behind a work have to be fetched "in" the individual contributor, in that *la raison d'être* of the product portrays the personality of the producer.

In this chapter, which I might have entitled "An Introduction to Gibran," I will depict the essential themes of Gibran's philosophy through his printed literature, in as much that I will attempt to outline the influences he bore, and the impact he left on his readers.

1. *The Meaning of Gibran's Publications*

Gibran has conveyed his thoughts through many literary forms of expression. He wrote many books ranging from poems, aphorisms, short plays, parables, to essays, and novels.

The very first appearance of Gibran as a writer is that of rebellious youth disenchanted with anything called "organization." *Spirits Rebellious* was composed in Arabic while studying in Paris in 1903. The book argues that the institutionalized laws of the church, as well as man-made social laws are decayed, for none of them enaid the individual to develop a self-identity. Rather, like Kierkegaard would say, they are "universal," and therefore, they appeal to the common mass, and mold patterned or stereotyped personalities. The book especially denounces the Maronite clergy's conduct toward the poor peasants as "simoniac," and declares human laws as unethical oppressions exercised in the name of moral justice. This work is meaningful in many respects. (1) It reveals the political and religious situations of Lebanon at the time of its publication, in that it clearly underlines that the spirit of feudalism under the Turks was detrimental to the poor for it introduced the class struggle. (2) It represents Gibran's moral philosophy.[2] Though the tone of it sounds a bit rebellious, Gibran's ethic, however, should not be identified with nowadays revolutionary radicals who abhor unconditionally whatever is called "establishment," meaning a complete rejection of rules and order in society. On the contrary, like Rousseau, Gibran is a "reformer" of the social woes caused by injustice, ineffective traditions, and the unnatural laws that hurt the innate laws of human nature. His reform asks that kindness, forgiveness and love be the guidelines of social intercourse between citizen and government. (3) Finally, the novel anticipates Gibran's later writings. In the theory-building of many philosophers, historians detect an evolution of ideas that involve contradictions and ambiguities, but, Gibran really never relinquished his very first ideas and never raised paradoxes in his system.

Soon after its publication, *Spirits Rebellious* was burned in the mid of Beirut. For punishment Gibran was excommunicated from the Catholic Maronite Church and was exiled by the Turkish officials from Lebanon. In a letter he wrote to his first cousin, Nakhli Gibran, he expressed his melancholy for what his countrymen did to him.

. . . I am not sure whether the Arabic-speaking world would remain as friendly to me as it has been in the past three years. I say this because the apparition of enmity has already appeared. The people in Syria are calling me heretic, and the intelligentsia in Egypt vilifies me, saying, "He is the enemy of just laws, of family ties, and of old traditions." Those writers are telling the truth, because I do not love man-made laws and I abhor the traditions that our ancestors left us. This hatred is the fruit of my love for the sacred and spiritual kindness which should be the source of every law upon the earth, for kindness is the shadow of God in man . . . Will my teaching ever be received by the Arab world, or will it die away and disappear like a shadow?[3]

However, when in 1908, the Young Turks, headed by Niyazi, overthrew the Sultan Abdul-Hamid II, the new government pardoned all the exiles including Gibran who was then in Paris studying painting with Auguste Rodin.[4]

His next novel is *The Broken Wings* (1912). Personally he writes: "This book is the best one I have ever written."[5] Best, indeed it is, yet with some reservations for *The Prophet* was not yet. In my opinion, the philosophy outlined in this book is in continuation with the philosophy of marriage stressed in *Spirits Rebellious*. Nonetheless, Gibran seems less preoccupied with polemic than trying to describe to us the human predicament of love, which constitutes the central topic of the whole novel. His definition of love hither is neither Platonic nor Freudian, but between romantic and spiritual.[6] Furthermore, he insists, after the manner of Blaise Pascal, that love is not the work of reason but of the heart; not the carnal or bodily sensation heart, but of a heart that still has a logic. *La logique du coeur* is the correct expression. What the emotions know logically, the logic of abstract reason cannot reason about unless it falls prey to one of Freud's defense mechanisms: rationalization.

The story that Gibran narrates is autobiographical[7]; it is about his first romance with Miss Hala Daher, whom he met while studying in Lebanon. By the way, his matrimony to Miss Daher was impeded not by the girl's father, but rather by the town bishop who had imposed against the wills of the girl and her father, the decision of a marriage with his nephew. The nephew was an irresponsible man and the uncle bishop was most avid to inherit the wealth of the Dahers. By the way, a movie has been made about *The Broken Wings*.

A Tear and a Smile (1914), argues through poems and prose poems that human existence oscillates between two metaphysical predicaments, viz., joy and suffering. These are metaphysical, because they express human dimensions, and impregnate the core of the being of man. Somehow, the philosophy that he expounds in this book is neither Schopenhauerism nor Leibnizian. The former thought that everything is evil and that our world is the worst one that God could have ever created. To the other extreme, Leibniz taught an exaggerated optimism, saying that if opportunity was presented, God could not create a better world than this one. Gibran is mid-way. Life is both a "tear" and a "smile." The tear has an intrinsic or extrinsic motive; the extrinsic is, however, the motive of the former. This amounts to saying, evil that surrounds us out-there in society, in politics, or in my other fellowman, is what tortures and hampers my existence, thus, affecting me from within. This being the case, we understand why Gibran has included in the book some short essays that portray the cupidities of society. Yet, Gibran does not stop at the iniquities of life, he also acknowledges the reality of happiness, joy and love. To put it bluntly, he approves of the philosophy of stoicism. The stoics bear courageously their cross; a lamentation which is not followed immediately by a pursuit of an intellectual meditation, *abases* man's intellectual capacities whose teleologic is to overcome meaningfully the pain. However, this should not make us think that Gibran's philosophy is an escape from life's frustrations through a calculative thinking process. Maybe, existentialism is the closest philosophy with which his system finds affinities. Indeed, like the existentialists, he assumes that pain and joy are complementary and interrelated. For instance, love is not without some sacrifices; there are no roses without thorns; there can be no appreciation of happiness unless the soul has first drunk of the cup of bitterness. Somehow, the book surmises that it is utopia to want a world exempted from psychological stress, in as much that it is untrue that human life knows nothing of joy, friendshipness, happiness. Finally, it is my personal conviction that *A Tear and a Smile* is not of a "Nietzschean inspiration," as said Andrew Dib Sherfan.[8] The overtone is similar to the British poet William Blake, whom Gibran imitated a great deal. For example, the so many articles about the function of the poet in society reflect a resemblance with Blake's conception of the authentic poet: a messenger sent from Heaven to lead people on the right path of God's love.

In 1918, at the age of thirty five, Gibran summed up his meditations in *The Procession*. The work was first written in Arabic verses. It communicates a dialogue between a youth full of vigor, an optimist, a believer in the native goodness of man, and worshipper of nature where he dwells—and an aged sage embittered by the inhabitants of the metropolis, where the rhythm of life is so mechanized and standardized that beauty, love, religion, justice, knowledge, happiness, gentleness, are veiled by false pretences. In the last page, the sage avows that if youth was granted to him, he would choose to run wild and free in nature. The poem reminds us of J. J. Rousseau's contrasts between the native goodness of human nature and the rotten constructed nature that civilization imparts upon us through its bad stimuli. Our author had a high esteem of Rousseau. On many occasions he spoke of the latter as a liberator of mankind from tyranny and "Bastille."[9]

Gibran's first publication in English is a collection of poems and parables with the title *The Madman* (1918). Here

41

we see Nietzsche's influence on Gibran's style. Like Nietzsche, Gibran expresses himself through parables. But also, his Madman following the trend of Zarathustra, introduces himself to others with a *"shout."* The cry of Zarathustra was the declaration of God's death; Gibran's Madman, however, does not proclaim the deity's death but asserts a relation of cooperation between man and God concerning Creation. As we turn the pages, we are struck by the attitude of irony and sarcasm that slowly builts up till it reaches its zenith with the last parable "The Perfect World." This essay, once more, denounces the hypocritic behaviors performed in the name of a "God of lost souls."[10] The Madman is not literally mentally unballanced; on the contrary, he is, in the language of psychosomatic medicine, perfectly healthy. His madness is only in the eyes of others, from whom he deviates in his right and just and logical doings. Gibran here agrees with the opinion held by the humanistic psychologists, namely, we tend to be what society expects from us, although these expectations could be detrimental for the development of our self-identity. Whence often times we veil our true self with masks, out of fear of being ridiculed by others. The ethics of Gibran's hero is quite simple: better be labelled madman by others, than hide my inner self with filthy social masks. The parables "The Wise King" and "The Blessed City" are significant in that they imbed at the manner of Aesop and La Fontaine, a moral lesson from which our contemporary world could learn something about sincerity.

With *The Forerunner* (1920) Gibran becomes more mysterious and more of a mature philosopher. The title he selected is quite appropriate for the type of philosophic thoughts he conveys through the parables. In his preface he defines man as a "forerunner" meaning that we foreran what we "are" today. His logic here is not much different from the historical dialectic of Marx or Sartre. Basically, he asserts that "man invents man" (Marx); we are our own product; "I am what I am because I have made of myself what I am" (Sartre). Nobody is to be blamed for our "being" and "having," but ourselves. Psychologically speaking, this is called self-actual-ization. Yet, this process is Heraclitian, i.e. it never ends for the tomorrow is always stretched out-there, untouched. In other words, Gibran makes clear that we are our own destiny, and not the toy of a blind fate. Moreover, the essay makes ample reference to intersubjectivity. A man's existence does not run parallel to another's. Existence is a coexistence. For better or for worse, man is not an island; he is a social animal.

The Prophet (1923) is his masterpiece; this book has become a second Bible for the readers. Priests don't mind to consult it during mass. James Kavanaugh for instance, when he was still part of the Catholic Clergy, cited during a matrimonial ceremony the lines of *The Prophet* on marriage instead of reciting the prayers of the St. Office.[11]

Now, it should be understood that Gibran had long meditated on *The Prophet* and rewrote it three times. He was just fifteen years old when he composed its first version. At the age of twenty, he revised *The Prophet* in Arabic. Then took it to his mother who was seriously ill,

> and he read to her what he had written of the young Almustafa. [The hero of the play]. The mother, wise in her son's youth as she had been in his child-hood, said "It is good work, Gibran. But the time is not yet. Put it away." He obeyed her to the letter. "She knew," he said, "far better than I, in my green youth."[12]

Then between 1917-1922, he rewrote the book for a third time; finally in 1923 he released it to the press.

Most particularly *The Prophet* is a direct copy of the style of Nietzsche's *Thus Spoke Zarathustra*. Yet, Almustafa does not share at all the philosophy of Zarathustra who is grim and pessimistic about the abilities of man. Here, like elsewhere, Gibran is simply fascinated by the style of Nietzsche; as to the content of Nietzsche's Zarathustra, Gibran is not the least under his spell. In my opinion the real straight forward influence on Gibran's thoughts of *The Prophet* is rather the Bible. Actually, Nietzsche himself was inspired by the figure of Jesus Christ, his speeches and style of expression, the parables. That is why we find many "numerical numbers" in Nietzsche's Zarathustra that were borrowed from the Holy Scriptures. For instance, Christ and Zarathustra both began their prophetic mission at the age of thirty.[13]

Fundamentally, all the sermons of the Prophet revolve around one dimension of human reality: the authentic social relations. Thus, Almustafa revokes all the intersubjective situations—marriage, law, children, friendship, giving, etc.— where people come in contact with each other. But also, the book teaches how these existential relations should genuinely be experienced. I know that I would not be exaggerating if for sake of comparison, I recalled to the attention of the reader that M. Heidegger, the leader of existentialism, has a somehow similar definition of the human predicament. Heidegger, following his teacher E. Husserl, characterizes man as a *Mitdasein*. That is metaphysically, man is a being-with-others, and in no instance could human nature be exempted from such a facticity; as for the case of solitude, isolation once more proves rather than disproves the "fact" of "togetherness." One may retract in his ivory tower either because he wants to reevaluate the meaning of his relations with his fellowmen, or because he has been hurt by others. But in all events we realize that the metaphysical predicament of being-with-others permeates man socially and psychologically, and not the other way around.

"Intersubjectivity" is not, however, the only kind of relation Gibran sought to express. Actually, *The Prophet* and two others, *The Garden of the Prophet* (1933) and *The Earth Gods* (1931) form a trilogy intended to outline the three-fold relational dimensions of the existential man. The corresponding technical philosophic expressions are *Mitwelt* (relation with other minds; synonymous, *Mitdasein*), *Umwelt* (relation with the world), and *Gotteswelt* (relation with God).

The Garden of the Prophet studies man's relation to nature

(*Umwelt*). The emphasis is that of "ecology" and "environmentalism," not with a scientific outlook but poetic. Gibran was a worshipper of nature and wild life. Had he lived long enough to witness to what degree our scientific inventors have intoxicated the air and polluted the rivers, there is no doubt that he would have sharply deplored our tyrannical attitude toward helpless nature. It is said that our primitive ancestors fought physically and intellectually to preserve themselves from cosmic calamities; well, today the role of master-servant relation is reversed; it is man now who presents a threat to nature. At any rate, the cosmology that Gibran propounds in the book is very much anthropomorphic. He describes human emotions with concepts borrowed from nature.

As for *The Earth Gods,* it explicates God's relation to man (*Gotteswelt*). Man has the desire to be close to the Divine. In Gibran's philosophy man ascends to God "in," "through" and "with" love only. The essay is a dialogue between three gods, two of whom consider that "man is food for the gods."[14] That is, man is meat for the glory and plans of the gods, and a toy that satisfies their whims. The third god, however, is all compassion; his speech is an attempt to change the despotic attitude of the two others; he reminds them that love is the virtue of the gods; finally, to win them on his side, in favor of the human, he reminds them that man is capable of practicing the very virtue of the gods: he gives them the case of the love of man for woman.

To revert back to *The Prophet,* Gibran has attained his zenith among the international scholars with "the little black book"[15], as he liked to refer to it because of its black cover. The thoughts contained in the work are so powerful and attractive that it has become one of the rare manuscripts ever to be translated in more than twenty languages. Every reader sees a bit of himself in the philosophic discourses of Almustafa. To many this "strange little book,"[16] still serves as a guide for their examination of conscience. The following stories are true happening; Miss Young relates:

45

There was a young Russian girl named Marya, who had been climbing in the Rockies with a group of friends, other young people. She had gone aside from them and sat down on a rock to rest, and beside her she saw a black book. It was *The Prophet,* which meant nothing to her. Idley she turned the pages, then she began to read a little, then a little more. "Then," said Marya, telling us the story, "I rushed to my friend and shouted, 'Come and see —what I have all my life been waiting for—I have found it—Truth!"

There was another man, a lawyer who sat through an hour of reading aloud from the same book in another bookshop in Philadelphia. He was a man full of years, with a benign countenance, and he listened with a quality of attention that could not fail to attract the reader's notice. When the evening was over this lawyer came to speak to me as others were doing, and he said, "I am a criminal lawyer. If I had read that chapter on *Crime and Punishment* twenty years ago I would have been a better and a happier man, and an infinitely better counsel for the defense."

I know a gentleman in New York City, the manager of a well-known real estate firm. He told me this: "My wife has three copies of *The Prophet* in our house. When we meet a new acquaintance who promises to be congenial, she lends him, or her, one of the copies. According to the person's reaction to the book we form our opinion of his worthwhileness." . . . You cannot read a page without being moved in the depths of your consciousness, if you are one of those "at all ready for the truth."[17]

Sand and Foam (1926) is a compilation of maxims and aphorisms similar to those of La Rochefaucault, William Blake, and F. Nietzsche. Each of these sayings could be used for intellectual meditation. But to consider them as good thoughts that could be wrapped in Chinese fortune cookies, I deem the project of bad taste.

Another major important work is *Jesus The Son of Man* (1928). Gibran has always been attracted by the majesty of Jesus' teachings and by the mystery of his life. He viewed Jesus as the great human exemplar who best fulfilled the metamorphosis of transmutation from human nature into God-like. As the title already implies, the Jesus that Gibran describes is not the Jesus of theology or dogmas of whom Revelation attests as the Son and Equal of God and the Holy Spirit in the Mystery of Trinity. Rather, he depicts to us a Jesus made of flesh, tormented by human passions, but who, however, has transcended the evil limitations of lust, injustice, and insensitiveness. At this point I remind the reader that Gibran had no attachment for organized religion. That is why he never meant to speak of the Jesus of the Christian, but of the Jesus of Nazareth, the man who had a mother and a father. His real concern is to make the image of Jesus accessible to the human. We know that the so-called intimidated mortals consider the life and deeds of Jesus unimitable because *a priori* they judge him not as a human but their God. Consequently, these souls remain unaffected by the exhortations of Jesus. Well, Gibran's new narration of the life of Jesus purposes to change our attitude toward this "extraordinary man, Jesus," who after all was not made of a different stuff than us, except that he had successfully developed to its peak the divine potentialities of love and compassion that God the Creator encompasses within our nature. Gibran recounts the life of Jesus through the testimony of seventy seven persons who knew him. The last personage is "A Man From Lebanon," most probably Gibran himself. I find it difficult to conclude that our author committed the heresy of the Jacobite Monophysites, or even of the Nestorians. The point he meant to get across to us is that the supernatural is implanted within each man, and it comes to each individual to realize the divinity of his nature. "The soul is a link in the divine chain."[18] For guidance in our pursuit of being worthy of God, he recommended to follow the path of Jesus.

Finally, the remaining of the works reiterate his thoughts already elaborated in his previous books. *The Wanderer* (1932) is a posthumous collection of fifty stories; *Secrets of the Heart* (1947) is an amalgamation of short stories, among which "The Tempest" sarcastically portrays at the manner of Nietzsche the lack of spirituality in modern society; *The Nymphs of the Valley* (1948) repeats once more his polemics against the social and ecclesiastical woes; *The Voice of the Master* (1959) speaks of the death of the prophet Almuhtada and gives an account of the teachings of the Master; *A Self-Portrait* (1959) contains some of his correspondences with his closest friends; *Thoughts and Meditations* (1961); *Spiritual Sayings* (1962); and, *Beloved Prophet* (1972) is a collection of Gibran's letters to Haskell; also this book contains Miss Haskell's private journal about Gibran's life and personality.

In conclusion allow me to express my discontent with some of Gibran's publishers. This man from Lebanon is widely read by the scholars and the laymen, and yet I personally feel that he is little understood by either of these readers. I have spoken to many of his admirers, to my surprise I discovered that they have a vague and confusing comprehension of what he meant to convey to mankind. After much thoughts I believe that the cause of the symptoms of ignorance among his readers are threefold. (1) Many get acquainted with just one or a few of his works, leaving their mind blank as to what he elaborates in his other books. And yet, no scholar can be enough appreciated intellectually unless a great number of his publications are absorbed. (2) A good part of the blame for people's ignorance has to be attributed most particularly to the publisher Alfred A. Knopf, who for monetary profit has made available *The Prophet* in three different kinds of lithography: purse feasable, medium, and gift wrap format. This "little black book" has become commercial. Friends will buy it as a Christmas or anniversary gift for other companions; and if it is the big edition they are offered, the wide white cover and precious sheets, the receivers will display it along with the painting books of Da Vinci on the table in their living room, where visitors will glance at it. Still, the latest and worst subjugation of Gibran to "intellectual prostitution," is Knopf's insignificant calendar-book *Kahlil Gibran's Diary* (1971, 1972) of which I am sure our author never dreamed of. (3) The last possible explanation for the reader's insufficient knowledge about Gibran's message, stems from the too poetical and musical phraseology employed by Gibran. Many enjoy reading Gibran because the lecture carries them to sleep in a beautiful concert of self-complacency; thereby they cease meditating upon the deep philosophical meaning hidden beneath the sound verses.

I hope that this present manuscript will conteract successfully the epidemic of ignorance blurring the intellectual vision of the reader. This is the very reason I am endeavoring here to explicate the most basic concepts that Gibran expounded, although he presented them in a scattering way.

2. *Gibran's Innovation in Modern Arabic Literature*

In the contention of the Russian Orientalist, Ignace Kratchovski, the Arab immigrants in America played an important felicitous role in the modernization of Arabic Literature.[19]

Till the turn of the nineteenth century, Arabic *belles-lettres* followed faithfully the conventional literary style laid down by the Koran and the Traditions of the Middle Ages. Thus, "in poetry—notes Professor Cachia—by far the commonest form was the panegyric. . . . In all the sentiment expressed was conventional. . . . Poetic compositions were overlaid by far-fetched similes, metaphors, and allusions, with elaborate paronomasias and ambilogies. . . . [On the other hand in] fine prose . . . the narrative element became no more than a framework on which to hang verbal *tours de force*."[20] All this amounts to saying with Sir Hamilton Gibb, that "conservatism was too deeply bound up with the entire heritage of Arabic literature to allow any kind of simplification,"[21] novelty, and originality in stylistic expressions and content.

However, when Napoleon came to Egypt in 1798, and translations of eminent European thinkers were made available to Middle-East intellectuals, a sort of rejuvenation and improvement was born in Arabic literature. Yet, to a large extent, the immigrants *(Mahjar)* also concurred in emancipating modern literature from the sterile and decadent literary style of scholasticism. Most particularly, Gibran's new writing's form and content inspired his fellow country authors to adopt the "free verse" as their new stanza.

Already as early as 1913, Gibran along with other immigrant writers, Amin Rihani and Nasseeb Arida, began to publish in the New York monthly newspaper *al-Funoon,* essays, articles, poems that were drastically different from the classical metric schemes *(Sadj).* The literary style that they employed was *Prose Poem (Shir manthur).*

Also, on April 20, 1920, the immigrant Arab writers, headed by Gibran as their president, formed a literary circle called "Arrabitah" (Pen-Bond), whose purpose was to update Arabic Literature "from the state of sterility and imitation to the state of beautiful originality in both meaning and style."[22] Soon "Arrabitah" impressed the Arab world. In the words of Muhammad Najm, this new school "characterized by power, modernity and revolt against all that is traditional and rotten, is the strongest school that modern Arabic literature has known until the present day."[23]

And precisely, through the society of "Arrabitah" and the literary form of "Prose Poem," Gibran contributed to the innovation of Modern Arabic literature. During his time he set the example as to how to combine prose with poetry and vice-versa. In depth his writings are poetical, though the verses are proses. The strophes have rhythm and rhyme.

Of course, it is Friedrich Nietzsche, the Psalms, and the Bible filled with parables, that gave a definite literary direction to Gibran's style of expression. From Nietzsche not only he borrowed Zarathustra's form of expression which is quite similar to the Christian Gospel, but he also acquired from Nietzsche the flair for mingling emotions and thoughts, sorrow and happiness. As from the Bible he learned the old semitic literary figure of parables, metaphors, anthropomorphism and cosmomorphism.

In summary, Gibran is hailed today by all the commentators of Modern Arabic *belles-lettres* as an innovator in Middle Eastern literature; and in my opinion, his writings can teach something to Western authors. To the Arabs he showed them how to break away from classical rhymed poetry *(Sadj)* and to feel free with the rhythm (prose-poem). To the Westerners, he is a lived example, as to how to make of philosophy a pleasant literature, and not a boring, eyes-tiring lecture of an incomprehensible language.

3. *The Foreign Influences*

No thinker can totally sever himself from the past and present ideologies. Not even the French philosopher, René Descartes, who planned in breaking the ties with traditional philosophy, did succeed in keeping his system virgin from foreign influences. Well, Gibran too bore some influences in his art work, poetry and philosophy. It is not possible for us to estimate accurately all the influences that shaped his art and thoughts. Nor is it possible for us to draw chronologically the evolution of influences on Gibran. Nevertheless, we do in fact detect a few major currents that attracted him as an artist and a writer.

Thus, Gibran's *paintings* reflect the impact of the Paris schools, *Academic Julien* and *Ecoles des Beaux Arts,* and most especially, that of his teacher Auguste Rodin under whom he studied in 1908 in France. But also, as the critic of his *Twenty Drawings,* Miss Alice Raphael noted: "In painting he is a classicist and his work owes more to the findings of Da Vinci than it does to any modern insurgent."[24]

51

Gibran's interest in Da Vinci dates back when at six years old he was given by his mother a volume of Leonardo's reproductions.

On the other hand, in his *literature,* Gibran was impressed by the early-Islamic poet Mutanabbi,[25] and the notorious Persian Ibn al-Muqaffa, who is best known for his translations of Pahlavi works into Arabic. Ibn al-Muqaffa employed a lavish rhetorical style for recounting fables which encompassed a moral lesson.[26] Gibran in his turn, used the style of fables in order to communicate to his reader a moral teaching. Also, Amin Rihani, Mikhail Naimy, Nasseeb Arida, the Egyptian woman author May Ziadeh, and many other Arab literati left deep imprints on Gibran's expressionistic literature.

Yet, it seems that his exposure to European culture refined by far his prose-poetry and provided him with philosophic ideas. Lest I repeat the names of those who influenced him in both his literary form and philosophical content, let's outline in brief the main Eastern and Western ideological movements that gave a special orientation to his philosophy and style of expression.

1. FRIEDRICH NIETZSCHE

This German philosopher (1844-1900) has probably next to the Bible the most influenced Gibran's thoughts and style of expression. Miss Haskell reports that Gibran had read Nietzsche since "he was twelve or thirteen."[27] Gibran had a high respect for Nietzsche. He would call him: "the loneliest man of the nineteenth century and surely the greatest."[28] At other occasions Gibran depicted him as "a sober Dionysus —a superman who lives in forests and fields—a mighty being who loves music and dancing and all joy."[29]

Essentially, Nietzsche's philosophy denounces society for the despiritualization and demoralization in the world. He blames Christianity and the social institutions for the dehumanization of the individual, and the occurrence of "slave morality."

Of all the works of Nietzsche, Gibran liked most *Thus Spoke Zarathustra.* His books, *The Madman, The Forerunner, The Prophet* and *The Tempest* were written with a Nietzschean inspiration. From Nietzsche Gibran learned how to convey his ideas in a messianic overtone, while at the same time using a flammatory style for criticizing the organized religion and the social establishment.

Now, to be precise, I call your attention to the fact that although Gibran was attracted by Nietzsche, he was not, however, in complete agreement with his teacher's philosophy. For one, Nietzsche was a pessimist and an atheist. His Zarathustra declared the death of God, and denied the immortality of man.[30] But Gibran's Almustafa is theocentric and believes that Good will prevail over Evil. Of his own, Gibran confesses: "His [Nietzsche's] form [style] always was soothing to me. But I thought his philosophy was terrible and all wrong. I was a worshipper of beauty—and beauty was to me the loveliness of things."[31] In the text, I will, when needed, further elaborate on the similarities and dissimilarities between the two.

2. THE BIBLE

When I visited the private library of Gibran located in the Museum in Bsherri, I noticed many editions of the Bible and in different languages, among his few other readings. This indicates, in contrast to Nietzsche's *The Antichrist,* that Gibran is a firm believer in the teachings of the Gospel. And indeed, his philosophy of love recapitulates in its fullest details Christ's sermons on "Agape." Actually, it is my understanding that Gibran's hermeneutics of life is his personal paraphrasing in a simple and highly emotional language, of the Holy Book. Besides the parabolical figure of speech that he borrows from Jesus and the anthropomorphism of the Gospel's metaphors, I find it interesting that he makes ample use of the biblical numbers 3, 7, 12 and 30, whenever he wants to convey a messianic or prophetic numerology of events. About these numbers, he once attempted to explain them in the following way: "7 is probably from the five planets the ancients knew, and the sun and the moon. And 12 was sacred too, from the months of the year, and 4 from the four seasons and the four points of compass. And 3 we can never get away from."[32]

3. BUDDHISM

In *The Poet From Baalbek, The Nymphs of the Valley,* and "The Farewell" of *The Prophet,* in as much as in many other passages, Gibran speaks of the reincarnation of the soul and Nirvana. Undoubtedly, through reading his predecessors the Middle-Age philosophers Avicenna, Al Farid and Al Ghazali on whom he wrote articles[33], he got acquainted with the doctrine of transmigration.

A brief expose of reincarnation as propounded by Buddhism will help us to understand the spirit of Gibran.

The term used in Buddhism for transmigration or rebirth is *samsara,* that is, moving about continuously or coming again and again to rebirth. The term refers to the notion of going through one life after another. The endlessness and inevitability of *samsara* are described in *Samyutta - Nikaya,* II. (A portion of the Buddhist scriptures.)

The idea of rebirth in Buddhism receives its most essential meaning from the Buddhist truth of the *dukkha* or suffering entailed in all existence. To understand suffering, it is not enough to consider one single lifetime, wherein *dukkha* may or may not be immediately evident; one must have in view the whole unending chain of rebirth and the sum of misery entailed in this whole seemingly endless process.

One of the great affirmations of Buddhism is that human consciousness cannot be transformed in a single lifetime. The

54

first conviction of Gautama was the conviction that became known as first of the Four Holy Truths, namely: "now this, monks, is the noble truth of pain; birth is painful, old age is painful, sickness is painful, death is painful, sorrow, lamentation, dejection, and despair are painful. Contact with unpleasant things is painful, not getting what one wishes is painful." Suffering or *dukkha* means more than just physical pain; it is the pain of heart and mind. Conflict, alienation, estrangement is at the very root of man's existence. It is claimed by Buddha that to appreciate properly the truth of *dukkha* entailed in all existence one must keep in mind this whole frightful chain of rebirth.

But *samsara* refers not only to round after round of rebirth in human forms. The whole range of sentient beings is included from the tiniest insect to the noblest man. This range forms an unbroken continuum.

The good news of Buddhism, however, is that the continuum can be broken and has been broken. At the stage of human existence *samsara* can be transcended, and released and Nirvana (or the Pali word, Nibbana) be attained. Nirvana was the final peace, the eternal state of being. But how to describe for his followers the state in which all identification with a man's historical finite self is obliterated while experience itself remains and is magnified beyond all imagination did not occupy the mind of the Buddha. When he was asked by a wandering monk if it was possible to illustrate by a simile the place called Nirvana, the Buddha replied:

> If a fire were blazing in front of you, would you know that it was?
> Yes, good Gautama.
> And would you know if it were to be put out?
> Yes, good Gautama.
> And on its being put out, would you know the direction the fire had gone out to from here—east, west, north, south?
> This question does not apply, good Gautama.

The Buddha then closed the discussion by pointing out that the question the ascetic has asked about existence after death was not rightly put either. "Feelings, perceptions, those impulses, that consciousness" by which one defines a human being have passed away from him who has attained Nirvana. "He is deep, immeasurable, unfathomable, as is the great ocean." *(Samyutta-Nikaya).*[34]

Later on, in Chapter Seven, I will come back to this issue.

4. WILLIAM BLAKE

Among the Anglo-Saxon authors, Blake (1757-1827) played a special role in Gibran's life. Most particularly Gibran agreed with Blake's *apocalyptic vision* of the world as the latter expressed it in his poetry and art. Also, Gibran followed the path of Blake in becoming a "poet of the Bible." Blake who was deeply touched by the life and teachings of Jesus, believed that in this world we could perceive the direct manifestation of the Divine presence, if we took away the scale of our eyes. Accordingly, the Divine is incarnated in everything. And the material world of our sense perceptions corresponds to the spiritual world. This correspondence is not a Platonic copy of a shadow to its light, but real for Blake, as it became for Gibran. The reason we lack this vision or enlightenment for seeing the unity between the material and the spiritual, is because, concluded Blake, as would later say Gibran, the vision of modern civilization is encrusting; symbolically speaking, we are caught up in the old Jerusalem and fail to see the new Jerusalem.[35] The man of the world creates polarities, social class differences, moral disparities, and speaks in a double language logic. Blake stresses this point in his two well-known metaphysical poems "The Little Black Boy," and "The Tyger."[36] But to the man of vision the polarities come together in the unity of God, who indwells in the tiniest matter as in the superior intelligences. Jesus, for Blake and Gibran, is a lived exemplar

56

who realized the Christian enlightenment, by perfecting through self-discipline and inner struggle his human and divine nature. But also, the poet—considered Blake and Gibran—is a man who has an apocalyptic vision of the world, seeks the correspondence between the transcendence and immanence of God, and who has a messianic mission in leading the people back to Truth.

No wonder that Gibran spoke favorably of Blake. "Blake is the God-man," he wrote. "His drawings are so far the profoundest things done in English—and his vision, putting aside his drawings and poems, is the most godly."[37] On the other hand, I find it true what Miss Haskell wrote in January 25, 1918 to Gibran: "Blake is mighty. The voice of God and the finger of God are in what he does.... He really feels closer to you, Kahlil, than all the rest."[38] This closeness in thinking and painting even Auguste Rodin noticed; that is why he called Gibran "The twentieth century Blake."

Finally, let me add, that Nietzsche, the Bible, Buddhism, and Blake were not the only foreign influences on Gibran. I think that Rousseau, Hugo, Lamartine, Voltaire, Bergson, Freud and many others, have provided Gibran with some insights. Since the scope of my research is to bring to light both the meaning of Gibranism and its place in history, I will then, when needed, cross-examine our author's idea with those who influenced his trend of thought. However, it is important to keep in mind, that an influence is always partial and temporary. Gibranism is a *Weltanschauung* of its own.

FOOTNOTES

[1] *S.P.,* p. 34.

[2] *See* "Chapter Five".

[3] *S.P.,* p. 14.

[4] Barbara Young, *This Man From Lebanon,* New York: A. Knopf, 1970, p. 186.

[5] *S.P.,* p. 20.

[6] I am in complete disagreement with Andrew Dib Sherfan who considers that the kind of love Gibran displays in this narration is Freudian. (Kahlil Gibran: *The Nature of Love,* New York: Philosophical Library, 1971, p. 26). Freudian love is a far more intricate and unconscious type than the love Gibran describes in *The Broken Wings.* Sublimation, cathexis, and sex are the unconscious processes that underline Freudian love; a love which by the way substitutes the pleasure principle with the reality principle. Whatever were the carnal desires of Gibran in *The Broken Wings* —and they are not non-existent—express merely romanticism, youth and idealism, but hardly Freudism. In Chapter Six I will come back on this issue.

[7] Accordingly, Gibran once confessed to Miss Haskell that the experiences and the personages reported in *The Broken Wings* were not his own. (*B.P.,* pp. 50-51) Now, to us historians, Miss Haskell's information sheds confusion on the biographical credibility of the novel. Whom should we believe? Miss Haskell who was told by Gibran? or the gossip folks of Bsherri who till today vaunt with pride that the great philosopher Gibran fell in love with one of their daughters, Miss Hala Daher whose family is still alive? As a biographer, this is my answer: there is plenty of doubt about Miss Haskell's knowledge of Gibran's early personal life; for one, whenever Gibran spoke to Haskell of his family, he overexaggerated with lies the story. For example, he did tell her the lie, that his father was wealthy and a tax collector in the Lebanese Government who unfortunately was trialed one day and found guilty of "embezzlement of taxes", but was then granted pardon, exiled etc. . . . (*B.P.,* pp. 20 - 21). Another reason why Haskell was misled about the real autobiographical value of *The Broken Wings,* has to do with the fact that Gibran never revealed to Haskell the names of his early love affairs, though he spoke freely about their adventures. (*B.P.,* pp. 68-69). Most probably, I believe Gibran denied in front of Haskell the autobiography of the novel, in order that he makes the dedication of the book to Haskell more genuine. Yet, in conclusion, I do concur with the biographers J. Sheban, A. Dib Sherfan,

A. Otto, the natives of Bsherri, etc., that *The Broken Wings* is an auto-biography of Gibran's first romance with the Lebanese girl, Hala Daher.

8 Andrew Dib Sherfan, Kahlil Gibran: *The Nature of Love*, New York: Philosophical Library, 1971, p. 26. Also, it should be noted that Gibran titled his book *Tears and Laughter*, but H. Nahmad when he translated it from Arabic he preferred for sake of phonetic the word "Smile" instead of "Laughter". In *A Self-Portrait* Gibran referres to it twice. (*S.P.*, p. 7 and p. 35).

9 *S.P.*, p. 4.

10 *MM.* pp. 69-71.

11 *The National Catholic Reporter*, July 21, 1968

12 Barbara Young, *This Man From Lebanon*, New York: A. Knopf, 1970, p. 56.

13 Cf. *The Portable Nietzsche*, ed. by Walter Kaufman, (New York: The Viking Press, 1968), p. 121; and *The Gospel of Luke*, Ch. 3, verse 23. In *The Voice of the Master* the hero prophet is 30 years old. (*V.M.*, p. 7).

14 *E.G.*, p. 11. About the complete triology of the prophet the third book that Gibran planned to publish along the same lines of *The Prophet* and *The Garden of the Prophet*, was *The Death of the Prophet*—whose content was to be about man's relation to God. Unfortunately, this book did not appear. (Cf. Barbara Young, *op. cit.*, p. 119). Fortunately, how-ever, Gibran did ponder occasionally on the theme of man's relation to God. In the text I have taken the liberty of calling *The Earth Gods* a work that deals with man and God, with the exception that this time it is God's relation to man which is under speculation.

15 Barbara Young, *This Man From Lebanon*, New York: A. Knopf, 1970, p. 13.

16 Mikhail Naimy, Kahlil Gibran, *His Life and His Work*, Beirut: Khayats, 1964, p. 194.

17 Barbara Young, *This Man From Lebanon*, New York: A. Knopf, 1970, p. 64; pp. 16-17; and p. 65.

18 *N.V.*, p. 19.

19 Ignace Kratchovski, *Monde Oriental*, Tome XXI, Fasc. 1-3.

20 P.J.E. Cachia, "Modern Arabic Literature" in *The Islamic Near East*, ed. by D. Grant, Toronto: University of Toronto Press, 1960, p. 284.

21 Sir Hamilton Gibb, *Studies on the Civilization of Islam*, Boston: Beacon Press, 1968, p. 261.

22 Quoted in Nadeem Naimy, *Mikhail Naimy. An Introduction*, Beirut: American University Press, 1970, p. 121.

23 *ibidem*, p. 123.

24 Gibran, *Twenty Drawings*, with an Introduction by Alice Raphael, New York: A. Knopf, 1970, p. 3.

25 R.A. Nicholson, *A Literary History of the Arabs*, Cambridge, En-gland: Cambridge University Press, 1969, pp. 304-313.

26 A.J. Arberry, *Aspects of Islamic Civilization*, Michigan: The Univer-sity of Michigan Press, 1967, pp. 73-118.

27 *B.P.*, p. 83.

28 *ibidem*, p. 93.

[29] *ibidem*, p. 36.

[30] "Thus Spoke Zarathustra", in *The Portable Nietzsche*, ed. by W. Kaufman, (New York: The Viking Press, 1968), "Prologue", pp. 121-137.

[31] *B.P.*, p. 83.

[32] *ibidem*, p. 344.

[33] *M.S.*, pp. 46-50.

[34] *The Wisdom of Buddhism*, ed. by Christmas Humphreys, New York: Random House, 1961. See also, *The Teachings of the Compassionate Buddha*, ed. by E.A. Burett, New York: The New American Library, 1955.

[35] *Selected Poetry and Prose of William Blake*, ed. by Northrop Frye, New York: The Modern Library, 1953, pp. 264-316.

[36] *ibidem*, p. 25, and p. 43.

[37] *B.P.*, p. 260.

[38] *ibidem*, p. 296.

CHAPTER FOUR

GIBRAN'S PHILOSOPHY OF AESTHETICS

A S A POET and an artist Gibran experienced psychologically the metaphysics of aesthetics, and like William Blake he successfully penetrated into the depth of the being of the beautiful merging at the surface with a literature and an art oriented toward the disclosure of the meaning of aesthetics in the life economy of the individual. The following two sections "The Essence of Poetry" and "The Essence of Art," discuss the concept of beautiful in Gibran's philosophy.

1. THE ESSENCE OF POETRY

Truth, the Goal of Poetry

In the history of high learning, poetry has become part of the "liberal arts" and especially of rational philosophy ever since Aristotle included it in logic. Poetry is not a vain work of imagination, but an intellectual art; and though the weakest form of argumentation, poetry by its essence aims at disclosing truth and leading the reader to truth. As Heidegger says, poetic thinking is "the foundation of truth" *(Stiftung der Wahrheit)*.[1] This is also the objective of Gibran the poet. The poet in the writings of our author appears as a conscientious mind who knows that he has a mission to accomplish among his fellowman. His duty is to teach "truth" which "is the will and purpose of God in man."[2]

61

In what way does poetry convey truth? According to the traditional answer given by Aristotle, the poet presents his truth in terms of images, metaphores and similes, for men naturally delight in images.[3] Gibran too as a writer uses the means of representation, imitations and parables in such a pleasing manner that he leads one to agree with his philosophical judgments. Yet, the images he uses are not empty entities. Rather, I should say, Gibran describes poetically the *historic* events of reality in view to induce the reader to perform an action. As such, though the style of Gibran belongs to the movement of romanticism, the content of his stories remind us of the "realist." Like Kafka, Sartre, Camus . . . Gibran's heroes live in a concrete situation and at a certain period of the Twentieth Century. They are committed and engaged in the political, religious and social ideologies of the contemporary world. It is important to bear this in mind for it proves that literature according to Gibran ceases to be mere fiction intended to embellish romantically life situations. The difference between romanticism and realism lies in their difference of approach to the existential world of man. The former uses a style, form and content heavily imbued with self-obsession. The romantic poet simply writes about his egoistic inner struggles and sufferances with almost no heed of what goes on outside of him. On the other hand, the realist hardly speaks of life in the first person; his literature is an impartial description of life endured by concrete individuals in as many idiosyncratic ways. Such approach makes literature committed *(engagée,* would say Sartre) in helping mankind in its present predicament.

Also Gibran's poetry fulfills the second principle of poetry stated by Aristotle. That is, poetry has the obligation to represent good human action as good and bad human action as bad. Aristotle writes:

> The objects the imitator represents are actions, with agents who are necessarily either good men or bad —the diversities of human character being nearly

62

always derivative from this primary distinction, since the line between virtue and vice is one dividing the whole of mankind.[4]

Gibran too, in his attempt of representing human action presents a judgment bearing on the morality of these acts. These judgments are universal in their applications, even though the story concentrates on the action of one particular individual living in a set of situations. For example, Gibran induces us to accept the universal judgment that marriages contracted by force or tradition lead to the downfall of genuine love, by giving us a particular representation of this in the person and action of Rose Hanne in *The Spirits Rebellious*. It should be kept in mind, however, that Gibran does not "moralize" poetry in the sense of imposing morality upon art, but as a poet, he observes faithfully human actions in view to qualify some deeds as good and others as bad. It comes to the philosopher of jurisprudence only to formulate and promulgate behaviors of morality, and anticipate the moral worth of conducts. Meanwhile, *the ethics of the poet is truth*. Gibran once said: "I shall follow the path to wherever my destiny and my mission for Truth shall take me."[5] Still, however, the poet's truth is not a matter of opinion as much as a constant search for the apodic's. The teleology of the poem is to "portray" phenomenologically the meaning of genuine reality in the way reality manifests itself. Hence Gibran writes: "Poetry is not an opinion expressed. It is a song that arises from a bleeding wound or a smiling mouth."[6]

Inspiration, the Mode of Poetic Thinking

Does the truth communicated through poetry a matter of logical syllogism? In other words, should poetry be reduced to the games and rules of logic? Basically, Gibran considers poetry the work of the spontaneous "thought feelings." Like the existentialists he does not give priority to abstract think-

63

ing. "Poetry is a flame in the heart, but rhetoric is flakes of snow. How can flame and snow be joined together?"[7] And again,

> Poets are two kinds; an intellectual with acquired personality, and an inspired one who was a self before his human training began. But the difference between intelligence and inspiration in poetry is like the difference between sharp fingernails that mangle the skin and ethereal lips that kiss and heal the body's sores.[8]

Gibran distinguishes sharply between "abstract thinking" and "inspiration" because he personally feels that abstract thinking fails to comprehend the *Gestalt* of reality. To quote Henri Bergson who held a similar discrimination between these two thinking processes, I would say that the "here and now" falls outside the realm of abstraction but lies within the range of intuition which is a sympathetic mode of conversing with reality in its personality. After all, abstraction, etymologically as well as operationally, comprehends bits of reality; it is a focus of the mind upon one aspect omitting the other correspondent portions that comprise the unity of a concrete existence. While abstract disciplines, for instance, sciences, proceed by dissecting a whole into its parts, e.g. water is composed of hydrogen and oxygen, "poetry is the understanding of the whole."[9]

Now the thinking that poetry exercises is *inspiration*. It is a type of knowing other than the work of "reason." Inspiration is the thinking of the "heart." For Gibran as for Pascal, the heart has a way of reflecting upon the world which is quite different form that of reason. Pascal writes: "The heart has its reason that reason itself does not know."[10]

The emotions involve the whole of the person, mind and body, and render the individual aware of the intersubjective relation which is experienced in the given moment. Were man by his metaphysical nature asocial, there would be no emotions. Feeling signifies to experience a psychic surge in front of something or someone. Even in the case of solitude the one-to-many relation is realized; for ideas are atoms animated by emotions. The latter are the ones that vivify ideas with powers and invest upon them the energy for actions. All this amounts to saying that the thinking process of poetry is a thought that "feels" with the heart the Beauty, Love, Sorrow and Truth encompassed in Life. Gibranism may well be labelled "irrationalism," a tag by which the existentialists are today referred; yet, irrationalism is not synonymous to anti-reason; it merely suggests that one does not sever "reason" from "feeling." Bluntly put, irrationalism is rather combative against rationalism, that famous philosophical movement begun by Descartes who stressed the separation between subject and object, and divorced man from his world, this world where the individual dwells and depends upon psychologically and physically. Really, Gibranism and existential irrationalism blend "reason" and "feeling" in the human. Witness how Gibran unites the two:

> Poetry is wisdom that enchants the heart.
> Wisdom is poetry that sings in the mind
> . . . enchant man's heart and at the same
> time sing in his mind, . . .[11]

One way of distinguishing between poetic thinking, *la logique du coeur,* and abstract scientific thinking, *la logique de la raison,* consists in that the latter makes use of "explanation" and "proofs" to convey its truth to his audience; yet, the truth of inspiration lies beyond proof. When Gibran writes "Inspiration will always sing; inspiration will never explain,"[12] he has in mind his own sayings that state: "The truth that needs proof is only half true,"[13] and again, "Truth is the daughter of Inspiration; analysis and debate keep the people away from Truth."[14]

If we ponder seriously on the meaning of these words, we see how much sense they make. The truth of poetic thinking is metaphysical in contrast to being epistemological, in that it depicts existence *qua* existence and not *qua* in the mind. The Middle Ages philosophers used to say, *ens verumque convertuntur*. Existence and truth are correlated. Now, poetry being a faithful representation of reality itself, does not need to prove the truth of reality, for what exists "is" what it is. We don't demonstrate existence for nothing is prior to "existence." Still however, instead of aspiring to becoming rigorous and metempirical, poetry lives by the heart, the senses and singing. Poetic thinking understands life better than abstract thinking. In his parable *The Scholar and the Poet*,[15] Gibran emphasizes the superiority of the poet's knowledge and stresses the fact that inspiration is both a thinking and a feeling about the "is." In Heidegger's own words, poetic thinking and philosophy transcend scientific thinking because the former are able to represent the whole meaning of a given individual existence: "Poetry . . . has so much world space to spare that in each thing—a tree, a mountain, a house, the cry of a bird—loses all indifference and common-placeness."[16] With these words, Heidegger, who incidentally possesses a philosophy of literature much similar to that of Gibran, discriminates between scientific knowledge and philosophical or poetic knowledge, on the basis that only poetry and philosophy encounter each reality in its entirety, while the empirical sciences with their methods aim at discovering the universal, the eternal and the immutable. As we know, each specific science approaches reality from one angle and after repeated experiments enunciates laws that prove to apply unconditionally to any member of a given class group. In Gibran's and Heidegger's opinion such attitude makes the individual reality lose its unique traits that separate it from the rest of the mass. And far from disclosing the "meaning" of that reality, science rather shatters it. Take for instance the smile: in scientific terminology a smile signifies the contraction of the jaw muscles, period. Yet, for philosophical and poetic thinking, a smile is more than a physiological activity; it expresses "joy," "happiness" or maybe "irony," depending on the "meaning" projected by the individual smiler.

In brief, the inspiration of poetry is something divine and in essence, naturalistic, for it is accessible to anyone who leads the life of Truth, Beauty and Love.

The Function of the Poet

Who is the poet? What is his role in modern society? To answer to these questions we have first to distinguish between the authentic and inauthentic poet. The latter is typically motivated by ambition. His verses lack truth and moral directiveness for the people. His poems are "full of noise and empty sounds."[17] Sincerity is shattered by the spirit of profit. In this respect, Gibran complains about modern poetry because it has become "a lapdog of the rich," a means to acquire "wordly goods," "a commodity"[18] and a "mere arrangement of words."[19] When Jean-Paul Sartre writes in *What is Literature?* "poetry is the loser . . . the poet is the man who commits himself to losing,"[20] he has in mind contemporary poetry. And like Gibran, he attributes this to the poet who has become utterly wordly.

The authentic poet, on the other hand, feels that he has a messianic mission among his brethren. He is, in the opinion of Gibran, "a" prophet sent to "enlighten"[21] the people about the will of God, Truth, Love and Beauty. The poet is not for himself but for *others*. In *A Poet's Voice* Gibran writes:

> Heaven fills my lamp with oil and I place it at my window to direct the Stranger through the dark. I do all these things because I live in them; and if destiny should tie my hands and prevent me from so doing, then death would be my only desire. For I am a poet, and if I cannot give, I shall refuse to receive.[22]

It is interesting to know that also J. P. Sartre conceives the function of the writer to be the "voice of the people." Note the similarity between this quote from Sartre and that of Gibran cited above:

> It is not true that one writes for oneself. That would be the worst frustration. . . . The operation of writing implies that of reading as its dialectical correlative and these two connected acts necessitate two distinct agents. . . .
> There is no art except for and by others.[23]

Now for Gibran, the messianic mission of the poet does not stop at the national boundaries of his native country but extends to all mankind. "The universe is my country and the human family is my tribe."[24]

If the poet, by profession identifies himself with the whole of mankind, irrespectively of the color of skin, political ideologies and ethnological boundaries it is because as William Blake would say, the poet fulfills the same role as the priest, namely, he mediates between the Gods and people. Such definition of the poet's function is also found in Heidegger, for whom the poet is the mediator between the gods and the humans, and Heidegger calls this: "In-between" *(Zwischen)*. The poet shows the openness *(offene)* of this "In between" between the divine and the human.[25] Furthermore, the poet is the shepherd of "language" as much of the being of truth.[26] Similar ideas are found in the writing of Gibran too.

> The means of reviving a language lie in the heart of the poet and upon his lips and between the creative power and the people. He is the wire that transmits the news of the world of spirit to the world of research. The poet is the father and mother of the language, which goes wherever he goes. When he dies, it remains prostrate over his grave, weeping and forlorn, until another poet comes to uplift it.[27]

It is clear from this passage that poetizing is that which makes language possible. Every poet is in close relation with the language of a historical people. And so long history will continue, as long poets will be present to guide their listeners. Consequently, Gibran sees the poet as the custodian of language. "The poet is the father and mother of language." Also, the poet employs three means for unveiling the essence of language: (1) through "feelings," for he alone has noble sentiments, (2) through speech; and (3) through the activity of writing. "The means of reviving a language lie in the heart of the poet and upon his lips and between his fingers." If Gibran ascribes to the poet the responsibility for protecting language it is because he sees, as Heidegger would say, *"Sprache ist das Haus des Seins"* ("Language is Being's House"). Only through language does the Gibranian poet communicate the saying of the gods.

It is noteworthy to elaborate a bit more on the relation between "language" and "being." Today people have almost lost touch with the meaning of the words of language. We learn and practice it unconsciously, somehow believing the fallacy committed by the Middle Age philosopher Abelard who said, language is but a *"flatus vocis"* (i.e. empty sounds). And yet, according to Gibran language reveals "reality"; it states explicity "the what is," no matter whether it is a "real," "fictitious" or "rational" being. If we had to rely only on our sense perceptions for deriving epistemologically the nature of "being" *(Sein),* then our acquaintance with the real would be quite limited, since our senses have a narrow reach. For instance, we cannot perceive with our naked eyes what lies five miles away, nor can we hear beyond a certain distance. Nevertheless, it is a fact that we claim acquaintance, let us say, with the "reality" of South America, although we might have never travelled across the boundaries of our parochial cities. How is this possible? Here it is either the spoken or written language that disclosed the "reality" of South America; spoken, if we heard some friends recounting to us their journeys to such land; written, if we read some geographical

69

books about it. At any rate, it is always language that discloses to us there being a South America. It is equally true, furthermore, that "language" more than "thinking" is the guarantor of "being." Along with Gibran we do not deny the temporal priority of thinking, for we think before we speak; but this is not the point. Had we been incapable to utter adverbially and expressively our thoughts, it would have followed that the "realities" known by thinking would have remained imprisoned in the luggage of thinking as a dead log, ineffective and solipsistically. Each one of us would have been locked up in himself with his small baggage of knowledge of "being." But fortunately, language fulfills brilliantly the means of "communication", in breaking down the barrier of isolation between the humans. One of the major differences between the animal kingdom and the human sphere consists in that the latter has devised "language" which in its turn resulted in the formation of society, the advent of scientific progress and the welfare of mankind. Once more, let us say with Gibran that thanks to "language," the "beings" in the thoughts of the many human mortals are transmittable in the extramental world where each individual is presented with the opportunity of discovering a bit more about the facets of "being" that others have grasped. Language is a *dialogue*. This is how the "reality" of the past is treasured and known about. If we have now understood why "Language is Being's House", then it gets apparent also why the poet, according to Gibran is *par excellence* the guardian of "language"; poetry is the written or spoken "language" of "being" and of the *Zeitgeist* to which the poet participates.

From whom does the poet get his authority to lead the people and protect language? He is "sent by the Goddess",[28] replies our author. And his duty is to "preach the Deity's Gospel."[29] The major and unique theme of God's gospel is "Love"[30] with its twofold expressions of "Truth" and "Beauty." At this point I have to add that Gibran's consideration of the poet is different from his teacher F. Nietzsche. On one hand, Nietzsche calls the poet liar; on the other hand, he does not believe that poets hold their inspiration from the gods. Nietzsche rather ridicules the gods. "... All gods are ... poets' prevarications."[31] While Nietzsche adopts the atheistic standpoint, Gibran at the manner of W. Blake moves to name the poet "an angel"[32] an the "holy."[33] The poet is human like his mortal fellowmen, yet, he has a divine vocation. In the words of Victor Hugo, whom our author venerated passionately, the poet is the messenger of Heaven amidst men. And contrary to Kierkegaard's logical fallacy, not all the poets are attracted to describing Beauty in a sensuous Epicurean fashion; the authentic poet sees that God's Gospel is transmitted adequately to His people. By way of comparative philosophy, I remind the reader that Gibran's philosophy of poetry corresponds to the third stage of life, called faith, of which the Danish philosopher Soren Kierkegaard spoke, and not to the aesthetic stage. It was Kierkegaard's contention that there are three ways of leading life. One is the aesthetic; this is the life of sense-experience typified by Don Juan. The second stage is the ethical, wherein the individual adjusts his existence according to some universal principles of morality. Socrates is the hero. Finally, the third stage was known to Kierkegaard as faith. The individual is totaly related to God. Abraham is the exemplar. It is interesting to see the resemblance in thinking between Gibran and the founder of existentialism, Kierkegaard. In the next section, the concept of God will be once more underlined in reference to Beauty and the role of the artist. Gibran was deeply religious like Kierkegaard.

The Fate of the Poet in Society

One would presume that poets are appraised by their people because of their divine messages, yet, retorts Gibran this is not the case. People's incredulity and persistent ignorance have made of the poets solitary figures. In *The Broken Wings* we read: "Poets are unhappy people, for, no matter how

71

high their spirits reach, they will still be enclosed in an envelope of tears."[34] The poet sheds tears because people close their heart and mind to the teaching of God's gospel. In consequence, the poet is a perfect stranger in this world, among his people and to himself. His soul yearns to depart from his body and to rejoin the after life. Since "there is no one in the Universe who understands the language"[35] of the angels that he speaks. *The Poet's Death is his Life* argues that death is the deliverance of the poet from the bondage of human company. On earth, the poet is as good as dead for no one of the mob enables him to realize his sacred duty, namely, allows him to teach truth. What kills the poet, the precursor of humanity, is "man's ignorance."[36] This is indeed what has afflicted mostly all the prophets. Their body extinguished because of the psychological frustrations they suffered from their surroundings.

It is said that Gibran believed that poets commit sin only when they deny their own nature[37] which is Godlike. Actually, none of Gibran's heroes committed such a sin, in that none accepted to compromise the divine teaching imparted to him with the wordly pleasures and man-made social laws, if even this disaccord cost him his life.[38] And incidentally, all the poets of Gibran seem to disagree with the precepts of their politicians. They break the rules fabricated by the government or religious ministers. In simple words, the poets of Gibran are revolutionary ones. In depth, style, form and content, the literature of our author is rebellious. In his own words, ". . . I Like in literature; rebellion. . . . And the three things I hate in it are imitation, distortion, and conformity."[39]

2. THE ESSENCE OF ART

Gibran's Art

Gibran the artist and Gibran the poet philosopher are not two different persons; what Gibran conveys through his metaphysical poems, he succeeds in representing through his art. In his art work and writings he is a mystic with a special evangelic message. And as he imitates the biblical style in his prose, so he imitates the biblical approach in his paintings. According to Anni Salem Otto, Gibran employs the parabolical method in both his art and his paintings. Now, it is understood that the parable is characteristic of the Holy Scriptures. It is important to keep in mind that the Bible has always been for Gibran as it was for William Blake, a source of prophetic inspiration that presented a visionary narrative of the life of man between creation and apocalypse.

Far from being a mere collection of pencil drawings or papers brushed with some water colors, Gibran's art encompasses a message; in depth, line, shapes, shades, shadows and forms his paintings describe concrete human situations. They recount a story and hide a moral lesson. Typically, his art portrays only human forms. Gibran never painted an apple, a prairie or the sun down, but people. Even in the rare cases where the symbol of the drawing stands for a "rock" or the "earth" Gibran draws human bodies in such a way that they figurate the meaning of the material object.[40] Yet, on the other side, our author in his prose poems will borrow ample metaphors from nature to represent a human feeling or thought. Here are some expressions: "The tree of my heart is heavy with fruit," "My heart overflows with the wine of the ages," etc. . . .[41] His art and poetry confirm what I said previously about his anthropomorphic *Weltanschauung*. As a mystic of a school different from Plato or the ascetics, he does not regard matter as inferior to volatile spirituality. Nature has human shapes, and *vice versa* man has the shape of nature. The *Garden of the Prophet* abounds with this anthropomorphic view of reality.

> You and the stone are one. There is only a difference in heart-beats. Your heart beats a little faster, does it my friend? Ay, but it is not so tranquil.[42]

73

At this stage, we ought to remember that W. Blake held a similar philosophy of art and philosophy of poetry. Northrop Frye, in his lengthy introduction on Blake, repeatedly insists that Blake's "art is the attempt of the trained and disciplined human mind to present this concrete, simple, and outrageously anthropomorphic view of reality."[43] Now, the real motives for Gibran's anthropomorphic art are to be found in his cosmological ecology and environmentalism, much like what is happening today. His love for nature and belief that both nature and man are the creation of God, explain why he portrayed in his art and depicted in his poems the man-nature coexistence. Ecologists and environmentalists may estimate the essay *Nature and Man* of great importance. Here are some excerpts:

> One of the flowers raised her gentle head and whispered, "We weep because Man will come and cut us down, and offer us for sale in the markets of the city." ...
> And I heard the brook lamenting like a widow mourning her dead child and I asked, "Why do you weep, my pure brook?"
> And the brook replied, "Because I am compelled to go to the city where Man contemns me and spurns me for stronger drinks and makes of me a scavenger for his offal, pollutes my purity, and turns my goodness to filth."
> And I heard the birds grieving, and I asked, "Why do you cry, my beautiful birds?" And one of them flew near, and perched at the tip of a branch and said, "The sons of Adam will soon come into this field with their deadly weapons and make war upon us as if we were their mortal enemies ...
> . . . "Why must Man destroy what Nature has built?"[44]

Besides the portraits he made of many eminent figures,

Gibran painted a lot of human naked bodies. He never drew a body clothed. When Miss Haskell asked him why he painted bodies naked, Gibran answered,

> Because life is naked. A nude body is the truest and noblest symbol of life. If I draw a mountain as a heap of human forms or paint a waterfall in the shape of tumbling human bodies, it is because I see in the mountain a heap of living things, and in the waterfall a precipitate current of life.[45]

What the German existentialist Karl Jaspers said of art: "The fine arts make our visible world speak to us"—applies quite well to Gibran's art. The mission of authentic art according to our author, is not to be for the sake of the artist's satisfaction, but expresses cultural, historical and educational ambitions. For one, the artist "is" and "lives" in a historical context; his art records and projects the "climate of the age" which he shares; secondly, by profession the artist's work purpose to influence the thoughts of the viewers and to contribute along with the politicians and businessmen to the making of history. That is, artists influence fashions, styles and to a certain extent the behaviors of a people. For instance, movies, fashion designers, music composers, painters and architects do have an impact on people's conduct. Art is *creative* of something new which never existed. Gibran writes,

> If you think more deeply on the subject, you will find that arts reflect and influence customs, styles, religious and social traditions—every aspect of our life.[46]

Elsewhere Gibran states explicitly that art is not to be imitative, otherwise creativity fades away. To copy is to repeat what exists already, but creativity means originality.

Art arises when the secret vision of the artist and the manifestation of nature agree to find new shapes.[47]

The artist's secret vision reaches not the phenomenal appearances of the shell of reality but peeps into the noumenal of nature. For every phenotype level, there is the genotype; to every surface there must be a bottom; beyond every phenomenal manifestation there is the noumenal revelation. Art penetrates into the immanence of nature in order to unveil what our bare eyes cannot see. This is called the *meaning* of existence.

Furthermore, the purpose of art is to transport the audience toward the discovering of God the creator. Art portrays the beauty of humanity and reality with the intention of revealing the presence of the Maker of Beauty, although sometimes the artist's intention may be different. It takes courage and faith to experience through art the existence of the metempirical. Gibran writes:

Art is a step from nature toward the Infinite.[48]

and again

Art is a step in the Known toward the unknown.[49]

Finally, when Gibran published in 1919 *Twenty Drawings,* Miss Alice Raphael wrote an introduction in which she acknowledged that Gibran's art is an attempt to unify the East and West. In that he engages in the struggle of reconciling the old and the new, the past and the present fashions, traditions and novelties. Also, in Miss Raphael's opinion our artist's work "owes more to the findings of Da Vinci than it does to any of our modern insurgents."[50] However, this does not limit his scope in search for new themes and in their realizations. If we had to classify him in a school of art, he would be at the "dividing line of East and West, of the symbolist and the ideationist."[51] Indeed, as a symbolist, he is an intuitive artist who follows his instinctive flair for truth and while his art is concerned with the life of the inner-self, it projects a moral lesson; but as an ideationist or pre-Raphaelite, he goes into the minute details of the situation in which the human in question is entangled with a spirit of sincerity, and delicacy of finish. Here is the long text of Miss Raphael:

> The quality of the East and West are blended in him with a singular felicity of expression, so that while he is the symbolist in the true sense of the word, he is not affixed to traditional expression, as he would be if he were creating in the manner of the East, and though he narrates a story as definitely as any pre-Raphaelites, it is without any fanfare of historical circumstances or any of the accompaniment of symbolic accessories. In his art there is no conflict whether emotion shall sway the thought, because both are so equally established that we are not conscious of one or the other as dominant. They co-exist in harmony and the result is an expression of sheer beauty in which thought and feeling are equally blended. In this fusion of two opposing tendencies the art of Gibran transcends the conflicts of school and is beyond the fixed conceptions of the classic or romantic tradition.[52]

The Manifoldness of Beauty

In all of Gibran's portraits, as well as in his writing, *Beauty* is the incentive force and the final arbiter of his productions. What is the aesthetics and metaphysical import of the beautiful in his mind? Gibran gives many and varied definitions of Beauty. He defines it as "truth," "a timeless language," "solve the problem of human existence," "the visible, manifest and perfect handiwork of God," etc. . . .

77

These definitions of Beauty however, escape any etymological or nominal definitions of the logical textbooks. Frankly speaking, Gibran does not think that the essence of Beauty could be comprehended by means of the logical method of definition. Only the process of phenomenological description can unveil the meaning of Beauty. Applying Husserl's phenomenological method, I have found in the texts of Gibran many approaches to the problem of Beauty. At least three major methodological conceptions are elaborated. On one hand, Gibran speaks of Beauty in terms of psychology; on the other hand, he undertakes the analysis from the standpoint of theodicy; finally, he tackles the issue with a metaphysical outlook.

Psychologically speaking, Beauty is a matter of sensation, feeling and experience. Beauty bespeaks to the heart and the spirit without using the language of proof or analysis.

> Only our spirits can understand beauty, or live and grow with it. It puzzles our minds; we are unable to describe it in words; it is a sensation that our eyes cannot see . . .[53]

Moreover, the aesthetic experience in Gibran's philosophy of art, is not a privilege of artists solely; every mortal is liable to enjoy it. "Beauty . . . is a timeless language, common to all humanity."[54] Each one of us is at sometime an artist in his own way. The professional artists are merely those who experience Beauty longer than the average men and are capable to project in paintings, music or architecture the forms of Beauty.

As a psychological experience, Beauty could be either the result of joy or originate out of sorrow. Happy movies as well as sad movies always move us deeply emotionally. This is why for Gibran Beauty is found in both a tear and a smile combined. "Beauty is that harmony between joy and sorrow which begins in our holy of holies and ends beyond the scope of our imagination."[55]

Unlike Leibniz, Gibran does not profess an exaggerated optimism in that our world is the best, and unlike Schopenhauer he does not teach pessimism in that our world is the worst one. Gibran's philosophy is realistic. He knows that life is a mingle of happiness and suffering. But these two are not contradictory to each other, rather complementary. Hence, Beauty, the expression of life is

> a magnificence combined of sorrow and joy, it is the Unseen which you see, and the Vague which you understand, and the Mute which you hear—it is the Holy of Holies that begins in yourself and ends vastly beyond earthly imagination.[56]

As a general rule, Gibran consents with the philosophers of aesthetics that the aesthetic value is *subjective*. Hence Beauty is interpreted and defined in different ways and manners according to each individual's conception. In *The Prophet,* Gibran attributes these variations of experience to the pragmatic interests each individual has in life. Beauty at this point becomes an emotional drive for "needs unsatisfied."[57] In other words, psychologically, the value discovered in the object, event or person is an unconscious projection of the inner-self. "The appearance of things changes according to the emotions and thus we see magic and beauty in them while the magic and beauty are really in ourselves."[58] This means that ugliness too is a subjective quality. As the old adage says, Beauty and ugliness are in the eyes of the beholder. "Beauty is not in the face; Beauty is in the heart."[59] What is commonly termed ugly is a sentiment in a heart totally enslaved by prejudices, pride and selfishness.

> Is it not that which you have never striven to reach, into whose heart you never desired to enter, that you deem ugliness?

> If ugliness is aught, indeed, it is but the scales upon

our eyes, and the wax filling our ears.
Call nothing ugly, my friend, save the fear of a soul
in the presence of its own memories.[60]

Finally, in essence, the aesthetic experience for Gibran, in addition to bringing immediate pleasure and satisfaction by revealing certain experiential aspects of reality, it can also fortify us in various ways to meet the practical demands of life. Beauty is *therapeutic*. It stimulates or soothes us; it changes the rate of the heart beat, renews our spirits, exciting us and giving us courage to overcome the existential vacuum that dashes upon us at the time of despair. In *The Broken Wings* Gibran tells us that after his friend gave him some information about the misfortunes that Selma Karamy had to encounter in her life, Gibran's friend "turned his head toward the window as if he were trying to solve the problems of human existence by concentrating on the beauty of the universe."[61]

From the *metaphysical standpoint,* Gibran holds like the scholastic philosophers, the thesis which asserts that Beauty is a transcendental predicament of being. "When you reach the heart of life you shall find beauty in all things, even in the eyes that are blind of beauty."[62] This amounts to saying that what is called ugly is but a psychological subjective emotion aroused either in the presence of a deformed physiology or due to some personal indispositions; yet, existence *qua* existence is "pulchritude." In other words, real Beauty is not essentially what we experience through sense perceptions, for these may well be defective and thus yield false information about reality, as for example, blindness, color blindness or deafness. This point is most vital, for Gibran's philosophy concentrates more on delineating the metaphysical meaning of Beauty than on its psychological effect. In the parable titled "Faces" he writes:

I know faces, because I look through the fabric
my own eyes weaves, and hold the reality beneath.[63]

Somewhere else he explains that Beauty is in being in as much being is Beauty. He also distinguishes between the physical Beauty and ontological Beauty, rating the latter superior to the former. As I already said, Beauty defined only in terms of sense appreciations leaves room for possible error, since the senses are arbitrary and very subjective. Actually, rather than enlarging our horizon of the understanding, Beauty captured by the senses may eventually enslave us and later on torture us. For instance, this is the unfortunate happening of those who define love in terms of physical prettiness; in Ronsard poetic words, physical Beauty is momentary, the rose is not rose forever, it will fade someday. Whence arises disappointments, frustrations and infidelity. In Kierkegaard's vernacular sensitive Beauty belongs to the aesthetic stage. On the other hand, however, Beauty, experienced through the spectacles of metaphysics, is a resigning attitude of the mind in accepting existence for what it "is," such Beauty frees us from the spells of the domination of the physical contours of Beauty. Here it is the heart, namely the spontaneous thought-feeling in contrast to the calculative thinking and the senses, that is involved.

Great beauty captures me, but a beauty still greater frees me even from itself.

Beauty shines brighter in the heart of him who longs for it than in the eyes of him who sees it.[64]

Another way to show the transcendental relation between being and Beauty consists in correlating Beauty with truth. In the essay *Nature and Man,* we read: "Is Truth Beauty? Is Beauty Truth?"[65] Here Gibran is not so much questioning doubtfully the relation between Beauty and truth. For in his mind, to use Aristotle's terminology, the relation is not predicamental but transcendental. A predicamental term signifies that the term is restricted in its application to a certain "kind" of things; while the transcendental applies to "all" existences unconditionally, and is interchangeable with existence (being). Although Gibran does not make use of such technical language, he does nevertheless convey this meaning when in the poem *Song of Beauty* he writes: "I [Beauty] am a Truth, O people, yea, a Truth."[66] And again in the essay *Before the Throne of Beauty,* Gibran emphasizes that Beauty leads the investigator to truth. "A beauty . . . is a stepping-stone for the wise to the throne of living truth."[67]

It is worthwhile to ponder seriously on the meaning of these words in order to bring to light the depth of Gibran's philosophy. The metaphysics of truth in contrast to that of falsity entails that the mind asserts reality in the way reality is. For what exists is what it is itself, and not other than itself. Being is harmonious and congruent with itself. To acknowledge reality for what it is, is to know truthfully reality. Now, what is truthfully itself does not involve contradiction nor inconsistency with itself, but is well ordered and harmoniously structured in its very being. Hence, it is Beautiful, for Beauty "is" harmony, order and truthfulness. Such is the backbone of Gibran's logic which claims that metaphysically, "ugliness" is a subjective psychological emotional uptightness and never a possible characteristic of existence. Objective Beauty is not of the province of the sense perceptions.

> Beauty . . . is not the image you would see nor the song you would hear, but rather an image you see though you close your eyes and a song you hear though you shut your ears. It is . . . a garden for *ever* in bloom and a flock of angels for *ever* in flight.[68]

Finally, Gibran's third approach to Beauty is from the *standpoint of theodicy*. It is obvious to Gibran's mysticism as it was for Plato, that Beauty found in nature is the handiwork of God. In his short essay *Creation,* Gibran explains the mystery of Creation as a divine act of Beauty. "The God separated a spirit from Himself and fashioned it into Beauty"[69] Beauty on earth is the reminder of God the Invisible. If someone wants a proof of God's existence, Gibran retorts let him see Beauty. In case now, he still doubts of the veracity of God, let him then take Beauty, answers Gibran, as his new religion. To worship Beauty is to worship God.

> Are you troubled by the many faiths that Mankind professes? Are you lost in the valley of conflicting beliefs? Do you think that freedom of heresy is less burdensome than the yoke of submission, and the liberty of dissent safer than the stronghold of acquiescence?
> If such be the case, then make Beauty your religion, and worship her as your godhead; for she is the visible, and manifest and perfect handiwork of God. Cast off those who have toyed with godliness as if it were a show joining together greed and arrogance, but believe instead in the divinity of Beauty that is at once the beginning of your worship of Life, and the source of your hunger for Happiness.[70]

I remind the reader that this quotation does not advocate a Rousseauian naturalistic religion, rather like Pascal Gibran is proposing a proof of God by playing the game of "Wage." It is better at least to worship Beauty in nature than to be an arrogant atheist, who may lose everything if after death God should exist. Also, this quote suggests a proof of God reminiscent of the early Greek philosophers who believed in the Divine because of their amazement and admiration in the face of the harmony and Beauty found among the celestial and terrestrial systems. The intention of Gibran being an attempt to unravel the presence of God, we understand now why in all his art work and literature he pursues Beauty. Beauty is the acid test of God's existence.

FOOTNOTES

[1] Heidegger, M., *Holzwee,* Frankfurt am Main: Klosterman, 1957, p. 62.

[2] *S.S.* p. 59.

[3] Aristotle, *Poetica,* 1448b 4 - 24.

[4] *ibidem,* 1448a 1 - 5.

[5] *S.S.,* p. 59.

[6] *S.F.* p. 21.

[7] *S.S.,* p. 15. Elsewhere he writes: "Thinking is always the stumbling stone to poetry." (*S.S.,* p. 24).

[8] *S.S.,* p. 33. From this passage it is apparent that Gibran would never classify poetry among the treatises of logic as Aristotle did.

[9] *S.S.,* p. 15.

[10] Blaise Pascal, *Pensée,* Paris: Librairie Generale Francaise, 1962, p. 236, No. 477. "Le coeur a ses raisons, que la raison ne connait point." (Engl. transl. by the author).

[11] *S.F.* p. 23. That Gibranism is not anti-intellectualism can best be seen in the essay "Of Reason and Knowledge", which stresses the importance of reason in our life. If a man lets himself be governed by "impulses" and "passions" alone, then his existence becomes animalistic and impetuous. Hence he writes: "Reason is a prudent minister, a loyal guide, and a wise counsellor ... Be wise—let Reason, not impulse, be your guide." (*V.M.* p. 53).

[12] *S.F.,* p. 23.

[13] *S.S.,* p. 18.

[14] *S.S.,* p. 7.

[15] *F.R.,* pp. 47-49.

[16] Heidegger, M., *Introduction to Metaphysics,* Garden City, New York: Doubleday & Co., Inc., 1961, p. 22. The reason I make ample references to outside writers, is simply to show the relevance and depth of Gibranism.

[17] *V.M.,* p. 31.

[18] *Th.M.,* pp. 72-73.

[19] *S.S.,* p. 29.

[20] Robert D. Cumming (ed.) *The Philosophy of Jean-Paul Sartre,* New York: Random House, Inc. 1966, p. 370.

[21] *S.S.,* p. 29.

[22] *T.L.,* p. 81

[23] Robert D. Cumming (ed.), *The Philosophy of Jean-Paul Sartre,* New York: Random House, Inc., 1966, p. 375.

[24] *T.L.,* p. 81.

[25] Heidegger, M., "Holderlin" in *Qu'est-ce-que la Metaphysique?* Paris: Gallimard, 1951, p. 250.

[26] *ibiden,* pp. 243-244.

[27] *S.S.,* pp. 51-52.

[28] *T.L.,* p. 28; p. 44.

[29] *ibiden,* p. 44. See also *V.M.,* p. 31. For Heidegger the poet and the thinker *(penseur)* have some commonesses, but, are not identical. "Only poetry stands in the same order as philosophy and its thinking, though poetry and thought are not the sense thing." *(An Introduction to Metaphysics,* Garden City, New York: Doubleday & Co., Inc., 1961, p. 21). Gibran too makes this distinction, however, for him poetic thinking surpasses philosophic thinking. According to Gibran, philosophy is metempirical *(S.S.,* p. 13), is an "intellectual prostitute" *(S.F.,* p. 64). finally, but not the least, an intellectual perusal of "man's mind, his deeds and his desires" *(S.F.,* p. 65).

[30] See "A poet's voice" in *T.S.,* pp. 167-174.

[31] Nietzsche, F., "Thus Spoke Zarathustra," in *The Portable Nietzsche,* ed. by Walter Kaufman, New York: The Viking press, 1969, Part II, sec. 17, p. 240.

[32] *T.L.,* p. 44.

[33] T.S., Introduction by Robert Hillyer, p. V.

[34] Quoted in *The Wisdom of Gibran,* ed. by Joseph Sheban, New York: Philosophical Library, 1966, p. 59.

[35] *S.H.,* p. 47.

[36] *T.L.,* p. 29.

[37] *T.S.,* Introduction by Robert Hillyer, p. V.

[38] In his short play "Assilban" we are told how a poet may commit the sin of renegation against his divine vocation. The following passage enumerates the possible ways of derogation: "There are . . . many poets . . . They all sell their voices, their thoughts and their conscience for a coin, for a meal, for a bottle of wine. . . . They are like talking machines of sorrow and joy. If the occasion does not call for then, these machines will be set aside like used utensils. . . . I blame them for not scorning the pretty and trifling. I blame them for not preferring *death to humiliation.*" *(S.S.,* pp. 89-90. The italics are mine).

[39] *S.S.,* p. 8.

[40] See the paintings in *The Parables of Kahlil Gibran* (by A. Salem Otto, New York: The Citadel Press, 1963), p. 108 and p. 142.

[41] *V.M.,* p. 22.

[42] *G.P.,* p. 36.

[43] Frye, N., (ed.), *Selected Poetry and Prose of Blake,* New York: Random House, Inc. 1953, Intr. xxviii.

[44] *V.M.* pp. 86-87.

[45] Naimy, Mikhail, *Kahlil Gibran. His Life and His Work,* Beirut: Khayats, p. 59.

[46] *S.S.,* p. 78.

[47] *S.S.,* p. 24.

[48] *S.F.,* p. 83.

[49] *S.S.*, p. 20.

[50] *T.D.*, Introduction by Miss Alice Raphael, p. 6.

[51] *ibidem*, p. 9.

[52] *ibidem*, p. 9.

[53] *B.W.*, p. 24

[54] *ibidem*, p. 23.

[55] *T.L.*, p. 69.

[56] *ibidem*, p. 69.

[57] *P.*, p. 75

[58] *B.W.*, p. 41.

[59] *M.S.*, p. 75.

[60] *G.P.*, pp. 26-28.

[61] *B.W.*, p. 16. In the poem "Song of Beauty," Gibran once more recognizes the psychotherapeutic effect of Beauty on a soul filled with anguish. "Youth beholds me, his toil is forgotten, and his life becomes a stage for sweet dreams." (*T.S.*, p. 161). Many times it is enough to glance at a field of beautiful roses or listen to a beautiful music in order to distract the mind from an idea that causes anxiety.

[62] *S.F.*, p. 26.

[63] *M.M.*, p. 52.

[64] *S.F.*, p. 67.

[65] *V.M.*, p. 85.

[66] *T.S.*, p. 161.

[67] *ibidem*, p. 52.

[68] *P.*, p. 76 I have underlined the words "ever" for it emphasizes that Beauty like being are unchangeable, universal and eternal. Since Gibran is a poet he uses the term "nature" to mean "being," the concept of the metaphysicians. Here is the passage where he explicates the transcendental relation between "nature and Beauty:" My life [it is the Nymph who speaks] is sustained by the world of Beauty which you will see, wherever you rest your eyes, and this Beauty is Nature itself" . . . (*T.L.*, p. 68).

[69] *T.L.*, p. 15.

[70] *V.M.*, pp. 27-28.

CHAPTER FIVE

GIBRAN'S PHILOSOPHY OF LAW AND SOCIETY

F OR MOST contemporary poets, and not for Sartre alone, literature ought to become "committed"—*Une littérature engagée.* Literature which is not committed is not literature at all. As an "engaged" writer, Gibran has composed many poetries and parables that are social in depth.

He mainly developed a hermeneutics of law, wherein he portrays the pathos of present day society. Methodically speaking, however, Gibran likes to introduce us to his study of legalism through the narration of concrete life-events.

But also, Gibran had a historical and nationalistic motive for tackling the issue of "justice" as practiced within the field of the legislative branch of government. With his lucid analysis of legality he aimed at attacking the types of decayed laws that the Ottoman Turks were enforcing in Lebanon his native land.

To insure a good presentation of Gibran's thought, I proceed to divide this chapter into three sections. (1) Humanistic Social Contract; (2) The Issue of Law; (3) Parables on Authority.

1. HUMANISTIC SOCIAL CONTRACT

The Zeitgeist of Modern Society

Like J. J. Rousseau's *Social Contract* Gibran did not extoll our social ways of behaving. To do this would be easy for him. The mission of the critic is not to praise virtues already acquired but to exhort people as to what should be done in order that imperfections be removed.

Gibran, the social philosopher instead of concentrating his polemic around the evils of technology as do most existential thinkers, v. g. Heidegger, Jaspers, Marcel and Erich Fromm —he prefers to attack people's social ways of behaving. Yet he agrees with the existentialists that technology is being misused to the point that nowadays the machine is no more a mere means for higher ends, but has become the supreme value, and man, the inventor, is the slave of his own invention. Definitely, Gibran is not suggesting us to close down the factories, as if the realm of the technical was evil in itself or that progress at the technological level were the very reason of all types of social inequalities, and sins against clean Mother Nature. On the contrary, to pretend that this were the solution for solving the present crisis mounting up in the human and environmental spheres, would be to relapse into the superstitious ways of our ancestors. The real blame comes to man alone who abuses intentionally of the merits of technology for the satisfaction of his egoistic desires. Thus, the spirit of technocracy affects psychologically the technocrat's *Weltanschauung*. In his relation with others, he treats them as subordinates, less valuable economically than his industrial plant. In his relation with his Creator, he wishes to occupy God's place, to repeat His deeds, to reorganize a man-made cosmos according to man-made laws of reason, efficiency and foresight—this is the ambition of the twentieth century technocrat that Gibran denounced vehemently when he wrote

> when man invents a machine, he runs it; then the machines begin to run him, and he becomes the slave of his slave.[1]

One mischief that he attributed to the misuse of technological invention is the manufacture of technological weapons.

He immensely deplored their discovery and considered them an indication of a step backward into primitiveness; killing one another is no sign of progress, civilization or education, but a direct manifestation of regression to the barbaric stage.

> The world has returned to savagery. What science and education have created is being destroyed by the new primitives. We are now like the prehistoric cave dwellers. Nothing distinguishes us from them save our machines of destruction and our improved techniques of slaughter.[2]

For Gibran, a Christian philosopher, the world of the technocrat has rejected theocentrism and replaced it with anthropocentrism. For example, what religion teaches about "procreation," the technocrat preaches as "fabrication." In contemporary vernaculars, "idolatry," "pantechnism," "autolatry," "technolatry," and "technomia" are all rubrics that describe the *behaviors* of the technocrat.

But asides the technocrat's wrongdoings, Gibran elaborates on the lack of spirituality in modern society. In a short essay *The Tempest*, we read the story of a man called Yussif El Fakhri who at thirty years of age withdrew from the tumult of society and took residence in a hermitage away from the town. The name of Yussif was a subject of conversation among the citizens of the city, especially since Yussif never left his solitude. One day a young man hearing the tales advanced by the gossips of the town decided to go and visit Yussif. While he was on his way, a tempest of rain, wind and thunder arose. Instead of discouraging, the young lad thought that the storm was a good excuse for him to ask refuge at Yussif's house. When he reached the hermitage, he knocked at the door and pleaded to be received inside the house until the tempest calmed down. Once accepted inside, in a cold way by Yussif, the adolescent asked the man what made him flee society. Yussif's reply was straight

89

and explicit. Yussif first denied that he retreated in the mountains in order to meditate on religion or God. God can be worshipped anywhere, even in the midst of the turmoils of the city. By such token, Yussif, who personifies Gibran, refused to call himself a *misanthrope*. (It is capital to keep this in mind, for none of Gibran's heroes are haters of human company. At this point Gibran agrees with the Danish philosopher Soren Kierkegaard in that "It is dangerous to isolate oneself too much, to evade the bonds of society.")[3]

Yet, the reasons Yussif enumerated to his unexpected visitor reflected the same reasons that have irritated today's European existentialists, most particularly Kierkegaard, Dostoyevski, Tolstoy, Gabriel Marcel and Franz Kafka—namely, it is the lack of spirituality, human understanding and responsibility on the part of the people. Thus, Yussif exclaimed,

> I left civilization because I found it to be an old corrupt tree, strong and terrible, whose roots are locked into the obscurity of the earth and whose branches are reaching beyond the cloud; but its blossoms are of greed and evil and crime, and its fruit is of woe and misery and fear. . . .

> . . . . No, my brother, I did not seek solitude for religious purposes, but solely to avoid the people and their laws, their teachings and their traditions, their ideas and their clamour and their wailing.

> I sought solitude in order to keep from seeing faces of men who sell themselves and buy with the same price that which is lower than they are, spiritually and materially.

> . . . . I deserted the world and sought solitude because I became tired of rendering courtesy to those multitudes who believe that humility is a sort of weakness, and mercy a kind of cowardice, and snobbery a form of strength.

. . . . I ran from the office-seekers who shatter the earthly fate of the people while throwing into their eyes the golden dust and filling their ears with sounds of meaningless talk.

I departed from the ministers who do not live according to their sermons, and who demand of the people that which they do not solicit of themselves.

. . . . I came to this far corner of God's domain for I hungered to learn the secrets of the Universe, and approach close to the throne of God.[4]

This lucid litany of societal woes acclaimed by Gibran is so relevant in itself, because it portrays the misconducts of our culture and echoes the cry of our youth. To limit myself to one geographical spot, I see, for instance, great similarities between Gibranism and today's American youth who are totally dissatisfied with the traditional sets of values of their forefathers. The U.S. youngsters are searching for spiritual values in contrast to the material aspirations of the previous generations to the cost of trespassing the social laws established for centuries, and renegating if needed their parental ties concluded in the generation gap. Wouldn't you admit that many of those sincere hippies resemble to Yussif?

In another story *Khalil the Heretic,* we are told that a youth abandoned the convent life, because of his discontentment with "this age of falsehood, hypocrisy and corruption"[5] practiced by the very priests, supposedly the emissaries of God. Gibran calls his present society "sick."[6] And elsewhere he labels figuratively society with all its inventions and masks: "decayed teeth."[7] Gibran's terrible indictment of society finds ground among many philosophers; thus, Buber, a contemporary philosopher, recognizes that the trouble with our society consists in the phenomena of "lie" which modern man has invented and "introduced into nature,"[8] as synonymous to truth.

91

So far I have compared Gibran's social analysis to the existentialists mode of thinking about our technological world. However, from the historical standpoint of view, Gibran is closer to Rousseau than to any other philosopher when it comes to his hermeunetics of the *Zeitgeist* of present society. I may even say without fear of historical error that Gibran was immensely inspired by Rousseau when he undertook his criticism of society. Actually, many of the contemporaries were themselves influenced by Rousseau's social philosophy. For instance Leo Tolstoy and Fyodor Dostoyevski, to whom I have alluded in the previous pages, were in the words of the Russian historian V. V. Zenkovski, followers and worshippers of Rousseau.[9] Gibran too often expressed in his letters[10] his admiration for Rousseau. And every-time he dreamed to return for a second time to Paris, he related us his desire to be "enlightened by the social studies . . . in the capital of capitals of the world where Rousseau . . . lived."[11] Rousseau's inspiration can best be seen in *The Procession*. This work of his reminds us of Rousseau's two well known manuscripts *Discourse on the Origin and Foundation of Inequality among Man* (1758) and *Social Contract* (1762). It is worthwhile at this point to give a brief explanation of this French author of the Enlightenment period and draw a parallelism between Gibranism and Rousseaunism.

In 1749 the Academy of Dijon announced that it was giving a prize for the best article on the question whether the sciences and arts had contributed to the advancement of, or rather introduced corruption in morality. Jean-Jacques Rousseau then submitted his *Discourse on the Arts and Sciences* which won the prize. Instead of praising the progress of sciences and arts, Rousseau oriented his pen toward an attack on the so-called civilized society, naming it "artificial social life." In such society human nature is not fundamentally better than it was during the primeval. Now, he writes, "we no longer dare to seem what we really are, but lie under a perpetual restraint."[12] This "perpetual restraint" are the masks that artificial society fabricates under the assumption of conventionality, and forces upon us as a second nature intended to replace our native nature. Prior to artificial civilization man was *l'homme de la nature,* "satisfying his hunger at the first oak and slaking his thirst at the first brook; finding his bed at the foot of the tree which afforded him a repast; and, with that, all his wants supplied."[13] Such a primitive man wandered up and down the forest, without home, without industry, and was an equal stranger to war and violence. His native nature was goodness. Evil came later with the establishment and development of cultures. In the eyes of Rousseau, the transition from the state of nature to the state of civilization, lies in the phenomenon of "private property." "Private property" is the removal of equality and the cause of inequality among men. And, with the advent of the insecurity and other evils that "private property" introduced in life, and moved by the desire to preserve their liberty, Rousseau contends that man created governments, states, and political institutions. Yet, adds Rousseau, political institutions "bound new fetters on the poor and gave new powers to the rich; irretrievably destroyed natural liberty, fixed eternally the law of property and inequality, converted clever usurpation into unalterable right, and, for the advantage of a few ambitious individuals, subjected all mankind to perpetual labor, slavery and wretchedness."[14]

Two centuries later, Gibran attacked with the same vigor the institutionalized society, and developed his logic of the evils of civilization on the same lines as Rousseau. For instance, he too does contrast the two types of nature called "native" and "artificial." This is best revealed in the youth and the sage, reported in *The Procession,* where the youth constantly emphasizes the life "in the wild" as being void of illusions, confusions, disbelief, injustices, slavery, unhappiness, despair and death; "in the forest" there is only love, eternity, fertility, hope and freedom. On the other side, the sage complains about the evil social ways that civilization introduced in the behavior of the people in the cities. The primordial law of existence "in the wood," is the belief in the native goodness of "Nature," whereas the philosophy of culture reiterates the British Thomas Hobbes' axiom of *Homo homini lupus,* i.e., each man is to another as a wolf. Most suggestive is the epilogue of the old sage who expresses the wish to rejoin the youth in his freedom in the wilderness.

> Had I the days in hand to string,
>   Only in forest they'd be strewn,
> But circumstances drive us on
>   In narrow paths by Kismet hewn.
>
> For Fate has ways we cannot change,
>   While weakness preys upon our Will;
> We bolster with excuse the self,
>   And help that Fate ourselves to kill.[15]

At this point I remind the reader that the concepts "forest" and "society" that Gibran contrasts should not be defined according to their strict nominal definitions, as if our author is advocating a return to peasant life or sublimating the attitude of misanthropy. Gibran is aware of the corruption nurtured in society, but he is not implying a total renunciation of society or a retreat to a hermitage in the forest. On the contrary, as he wrote on April 15, 1914 to his benefactress Miss Haskell,

> Personally, I can get along with the two extreme links of the human chain, the primitive man and the highly civilized man. The primitive is always elemental and the highly civilized is always sensitive.
>
> (*B.P.,* pp. 182-183)

Human nature by its very ontological structure discloses the *a priori* of "sociability." Men are bound to live together.

As I will show later when I will tackle the issue of intersubjectivity in the Chapter on Love, Gibran did emphatically stress the idea that no individual could fulfill his personality all by himself, for the other part of the self is found in the other fellowman. Hence, it is not "togetherness" that Gibran discredited. He was rather antagonistic against false communal life. And this is the very reason he uses the concept "forest" *symbolically* as an indication of simple, innocent, pure, free, uncorrupted, unprejudiced, ethical existence. Conversely, the notion "society" with its "culture" and "civilization" denotes symbolically the inauthentic existential conducts that conventionality, traditions, customs and man-made laws introduce in the life economy of the individual person. Human existence oscillates between two diametrically opposed existential behaviors. One is the authentic that embalms a freshness, purity and naturality similar to the fragrance that Mother nature proliferates. The other, the inauthentic, is not in accordance with the natural inclinations of goodness but a deviation from nature. In an essay titled *Your Lebanon and Mine* Gibran parallels phenomenologically the *Geist* of these two types of behavior.

. . . Your Lebanon is two men—one who pays taxes
and the other who collects them.
My Lebanon is one who leans his head upon
his arm in the shadow of the Holy Cedars, oblivious
to all save God and the light of the sun.
. . . Your Lebanon is appointees, employers, and
directors,
My Lebanon is the growth of youth, the resolution
of maturity, and the wisdom of age.
. . . Your Lebanon is disguises and borrowed ideas and
deceit,
My Lebanon is simple and naked truth.
Your Lebanon is laws, rules, documents, and
diplomatic paper,
Mine is in touch with the secret of life

which she knows without conscious knowledge, . . .

Your Lebanon is a frowning old man, stroking
his beard and thinking only of himself,

My Lebanon is youth erect like a tower, smiling
like dawn and thinking of others as he thinks of
himself.

. . . But who are the sons of your Lebanon?

. . . They are free and ardent reformers, but only
in the newspapers and on the platform.

. . . They know no hunger unless they feel it in
their pockets. When they meet with one whose hunger
is spiritual, they ridicule him and shun him saying,
"He is not but a ghost walking in a world of phantoms" . . .

. . . Now let me show you the sons of my Lebanon:

They are peasants who turn the stony land into
orchards and gardens.

. . . The sons of my Lebanon are the vinedressers who
press the grapes and make good wine,

The fathers who raise mulberry trees and the
others who spin the silk,

The husbands who harvest the wheat and the
wives who gather the sheaves, . . .

. . . They walk with sturdy feet toward truth, beauty
and perfection.[16]

Lebanon in this context is not necessarily the geographic and
ethnographic spot, but represents symbolically the ways of
authentic and inauthentic *communal* behaviors.

Now Gibran's social philosophy is not as detailed as that
of Rousseau's, nonetheless, like his predecessor he knows how
to tap down the real cause of all social trauma. In his eyes,
the superego of civilization disturbs the natural equilibrium
of the psyche because it conflicts with the native aspirations
of goodness. If for Rousseau "private property" begets inequalities, and if Nietzsche attributes the reality of despiritualization to the will-to-power, Gibran sums up in one word
all the evil pathos of cultural superego: *hypocrisy*. This was

the one human vice that he could not tolerate. He blamed society, culture and civilization for having created hypocrisy. Hypocrisy is at the root of inequality, injustices, class struggles, materialism, irreligiousity, selfishness, restraint of freedom etc. . . . Hypocrisy disguises itself under the garments of man-made laws, customs and corrupted traditions.

From the literary, psychoanalytical and socio-cultural standpoints, it is interesting to note that Gibran associated all the rich with the spirit of hypocrisy, although, he admitted that the poor were also capable of concealing their corrupted disguised intentions behind gentle smilings, soft words and loving gestures. In all his novels, essays and poems he depicted the rich as self-centered persons, unsatisfied with the wealth they stole from the poor. After all, it is true that money breeds the worst social conducts. However, there was only one wealthy personage of whom he spoke with compassion: the father of Selma, Farris Effandi, who was not affected by the disease of hypocrisy.

> I do not know any other man in Beirut whose wealth has made him kind and whose kindness has made him wealthy. He is one of the few who comes to this world and leaves it without harming anyone, but people of that kind are usually miserable and oppressed because they are not clever enough to save themselves from the crookedness of others.[17]

In short, Gibran condemned like Rousseau the Pharisaic social philosophy. And in the words of his biographer Barbara Young,

> He had intolerance only for hypocrites. All other forms of wrongdoings or misdoings he accepted either as explainable or stupid. And of all these he said, "Leave them be." But against hypocrisy he raged.[18]

97

It is said of Rousseau that at one time he was so disgusted with the decadence of social life that he gave up everything he had received as clothes from society and retreated in the mountains. Some of Rousseau's followers likewise discovering the evil of societies decided to live like a hermit. For example Tolstoy, refused to eat and drink, and dedicated himself to meditations in the desert. Gibran too experienced the same feeling of uneasiness. True, he spent the rest of his years in the busy city of New York. Yet, there, he would seclude himself for days and nights in his studio. And in 1922, he wrote confidentially to his friend the philosopher Miklail Naimy, who was then living in a hermitage on Mount Sanin, in Lebanon,

> Your thoughts on "repudiating" the world are exactly like mine. For a long time I have been dreaming of a hermitage, a small garden, and a spring water. Do you recall Youssif El-Fakhri? Do you recall his obscure thoughts and his glowing awakening? Do you remember his opinion on civilization? I say, Meesha [nickname for Mikhail], that the future shall place us in a hermitage on the edge of one of the Lebanese valleys. This false civilization has tightened the strings of our spirits to the breaking point. We must leave before they break. But we must remain patient until the day of departure. We must be tolerant, Meesha.[19]

Spiritual Awakening, A Remedy

In Gibran's opinion, modern man lives in shadows and not in genuine reality. What man holds to be true is nothing but a shadow and a projection of his ill-desires. Modern man believes that he is awake and acts consciously in each concrete situation, but this is a delusion; like the man of Plato, modern man is found at the very bottom of the "cave" where only shadows of the True Light reach him. He lives his life, not to its fullness or genuiness. Hypocrisy masks and hinders the natural course of his social growth. Though, now, our author is aware of the present plight of society, he does *not,* however, assume a *nihilistic attitude.* There is a remedy for society; it will redeem itself if it reawakens from the slumber and semideath that false civilization plunged it into. The nature of such awakening is the revival of the belief in the spiritual. What distinguishes man in his very existential structure from the kingdom of organism, is not biology but the spirit. Therefore, to be oneself one must accept his ontological existence as it is structured and live up to the ways nature has fathomed man. That is, man's existence and behaviors ought to focus on the spiritual. "The spiritual awakening is the most essential thing in man's life, and it is the sole purpose of being."[20] This spiritual awakening of which Gibran speaks is something that cannot be attained through the five senses. It is a type of awareness, not logical or mathematical, but of communion. It is *"love," Agape* the golden rule *versus Eros.* And here he gives us a personal experience as to how love, the spiritual awakening, works,

> Man finds . . . pleasure . . . through the five senses. But Gibran's soul has already grown beyond that to a plane of higher enjoyment which does not require the mediation of the five senses. His soul sees, hears, and feels, but not through the medium of eyes, ears, and fingers. His soul roams the whole world and returns without the use of feet, ears, and ships. I see . . . far near and I perceive everything around . . . as the soul regards many other invisible and voiceless objects. The subtlest beauties in our life are unseen and unheard.[21]

It is not blood-shedding revolutions nor communistic control of the inequalities among man that will save mankind, but this spiritual consciousness, called love, when it becomes general and practiced by all societies. To discover "love," we need not search for it with the most sophisticated technological instruments; for really such spiritual awakening is not of the realm of scientific or philosophic reasoning. It lies in the province of feeling with the whole body and mind. The success of this feeling consists in returning back to Nature where goodness resides. And the goodness of Nature awakes itself in love. Love, understanding among people and respect for each other, is what Gibran proposes as medicinal for curing the shortcomings of modern society. Historically, Gibran is not the first philosopher to make of "love" the unshakable foundation for erecting authentic societies. From time immemorial philosophers, religious men, poets and politicians have preached or defended with wit the forcefulness of the power of love.

Here, Gibran's hermeneutics of society finds plenty of support from the part of many leading international figures. For example, I was personally fascinated to notice the great resemblance between his Social Contract and the social theory of the Mexican philosopher Antonio Caso (1883-1946), who was, incidentally, born the same year (and most probably acquainted with our author). Caso's philosophy distinguishes two types of existences much like Gibran, viz. *La existencia como economía* (existence as economy), and *La existencia como caridad* (existence as charity). In the former situation, the individual relates to others with the intentions of using them as means for the attainment of his personal interests. Furthermore, he does nothing without previously calculating and prerating the revenue of his actions. Simply worded, he is an economist. In Caso's vernacular, people who lead such a life are "primitive" even though they happen to inhabit a highly conglomerate technological environment. For after all, to think always in terms of "maximum gain with minimum of effort"[22] is to revert back to the primitive law of seeking preservation of the biological principle of homeostasis by avoiding pain. What is catastrophic in a society of *existencia como economía,* is that the human relations degenerate to pure egoism.

100

On the other hand, *la existencia como caridad* is typical of the disinterested existence. In such situation the individual transcends his limited biological spatio-temporal egoism in order to encounter in a sympathetic attitude the other selves. He is like an artist. because "art is not an economic activity,"[23] but an innate disinterestedness expressed in sympathetic intuitions unto the nature and essence of the other, and from the other standpoint. The society of *La existencia como caridad* breeds a spiritual human society composed of persons wherein each one treats one another with respect, and follows the precept of "maximum of effort with minimum of [personal] gain";[24] its motto of life ascribes to the following:

> . . . *The table of human values is this: the more you sacrifice merely animal life to disinterested ends, and the more difficult it becomes to make the sacrifice, until you arrive, from esthetic contemplation and simple good deeds, to heroic action, the more noble you are.*[25]

The conclusion we arrive at reiterates what we have been stating all through these pages about the internationality and ingenuity of Gibranism. Gibran like many other humanists is a *problem-center* thinker very much concerned with the welfare of society. Not only is he critical of the wrongdoings, but also exhorts what has to be done so to counteract the mischiefs. Fortunately, the solution he proposes is the very same that Christ, the right wing of existentialism, Antonio Caso and a host of other humanists have taught about "love," the spiritual awakening. In Chapter Six I will dwell more explicity on the phenomenon of love, thereby reinstating the social message of Gibranism.

Historical Implications

None of Gibran's writings have fairytale inspirations, especially the stories found in his philosophical essays. He be-

101

long to the movement of "committed literature"—*la litterature engagée*. This is mostly manifest in his articles on social ideas. To put it bluntly, our author developed his Social Contract because of some contemporary historical events that afflicted his society.

In the previous pages I have delved abstractly on the meaning of authentic and inauthentic society; it is time to narrow the concept to his native country and dig up all the historical facts that led him to pronounce his terrible indictment against the corruption of modern age culture.

Researching about this topic, has not been easy, for Gibran appears here and there with different personalities, confused and confusing the reader. Joseph Sheban has made an accurate estimate when he called Gibran a "dual personality."[26] Instead of defining this accusation, let us show how the dual Gibran has enacted passionately toward the Middle East societies.

a). OTTOMAN CORRUPTION AND FRENCH EXPEDITION. Readers should not forget that Gibran was an Arab, knew perfectly his mother tongue, and was always kept informed of the political developments in the Middle East. Now, the situation in the Middle East was quite different from existence in America. The Turks had conquered the Arab lands from the fifteenth century and remained sole rulers till the first World War. The invasion of the Ottomans had never been favorable to the Arabs, either militarily, intellectually, economically, geographically, socially or in matters of legality. The one time glory of the Arab Empire, Arab wisdom, Arab knowledge in the fields of mathematics, astronomy, philosophy, medicine and architecture that enlightened Europe from its dark ages, was jeopardized and eclipsed with the advent of the big bulk of ignorance, illiteracy and savagery of the Turks. For five centuries the Arab world suffered the Turkish heavy yoke of injustices, usurpations, ignorances and slavery. Fate was slightly changed when a Turk-revolted Pasha, Muhammad Ali, sent to Egypt (1799) to appease the natives insurrections, turned later on against his own government. Muhammad Ali is today acclaimed the liberator of Egypt. However, Lebanon, Syria and many other Arab countries were not so successful in resisting the burden of the Turks as Egypt, who by the way was not so completely free.

The coming of Napoleon in 1798 to Egypt was a break for the Egyptians and the surrounding lands. The expedition was a happy event. The European knowledge which was at one time carved on Arabian erudition was brought back to the people with a far richer treasure of literary, philosophical and scientific insights. Also, the first Arabic printing that Napoleon seized from the Collegio Propaganda in Rome, now enabled translations from French into Arabic. Europe *awakened* the Middle East from its slumber. Yet, such awakening aroused different reactions from the few thinkers there were.

1. To the *ulema* (educated) conservatives, it merely awoke in them a "response of reaction," i.e. the feeling that Islam is higher than any other culture because it alone possesses the Koran which is Truth incarnated. These traditionalists set themselves to revive early Islamic thinking as a shield against the intrusion of Western new ideas. Politically they remained obedient to the Turkish Sultan.

2. To the *ulema* reformists, the French on the scene instigated them to revise their traditional thoughts along with a spirit of reformation. They rejected the stagnant thinking *(taqlid)* of the conservatives and propelled the *ijtihad* or independent judgment. The champions of this movement were the leaders Jamal ad-Din al Afghani (1839-1897) Muhammad 'Abdu (1849-1905), Muhammad Rashid Rida (1865-1935), and, Abd al-Qadir al-Mughrabi (1867-1956). The West provided them with many ideas about social reforms, and above all made them conscious to fight against the decayed politics of the Ottoman whom they judged was the cause of the degradation of Muslim faith. Because of their political dissension, the reformists were

many times exiled like Gibran himself. Their main emphasis was put on the reform of spirituality *versus* the cultural materialism of the Ottoman and Europe (somehow like Gibran except from that Gibran was Christian). Al-Afghani writes on this matter: "Every Muslim is sick and his only remedy is in the Koran."—"Muslim backwardness was not caused by Islam but rather by the Muslim's ignorance of its truth."[27] The new political system they sought was the reunification of all Islamic states under the standard of Pan-Islamism.

3. To a third group of Muslim *ulema,* Europe awoke in them a stronghold for secularist intellectualism. Reason was proclaimed the sole agent for truth. And in contrast to the Muslim reformists, the secularists were not religiously oriented. They appealed to secular values and norms, especially with regard to politics. Political liberty consisted not in seeking advice from religion but in fighting tyranny and oppression with enlightenment and education. Knowledge dissipates political fear. One of the secularist axioms for cultural reform was economic balance and equitable distribution of the goods between poor and rich. Also, they violently opposed ill-traditions. (Note the similarity with Gibran Social Contract.) Qasim Amin (1863-1908), the pioneer, writes: "Among the causes of our suffering is the fact that we base our life on traditions which we no longer understand, which we preserve only because they have been handed down to us . . ."[28]

4. To the Arab Christians, the West made them become totally free thinkers. Most of the Christians were then educated in the Universities of Paris and The Propaganda (the Maronite school) in Rome. At home they were a source of inspiration to the Muslim secularists. In their political stand, they were anti-Ottoman corruption. Here, the study of Gibran's Social Contract is appropriate for twofold reasons: on one hand, he informs us quite well

about the Arab societies, on the other hand, he expresses more or less the same feelings that other Arab Christians nurtured toward the Middle East of the Early Twentieth Century.

b). "DECAYED TEETH." Gibran has much in common with the *ulema* reformists and secularists. With the former he agreed that Arab nations were "sick" for accepting benevolently the oppressions with no attempt at changing their fate nor to cultivating the spiritual richness of their fore-fathers. His political polemic *Decayed Teeth* denounces the slumberness into which the Syrian (*N.B.* Lebanon and Syria were one then) people lived in. The essay portraits the injustices, hypocrisies, and wrongdoings of the Syrians under the Ottoman Government. Ironically, he calls his country "rotten, black, and dirty teeth that fester and stink."[29] And then he gives some instances where mostly the deterioration is experienced.

If you wish to take a look at the decayed teeth of Syria, visit its schools where the sons and daughters of today are preparing to become the men and women of tomorrow.

Visit the courts and witness the acts of the crooked and corrupted purveyors of justice. See how they play with the thoughts and minds of the simple people as a cat plays with a mouse.

Visit the homes of the rich where conceit, falsehood, and hypocrisy reign. But don't neglect to go through the huts of the poor as well, where dwell fear, ignorance, and cowardice.

Then visit the nimble-fingered dentists, [metaphorically the leaders], possessors of delicate instruments, dental plasters and tranquilizers, who spend their days filling the cavities in the rotten teeth of the nation to mask the decay.[30]

105

What mostly irritated Gibran was that the Syrians were contented with the filth in which they lived. Instead of extracting completely the "decayed teeth," they rather preferred to conceal the teeth with gold fillings. In other words, the Syrians concealed their inner-self with the garment of "hypocrisy."

> And if you suggest "extraction to them, they will laugh at you because you have not yet learned the noble art of dentistry that conceals disease.[31]

In another essay *Narcotics and Dissecting Knives,* once more Gibran takes the defensive position against the weaknesses of the Orient at the manner of the Muslin reformers and secularists. He sees the greatest threat to the downfall of the Arab nation, not only in the perspective of the Ottoman, but mostly he blames the so called Arab leaders who instead of ameliorating their destiny, rather concurred with the oppressors to administer "narcotics" (metaphorically speaking), so that the Orient remains in its slumber

> The Orient is ill, but it has become so
> inured to its infirmities that it has
> come to see them as natural and even
> noble qualities that distinguish them
> above others. . . .
>
> Numerous are the social leaders in the Orient,
> but many are their patients who remain uncured
> but appear eased of their ills because they
> are under the effects of social narcotics.
> But these tranquilizers merely mask the
> symptoms.[32]

The leaders whom he blames are the native politicians and the religious. He recognizes that the former begin well when they incipiently revolt against their Turkish superiors. But, he also acknowledges that many of them later on prostitute

106

their ideals with the silence of money or official promotions offered by their enemy. (This event was current in the whole Middle East.)

> A group or party revolts against a despotic
> government and advocates political reforms . . .
> But a month later, we hear that the government
> has . . . silenced him [the leader] by giving him
> an important position. And nothing more is heard.[33]

On the other hand, the religious leaders of the Middle East were not spared from his critics. Gibran often held them responsible for the ignorance, exorbitant taxes and legal injustices to which their faithfuls were subjugated. Historically, the clergy at that time enjoyed many privileges from the Ottomans.

From what has been said up to now, it is clear that Gibran was calling for drastic changes; also, the tone of the appeal was not gentle but that of an exasperated social engineer. Indeed temper was his personality.[34] In his political essays we see him *raging against his countrymen* for being afraid of changing their sour existence. The poem *My Countrymen,* was written in great angriness against his own people.

> I have cried over your humiliation and submission;
> and my tears streamed like crystalline, but could
> not sear away your stagnant weakness; . . .

> My tears have never reached your petrified hearts, but
> they cleansed the darkness from inner self. . . .

> Your souls are freezing in the clutches of the priests
> and Sorcerers, and your bodies tremble between the
> paws of the despots and the shedders of Blood, and
> your country quakes under the marching feet of the
> conquering enemy; . . .

Hypocrisy is your religion, and Falsehood is your life,
and Nothingness is your ending; . . .

I hate you, My Countrymen, because you hate glory and
greatness. . . .[35]

Despite all this, Gibran still was a real *Habbibi* (kind); he
felt sorry for the treacherous wretchedness that plagued his
beloved countrymen. Getting simultaneously angry and affable
is one indication of his dual personality. At any rate, he
showed deep sympathy for his people, when early in the winter
of 1916 famine stared the population in the face, and the
entire land became a paradise for disease germs as a result
of World War One, and the Turks exporting the material
goods of the nation leaving the natives starving to death.
Gibran then in the U.S., formed with other immigrants a
Relief Committee, and was elected its secretary. This Committee was to send to the people of Mount Lebanon food and
material goods; however, when the Turkish government forbade such enterprise, Gibran with the others appealed to
Washington to intervene; finally on December 17, 1916 with
the help of the United States Navy and the American Red
Cross Society the boat *Caesar* sailed with foodstuffs estimated
at a value of $750,000.00. Of this experience, Gibran writes:

> It is a great responsibility but I must shoulder it.
> Great tragedies enlarge the heart. I have never been
> given the chance to serve my people in a work of this
> sort. I am glad I can serve a little and I feel that
> God will help me.[36]

In the same year Gibran wrote the famous poem *Dead Are
My People* in which he lamented the miseries, the famines,
the diseases and the death of his countrymen. He felt remorse
that he was spared from the famine. Guilt pushed him to
wish in delerium that he were an "ear of corn," a "ripe fruit"
or a "bird flying" so that he could satiate the hunger of some:

108

Gone are my people, but I exist yet,
. . .
The Knolls of my country are submerged by
tears and blood, for my people and my beloved
are gone, and I am here . . .

My people died from hunger, and he who did not
perish from starvation was butchered with the
sword; and I am here in this distant land, . . .
. . .
My people died a painful and shameful death
and here am I living in plenty and in peace. . . .[47]

The amazing thing about Gibran as a concerned social engineer—and here I am getting deeper to the dual personality
—is that even during his moments of sympathy toward his
suffering people, he would burst momentarily with anger
against them wishing that they had died like rebels with the
sword in their hands fighting courageously their oppressors.[38]
In general, one of the direct implications Gibran was trying
to achieve with his social writings was to awake his countrymen from slumberness to rebellion. I am not too wrong in
suggesting that he was looking for a bloodshedding revolution.
Actually, he himself often used the word "revolution." For
instance, in 1913 Gibran was asked by some Syrians of New
York to be their representative at a Paris International European Conference, where the New Home Rule for Syria and
Lebanon was to be discussed. Gibran turned down the assign-
ment because he was asked to be patient, gentle and diplomatic
in his speeches about the Turkish regime; personally he
wanted revolution and war at all cost. This idea of revolution
motivated him to think organizing in New York "a July Conference between some of the men from Paris and the leading
Syrians in this country," during which they would plan a
military maneuver against Turkey; supposedly, the troops
were to be commanded by "Damascene Eresi (or some such
name)" and by his good friend the General Giuseppe Gari-

baldi, the grandson of the Italian hero. Of course, such a political gathering never took place. (*B.F.*, p. 127-129).

But most of all the kind of revolution he was preaching was a social *reform*. Like his neighbors, the Egyptian Muslim secularists, he wanted to inculcate in the attitude of the orientals, an open mindedness toward the West.[39] For that he undertook a strong criticism of the class inequalities, asking for a reform in economy. After all, there is nothing that the rich could claim to be his own. The product is never the complete work of the owner; the employees concurred in the production.[40] But also, like the Muslim reformers and secularists, Gibran submitted all the oriental traditions and customs to a revision of scrutiny, rejecting those that he deemed too old-fashioned. For instance, marriage contracted for sake of fame, social appearances or on the basis of parents' consents only, no matter whether the partners love each other or how aged is one in regard to the other. Gibran called such marriages adultery, irreligious and immoral, even if the engagement was concluded in the church.

In simple words, Gibran condemned what his teacher Nietzsche labelled "slave ethics" or "herd morality," because such morality breeds passive citizens, masses of ignorant sheep depersonalized and dehumanized, and who happen to be toys at the mercy of potent masters. Here is the famous Nietzschean inspiration on Gibran:

I found the blind slavery, which ties the people's present with their parents' past, and urges them to yield to their traditions and customs, placing ancient spirits in the new bodies.

I found the must slavery, which binds the life of a man to a wife whom he abhors, and places the woman's body in the bed of a hated husband, deadening both lives spiritually.

I found the deaf slavery, which stifles the soul and the heart, rendering man but an empty echo of a voice, and a pitiful shadow of a body.

110

I found the lame slavery, which places man's neck under the domination of the tyrant and submits strong bodies and weak minds to the sons of Greed for use as instruments to their power.

I found the ugly slavery, which descends with the infants' spirits from the spacious firmament into the home of Misery, where Need lives by Ignorance, and Humiliation resides beside Despair. And the children grow as miserables, and live as criminals, and die as despised and rejected non-existents.

I found the subtle slavery, which entitles things with other than their names—calling slyness an intelligence and emptiness a knowledge, and weakness a tenderness, and cowardice a strong refusal.

I found the twisted slavery, which causes the tongues of the weak
to move with fear, and speak outside of their feelings, and they feign to be meditating their plight, but they become as empty sacks, which even a child can fold or hang.

I found the bent slavery, which prevails upon one nation to comply with the laws and rules of another nation, and the bending is greater with each day.

I found the perpetual slavery, which crowns the sons of monarchs
as kings, and offers no regard to merit.

I found the black slavery, which brands with shame the disgrace forever the innocent sons of the criminals.

Contemplating slavery, it is found to possess the vicious powers of continuation and contagion.[41]

Once his fellow Arabs besought him earnestly to return to Lebanon in order to become a political leader, to which

111

Gibran exclaimed: "I am not a politician, and I would not be a politician. No. I cannot fulfill their desire."[42] Often times, however they reacted negatively against his harsh criticisms of the Orientals. And during his youth (1903), both the government officials and the Maronite Church, issued a joint *communiqué* proclaiming his exile and excommunication. Gibran suffered from being rejected by his homeland. Analyzing his own social philosophy, he laments:

> . . . If men and women were to follow Gibran's counsels on marriage, family ties would break, society would perish, and the world would become an inferno peopled by demons and devils. . . .

> Such is what people say of me and they are right, for I am indeed a fanatic and I am inclined toward destruction as well as construction. There is hatred in my heart for that which my detractors sanctify, and love for that which they reject. And if I could uproot certain customs, beliefs, and traditions of the people, I would do so without hesitation. . . .[43]

Let us, now, revert back to the "decayed teeth" and "sick society" and ask Gibran how does the law behave morally in relation to the individual citizen? Hence, we come to our next section.

2. THE ISSUE OF LAW

Scepticism Toward Man-Made Laws

From what will be said about Gibran-and-the-established-laws, we should not the least suspect that our author was a belligerent personality nor that his philosophy is anarchist. Actually, many are the contemporary writers who rebuked vehemently against the ineffectiveness of man-made laws. Take for instance, the German novelist, Franz Kafka, who after graduating in law and practicing for some time in an insurance firm, abandoned his profession on the account that it is utterly corrupted. Now Kafka's philosophy of law is much similar to that of Gibran. A brief presentation of Kafka will disclose what I mean.

Kafka's writings have for central theme the problematic of *authority*. In the novel *The Trial,* Kafka illustrates with a good understanding of the legal procedures, what really occurs inside and outside courtrooms, and, how most of the time legal authority inflicts on man more damages than it does to protect him. *The Trial* has been written simply to show the absurdity of legal authority. Also, in his parable "Before The Law," Kafka demonstrates the ignorance and the injustices done by all institutionalized authority. The parable portrays the case of a man who one day came to the Law to seek advice. Reaching to the domicile of the Law, he found a doorkeeper. The man asked the doorkeeper permission to enter through the door that leads to the Law; the doorkeeper insisted, in return, that the man could not be admitted at the moment. Then, the man, on reflection, inquired if he could see the Law later. The doorkeeper's reply was affirmative. Following such conversation, the man asked if he could wait in front of the door. The doorkeeper offered him a stool to sit on until the moment comes for him to enter inside. To the man's surprise, however, days, weeks, months and years passed, and he was still waiting to be received by the Law. Finally, Kafka concludes,

> his eyes grow dim and he does not know whether the world is really darkening around him or whether his eyes are only deceiving him. But in the darkness he can now perceive a radiance that streams immortally from the door of the Law. Now his life is drawing to a close. Before he dies, all that he has

113

experienced during the whole time of his sojourn condenses in his mind into one question, which he has never yet put to the doorkeeper. He beckons the doorkeeper, since he can no longer raise his stiffening body. The doorkeeper has to bend far down to hear him for the difference in size between them has increased very much to the man's disadvantage. 'What do you want to know now?' asks the doorkeeper, 'You are insatiable.' 'Everyone strives to attain the Law,' answers the man, 'how does it come about, then, that in all these years no one has come seeking admittance but me?' The doorkeeper perceives that the man is at the end of his strength and that his hearing is failing, so he bellows in his ear: 'No one but you could gain admittance through this door, since this door was intended only for you. I am now going to shut it.'[44]

The factual implication of this parable suggests that men who seek justice from the man-made laws, die before obtaining their rights. The doorkeeper represents the lawyers and the codified written laws, both of whom claim that authority has been invested upon them from the Almighty Law whom none has seen. Kafka at this point asks what guarantees us that man-made laws spring from the Law since no one has yet heard of him? The doorkeeper never received immediately and directly his job from the Law; only another doorkeeper from inside the courtroom had secured him the appointment. What Kafka resents most is that man-made justice treats the individual in an impersonal way. Kafka, himself a lawyer, knows that the laws are for the rich.

> . . . The laws were made to the advantage
> of the nobles from the very beginning,
> they themselves stand above the laws,
> and that seems to be why the laws were
> entrusted exclusively into their hands.[45]

In my opinion, Kafka's harsh criticism of human codes, explains why all his personages are in search of their self-identity in a society geared by stereotyped laws.

Now Gibran was not a professional lawyer like Kafka, yet, he has denounced in an identical manner the absurdity of man-made laws.

In *The Cry of the Graves,* Gibran tells us the story of three different individuals who are sentenced to death by a human authority for the good deeds they have fulfilled. *The first case* is that of a chevaleresque soul who killed in self-defense one of the Emir's officers who was trying to take advantage of a young girl of a poor family. *The second case* concerns a young woman accussed by her aged husband of adultery, merely because she met unintentionally one day her true beloved person and talked to him. *The third case* is the story of an old man who grew old and sick after dedicating many years of hard work in a religious convent. One day he begged from the priests some bread for his youngsters, but was repelled. To satisfy the natural hunger of his children he resolved to steal the food from the convent. Unfortunately he was caught; the priest who trapped him accused him in front of the judge of burgling the sacred vase.

In all these three stories Gibran revolts against the Emir who condemned innocent people without giving a fair trial to each one. The reason for declining a panel of self-defense is due to the fact that the accussers are all nobles and the defendants come from a low social economical class. And yet, as Kafka has said it, "The Law is whatever the nobles do."[46] In Gibran's opinion the prosecutors are far more criminal than the criminals. Hence, like Kafka, Gibran retorts sceptically to himself,

What is Law? Who saw it coming with the sun
from the depths of heaven? What human saw the
heart of God and found its will or purpose?
In what century did the angels walk among
the people and preach to them, saying,
'Forbid the weak from enjoying life, and

kill the outlaws with the sharp edge of the
sword, and step upon the sinners with iron feet?[47]

Absurdity of the Laws' Sanctions

The ethics of punishment is all together wrong and above
all self-contradictory for the law meets evil with evil, and
sanctions the criminals by becoming itself criminal. "Shall we
meet evil with evil and say this is the law? Shall we fight
corruption with greater corruption and say this is the rule?
Shall we conquer crimes with more crimes and say this is
justice."[48]

If even a man is guilty, society has no right to bring a
harsh sentence against him. Man is not man because of his
deeds, but because he was born man. Personhood is an
intrinsic value and characterizes essentially and existentially
the nature of man. The value of personhood is not quantitative in that it may augment or decrease. Also, it is not
true that one person "is" more valuable than another. Would
you say that a moron is less of a human than the normal
one? Or a poor less than the rich? Personhood, to reiterate
Nicolai Hartmans and Max Weber, is in itself a value and
the highest in the scale. This is the idea we read in *Kahlil
the Heretic,* where Rachel and Miriam rescuing in the mid
of the night a man in the snow, Miriam begins fearing that
he might be a criminal. But Rachel replying to Miriam says:
"It makes no difference whether he is a monk or criminal;
dry his feet well my daughter."[49]

At this stage, I have to say that Gibran's ethics does not
permit the sanction of capital punishment. For him no law
has the right to take premeditatively and willingly the life
of someone else. As for the lay murderers, they need mental
and social rehabilitation. The logic behind such assertions
is threefold. (1) Each man is a unique mystery in himself;
to really bring a judgment against the accused, requires on
the part of the outsider a complete knowledge of him and the

116

circumstances that made him—"And you who understand justice, how shall you unless you look upon all deeds in the fullness of light?"[50]—which is utopia for no mind can have full understanding of another person's idiosyncrasies; hence, writes Gibran: "You cannot judge any man beyond your knowledge of him, and how small is your knowledge."[51] (2) Secondly, when a good judge begins to scrutinize carefully all the circumstances that surround the deed of the criminal he will discover that these circumstances "forced" and "conditioned" the accused to perform his action. Furthermore, the analysis will disclose that the defendant is not alone responsible for the crime, but somehow, society with its righteous people bears part of the blame. No man is an island. If it is true that one's success owes to the contribution of others, it is equally true, that crimes are the work of participation of others. The Prophet says:

The murdered is not unaccountable
for his own murder,

And the robbed is not blameless in
being robbed.

The righteous is not innocent of
the deeds of the wicked,...

So the wrong-doer cannot do wrong
without the hidden will of you all.[52]

(3) Finally, the value "personhood" admits but one external criteria, this is God, the creator of the person. As for the authority of man-made laws, Gibran is sceptical since earthly laws see differences in the value of personhood; and yet, "The life of one man is as weighty in the scales of God as the life of another."[53]

Therefore, all sorts of legal punishments are injust. Here, Gibran is relying more on the Evangelic ethics than on speculated philosophical arguments. Somehow, he is repeating Christ who once said to an angry crowd raging against the adultress Magdalena: "whoever think he is pure of heart, let him cast the first stone"—to which the people dispersed for they were all sinners. Well, this is the same message he allots in the parable *The Saint*. A brigand came one day to a Saint and sought absolutions for the "countless crimes" he committed. To his surprise the Saint refused to be his judge before God, and replied:

> I too have committed crimes without
> number. . . . Then the brigand stood
> up and . . . went skipping down the hill. . . .
> At that moment we heard the brigand singing
> in the distance, and the echo of his song filled
> the valley with gladness.[54]

The thief was happy because he found that even Saints sin at least seven times a day. Also, the lesson of this parable implies that no human is an angel. As Blaise Pascal, the French philosopher, used to say: "who wants to play the angel, mimics it badly like a beast"[55]; so too, Gibran defines man a microcosm, limited in perfection; there is no shame in not being Perfection, otherwise we should be ashamed of being human. The poem *Perfection* emphasizes that man reaches to perfection when he accepts willingly his weaknesses, instead of boasting for what he is not.[56]

Man-Made Laws and the Plea of Uniqueness

I believe without fear of contradiction that Gibran's heroes rebel against the institutionalized stereotyped norms of conduct simply because they feel that these laws hinder to the growth of their individuality. However, none of them would follow the ideological path of an Abbie Hoffman or an Angela Davis. They are not anarchists; and Gibran himself was not a social rebel. Once he said to his fellow Lebanese of American birth that they ought to become good citizens and loyal to America, despite their being descendants of Lebanese. "I believe that it is in you to be good citizens. . . . You should be proud of being an American. . . ."[57]

The heroes of our author argue for a personality freedom, and their dispute is based on the same philosophical premises, that Tolstoy, Kafka, Dostoyesvski and Blake insisted in their writings.

In short, according to Gibran, man-made laws afflict great injuries to the individual by imposing fixed patterns of conduct and in seeing that these ways of thinking and doing be realized literally. After all it is true that human laws aim to have a wide range of application without consideration of the idiographic situation in which the person lived at the time he performed his deed. The so used expression by the police, politicians, lawyers, or bureaucratic administrators: "IT IS THE LAW," exemplifies how absurd man-made laws are when the accused seeks to justify his actions.

The psychological feeling that originates in a man who feels his personality oppressed and burdened by the institutionalized codes advanced either by society or the Church is that of "statistics" or being "a number among other numbers." Gibran is aware that the spirit of statistics is predominant in our technological society; people are becoming increasingly deindividualized. As for our education it does its best to mold us in conformism and totalitarianism. And yet, for Gibran the purpose of education is to enable each one to develop his innate endowments thereby one's self-identity. "Education sows not seeds in you, but makes *your seeds grow.*[58]

Gibran blames two categories of oppressors for robbing the subjectivity of the individuals. These oppressors have in common the privilege of being rich and of making laws to which the poor have to conform, while they themselves are exempted. As for their differences, one wears a cassock and is called priest and his norms are religious; the other is a layman who lives in palaces built with the tears and money of the poor and his laws are societal. Now, in Gibran's vernacular of words, priests are like ivies that climb high in the skies while their roots plunge in the ignorant kindness of the poor stealing from them in the name of God their individuality and finances. "I beheld priests, sly like foxes; and false messiahs dealing in trickery with the people".[59]

The consequences of man-made laws are detrimental to the uniqueness and dignity of man. Like his friend the Swiss psychoanalist Carl Jung, whose portrait he painted, Gibran acknowledges that in a world where the feeling of statistics prevails, morality tends to decrease. Jung writes,

> The individual is increasingly deprived of the moral decision as to how he should live his own life, and instead is ruled, fed, clothed and educated as a social unit, accomodated in the appropriate housing unit, and amused in accordance with the standards that give pleasure and satisfaction to the masses.[60]

Similarly, Gibran reckons the downfall of morality as a result of "institutionalized morality." For instance he pokes at the Superego's morality of present days politics. "Organized political duty" is false morality since it norms the good and the evil on a criteria invented by the politicians. The example is patriotism for whose sake people tear each other apart in war. I remind the reader at this point, that Gibran is not equating patriotism "with love of the native land."[61] In his opinion, patriotism at the expense of human life is a "construct" with no concrete foundations; it is an invented sentiment of attachment to the land; it is a rumor fabricated by politicians. Yet, "love of the native land" has no ethnological, social, juridical, geographical, political or religious connotations. My native land is the planet earth where humans survive, and eventually, the whole universe in which I am born as part of it. "Love of the native land" is a natural inclination, which, however, does not surpass the "love for/of others" which stands higher in the scale of values.

Beware, my brother, of the leader who says, 'Love of existence obliges us to deprive the people of their rights!' I say unto you but this: protecting others' rights is the noblest and most beautiful human act; if my existence requires that I kill others, then death is more honorable to me, and... I will not hesitate to take my life by my own hands for the sake of Eternity before Eternity comes.[62]

And again,

If duty exiles peace from among nations, and patriotism makes havoc of man's tranquility, then away with duty and patriotism![63]

Now, morality is shattered because the individual pressed by the codified conducts, gives up his existential freedom to assume a generic social and religious responsibility. "I beheld... true freedom walking alone in the street, seeking shelter before doors and rejected by the people."[64] In the final analysis, if there is someone to blame for the deterioration of the inner-self and freedom, this someone is man alone who

set for the God-given soul a limited and earthly law of his own. He made for himself strict rules. Man built a narrow and painful prison in which he secluded his affections and desires. He dug out a deep grave in which he buried his heart and its purpose.[65]

Natural Laws vs. Man-Made Laws

From the preceeding pages one would think that Gibran is an anarchist. Yet, to an alert philosopher, he really appears as a guarantor of laws. This is not only manifest in his work but also in his life. Gibran was never put in jail for violation of a social code nor has he ever participated in a demonstration rally. When he attacks man-made laws he does so not so much out of caprice as much as out of concern for his fellowman. He merely objects to man-made laws because he feels that these norms hinder the individual's search for the "spiritual awakening" that leads to happiness. After all he accepts the absoluteness of the "eternal law"[66] and its corollary, the natural law. A brief comment on these laws will disclose the thoughts of Gibran.

The distinction Gibran makes between the eternal law, natural law and man-made law is something commonly accepted by most moralists, especially the Thomists. Concerning the eternal law, many are the passages where Gibran mentions it.[67] The eternal law is the rule of divine wisdom, which is eternal, ordering all things to their end, man included. In Thomas Aquinas' own words to quote an outsider,

> ...Granted that the world is governed by divine providence... the whole community of the universe is governed by the divine reason. Therefore the very motion of the government of things in God, the ruler of the universe, has the nature of a law. And since the divine reason's conception of things is not subject to time, but is eternal...this kind of law must be called eternal.[68]

For Gibran too, the rule of divine wisdom whereby God provides for creatures from eternity is called eternal law. The existence of such law is founded on the divine attribute of wisdom in God. God directs creatures to Himself, who is the Highest Good of all. Moreover, this eternal law is universally knowable by man, and therefore, is not a prerogative of priests or educated man. Whoever lives on the paths of Love, Beauty and Truth, fulfills the eternal law.

As for the natural law this is the participation of the eternal law in both the rational nature and non-rational nature through the natural inclinations. In man, furthermore, the natural law participates to the eternal law through the first principles of practical reason. The light of reason is a natural inclination, proper to man. Man's nature is rational and he alone discovers the natural law by the light of natural reason in drawing conclusions about his nature. According to Gibran God promulgates the natural law to man through the endowment of the rational nature. It is written so to speak in our very beings. The laws of the universe are a replica of the eternal law. "Even the laws of Life obey Life's laws."[69] And the primordial precept of nature is "Love," along with those virtues that "love" entails, such as compassion, forgiveness, forbearance. Justice is a type of kindness.

What about man-made law? In Gibran's terminology this refers to the law that the religious or political legislative government decreed. But, in his opinion these laws are neither deduced from the natural law nor dictated by the eternal law. Contrasting the natural law to man-made law, Gibran exclaims, "the only authority I obey is the knowledge of guarding acquiescing in the Natural Law of Justice."[70]

His motive for considering the organized laws as contradictory to the natural or eternal law square with the fact that there is a discrepancy between human laws and "justice." Quite lucidly he is aware that these two are not interdependent in present society, not even among the professional guarantor of the law enforcement. Lawyers will try to be successful with their client's case not so much for justice sake as much as for personal social ambitions or professional duty. I myself often heard that lawyers have a professional duty toward their clients regardless of the worth of their deeds, and the interest of justice. This unbridgeable gap is best delineated in Gibran's satirical prose-poem *The Procession* (sometimes translated as *The Cortége)*, a long dialogue between an old sage and a youth concerning the differences between the earthly authority and the natural law. The sage represents a man who spent his entire life span in the turmoils of the city, and toward his society he feels bitter because of the corruptions, defamations, desecrations, injustices and hypocrisies that human laws have brought in the lives of the citizens. The youth, on the other hand, symbolizes innocence unspoiled by any of the amoral tricks of the social laws. The only law to which the youth abides is that of nature.

SAGE

Justice on earth would cause the Jinn
To cry at misuse of the word,
And were the dead to witness it,
They'd mock at fairness in this world.

Yes, death and prison we mete out
To small offenders of laws,
While honor, wealth, and full respect
On greater pirates we bestow....

YOUTH

In Nature there is no justice
Nor is there a punishment.
When the willows cast their shadow
O'er the ground without consent,
No one hears the cypress saying,
'This act is versus law and right!'
Like the snow, our Human Justice
Melts from shame in warm sunlight![71]

To condense what we have been saying, let us repeat that our author takes a harsh stand against man-made laws simply because these directives for living are inflexible, established on vicious customs, corrupted practices, conflict with the

idiosyncrasis of the individual and breed masses of depersonalized individualities. In a letter he wrote to his first
cousin in 1908 after the incidence of the burning of his *Spirits
Rebellious* in the market place of Beirut, Gibran confessed,

> People are saying that I am the enemy of
> just laws, of family ties, and old traditions.
> Those people are telling the truth. I do not
> love man-made laws and I abhor the traditions
> that our ancestors left us.[72]

A life-situation that grows on man-made law and which
Gibran mostly critized is the case of marriages in the Orient.
As a matter of fact at the time of Gibran, but less now,
marriages in the Mediterranean countries were conjugated
almost for material reasons without there being any genuine
love between the conjoints. Either the parents would pro-
mise the hand of their daughter, while still a young girl, or
one of the partners would consent to the other because of
his riches. Now, according to the Church-made law, once
the two were consecrated in front of a priest, there could
be no divorce and the two would be *legally* married. Here,
Gibran's ethics replies, could love be bought? Is love a mere
paper formality? What is the difference between the prostitute and the person who makes intercourse the same night-
after signing some official documents, that he or she thought
would be beneficial?[73] This is one way of showing the absurdity of institutionalized codes.

At this stage I would like to introduce an idea of mine
which reflects the intentions of Gibran. The purpose of any
type of law is to help the individual to develope to its peak
his personality. The success of the law resides in its understanding of all the concrete events that make the concrete
situation of a unique individual. The law should never become bureaucratic. But as Gibran says, "Kindness should
be the source of every law upon the earth, for Kindness is
the shadow of God in man."[74] Otherwise, the law will be-

come a mere dead written letter found in books on the shelves of a library. This is the idea that Almuhtada conveys in his sermons on *Of the Martyrs to Man's Law*.[75]

In conclusion, it is obvious to our author that who abides to the eternal law and natural law has attained moral happiness and a freedom similar to that of the birds. The bird symbolizes freedom.

> The bird has an honor that man does not have. Man lives in the traps of his fabricated laws and traditions; but the birds live according to the natural law of God who causes the earth to turn around the sun.[76]

3. PARABLES ON POLITICAL AUTHORITY

The purpose of this present section is twofold. On one hand, it serves as a *conclusion* for Chapter Five; on the other hand, it delves into the various forms of "political authority."

Accordingly, Gibran distinguishes three types of government. These are (i) weakened rulers; (ii) wicked rulers; (iii) Co-operative rulers. Also Gibran employs the parabolical style of expression in order to convey in a pleasant and direct way to his readers the moral lesson encompassed in the stories.

Weak Government

The parable "The Wise King" in *The Madman,* portrays a king who ruled over the city of Wirani with wisdom and might. The king and his subjects lived in mutual understanding until one night a witch came into the city and dropped seven drops of a strange liquid in the sole well which provided water to the entire populace, and cast a spell: "From this hour he who drinks this water shall become mad."[77]

126

On the next day, the inhabitants drew their water supply from the well and drank of it. Suddenly, they became mad, as the witch had predicted. However, the king and his lord chamberlain were not affected, because they had not yet touched to the water. Their behaviors were the same.

What was peace before, now turned to be uprising. For during the course of the day, the citizens gathered in small groups and murmured to each other: "Our King and his lord chamberlain have lost their reason. Surely we cannot be ruled by a mad King. We must dethrone him."[78] They knew of the madness of the monarch, because the latter did not behave as usual, according to their expectations.

Having heard of the rumor to overthrow him, the King afraid of losing his crown and power, commanded his soldiers to bring him in a golden goblet some water from the well. He drank the water and gave a portion to his lord chamberlain. From thereupon, concludes the parable, "there was great rejoicing in that distant city of Wirani, because the King and its lord chamberlain had regained their reason."[79]

Now, as we ponder seriously on the meaning of this fairytale, we understand that the King who was both "wise" and "powerful" accepted at the end to sell his wisdom in order to retain his authority. He consented to become mad like all his citizens, instead of finding a cure for healing the madness of the city. In other words, there are many political rulers—Gibran surmises—whose acts, thinking and decision-making are foolish, degrading, uncivilized, uneducated, backward, caught up with traditions but which nevertheless reflect the general consent of their citizens. These governments let themselves being ruled by their "mad" people instead of enlightening and guiding them according to the rules of contemporary social, cultural and educational progress. Might, power, authority is their preference over "wisdom." I believe that there exists among the underdeveloped countries some governments who resemble Gibran's "Wise King of Wirani."

127

In the parable "The Lion's Daughter," Gibran depicts another version of authority, known as autocratic, tyrannical, despotic and dictatorial.

The story revolves around four slaves fanning their old queen sleeping on her throne, and a cat sitting on the lap of the monarch. While the queen is sound asleep, each slave ridicules the queen's old age, ugliness, and complains about his destitution. The cat, on the other side, attempts to awake the slaves from their state of servitude and slumberness. The dialogue between the slaves and the cat reaches its heights, when the queen nodded her head in her sleep and "her crown fell to the floor."[80] At this moment one of the slaves exclaimed "that is a bad omen."[81] And the others unanimously agreed with the first slave. However, here, the cat purred: "The bad omen of one is the good omen of the other."[82] Meaning, that if the slaves wanted, they could now revolt against their queen, who is also made of flesh and blood. The crown which symbolizes "authority" is not a quality, a privilege, or a right with which she alone could be identified. For as a matter of fact, the crown, that is her authority, was fragile and could be dislocated from her. It fell on the ground.

Surprisingly enough, the slaves consented together to put back the crown on the head of the queen. They expressed fear that should the queen wake up and find the crown besides her feet, she might punish them, believing that they threw away her sceptre. To the slaves, the cat purred: "Only a slave restores a crown that has fallen."[83]

In brief, Gibran contends that in the political situation of despotism, it is not the dictator who should be blamed for exercising tyranny, but the people themselves who allow that their wicked government go into existence. The people's failure to revolt in order to change their fate, is to be condemned. Actually, it is understood, that no political revolution could be successful unless a few shed blood. Well, for Gibran it is better "Dying for freedom . . . than living in the shadow of weak submission."[84]

People's Government

Gibranian political philosophy discredits the two previous forms of government as ineffective and contrary to the welfare of the people. In his opinion only a government that cares for, is elected by, and functions directly with the *people*, deserves to continue into existence. Reading his parable *"The King"* one gets the impression that Gibran wrote it under the inspiration of President Abraham Lincoln's Gettysburg address, November 19, 1863. As Lincoln was a firm believer in a government "of the people, by the people, for the people," so too was Gibran. This point is well stressed in his story of the monarch who ruled over the Kingdom of Sadik.

One day, the people of the city approached the palace, and with one voice shouted down to the King of Sadik. His majesty promptly showed up on the scene, and hailed the people in a friendly manner; after which he yielded with no resistance his crown and sceptre to his audience, saying: "My friends, who are no longer my subjects, . . . I will be one of you . . . I would work together with you [in] the fields and vineyards. . . . All of you now are King."[85]

Yet—the story continues—the Kingdom of Sadik did not find peace and justice once the King abdicated. Rather, the people's discontent augmented everyday, because they were now cheated by their masters the rich. And so, as the people had dethroned the monarch, later it became their wish to restore the King by conferring upon him all the rights to govern them. "Now rule us—they told him—with might and with justice."[86] The King replied: "With might, I can, for any man is capable of this ambition. Yet with justice, it is difficult; for justice is a Divine quality and a gift of Heaven."

During the following days, the people voiced their com-

129

plaints to the King about three masters. (Note carefully the monarch's dialogue and sense of justice.) The first person whom the plebeian brought to trial was a baron; their grudge against the defendant was that he treated them as serfs and not as human beings. Straightway the King pronounced against the baron: "The life of one man is as weighty in the scales of God as the life of another. And because you know not how to weight the lives of those who work in your fields,"[87] you are hereby exiled from our Kingdom. Next, the people reported the cruelty of a countess. Instantly, the King ordered to bring to trial the countess. Again, he banished her from the city, laying down the reason: "Those who till our fields and care for our vineyards are nobler than we who eat the bread they prepare and drink the wine of their winepress."[88] Finally, the people denounced their bishop as inhuman and greedy for he made them build a cathedral without that he remunerated them for their hours of labor. To this the King called the bishop, and angrily admonished the prelate, saying: "That cross you wear upon your bosom should mean giving life. But you have taken life from life and you have given none. Therefore you shall leave this Kingdom never to return."[89]

From that day on—the parable adds—the people lived happily, because their ruler was always on their side.

In conclusion to this whole chapter, I believe that Gibran's social contract, legal philosophy and political system, does not advocate the ideology of democracy; for as I see it, democracy is an utopia, while in practical life it breeds capitalism and the class struggle. It is my contention that Gibran leans rather towards socialism; however, not the communistic type but towards a humanistic one; since communism proliferates atheism, and secretly practices the inequality between the governor and the governed. Only within the framework of *authentic socialism,* do the human laws conform to the Divine precepts. One indication of this correspondence between the human laws and the Divine Will consists in the perennial proposition to which Gibran whole heartedly ascribes, namely, *"vox populi vox Dei"* ("the voice of the people is the will of God"). Actually Gibran emphasizes this humanistic-socialistic-Divine argument in the conclusion of his parable *"The King,"* of which we spoke a while ago. In the words of the monarch, the hero of the story, the people themselves are the genuine rulers: "You yourselves are King." As for him, he is "but a thought in the mind of" all of them, and he exists not save in their actions. "There is no such person as governor. *Only the governed exist to govern themselves."*[90]

FOOTNOTES

[1] *S.S.*, p. 39. Gibran always condemned the ecological and environmental calamities of pollution. And on other occasions he favored a halt in technological progress, because he predicted that such advancements would endanger the peace among nations. Miss Young tells us, for instance, that Gibran was against the early productions of airplanes. He believed that air supremacy during wartime would cause grave disasters. Gibran once uttered: "If I could I would destroy every airplane upon the Earth, and every remembrance of that flying evil from men's mind" (B. Young, *op. cit.,* p. 26). This quote should not make us think that Gibran was against scientific or technical *Knowledge qua* such. It simply expresses Gibran's concern for his fellowmen who were someday to be slaughtered from the air. Remember the aircraft that carried the atomic bomb to Hiroshima, or the destruction from the air of the city of Hamburg, or the billions of tons of napalm dropped from the air over Vietnam and elsewhere. . . .

[2] *Th. M.*, p. 89.

[3] Soren Kierkegaard, "Journals:. quoted in *A Dictionary of Existentialism* edited by Ralph B. Winn, New York: Philosophical Library, 1960, p. 98.

[4] *S.H.*, pp. 17-19.

[5] *S.R.*, p. 58.

[6] *S.H.*, p. 19.

[7] *Th. M.*, pp. 27-29.

[8] Martin Buber, *Good and Evil*, New York: Scribner's Sons, 1953, p. 9.— It would seem odd to many intellectuals that I quote a Jewish scholar in a treatise dedicated to an Arab. But I have my reasons which are not political and aim at no politics. My intention is to draw the similarities between Gibran's thought and the classic thinkers acknowledged by the world.

[9] Zenkovsky, V.V., *A History of Russian Philosophy*, New York: Columbia University Press, vol. I, 1967, p. 391.

[10] *S.P.*, p. 4; p. 9.

[11] *ibidem*, p. 9.

[12] Jean-Jacques Rousseau, *Discourse on the Arts and Sciences*, London: J.M. Dent and Sons Ltd, 1947, p. 122.

[13] Jean-Jacques Rousseau, *Discourse on the Origin of Inequality*, London J.M. Dent and Sons Ltd, 1947, p. 163.

[14] *ibidem*, p. 205. Gibran's social philosophy is much closer to Rousseau's than to Nietzsche's. True, Nietzsche denounced the despiritualization and slave-morality that predominate in contemporary culture; however, it is

equally true that he entertained some grim ideas about the basic nature of man, which he considered to be ontologically evil. Nietzsche was pessimistic in his thoughts, much like Schopenhauer. He always depicted man as "merciless, greedy, insatiable, murderous," who hangs "upon the back of a tiger." ("On Truth and Lie," in *The Portable Nietzsche,* ed. by W. Kaufman, New York: The Viking Press, 1968, p. 44). This last statement is a good proof in itself, that shows the discrepancy between Nietzsche and Gibran who emphatically kept faith in the *goodness* of human nature unspoiled by the superego of culture. Of course, I am not implying that Gibran was not, somehow, inspired by Nietzsche's theory of the "superman." Quite the contrary, I have good reasons to suspect that Nietzsche enlightened Gibran about the "slave-morality" and the despiritualization prevailing in our contemporary society.

[15] *The Procession,* p. 74.

[16] *S.S.,* pp. 96-101. Although Gibran never asked us to flee from urban life in order to reestablish the now dying rural form of society, he does seem, nevertheless, attracted to peasant existence. I partially attribute this inclination to his boyhood period, when he lived in Bsherri with his father who was himself a shepherd, farmer and a man of nature. Still, Gibran had philosophical and psychological reasons for doubting of the benefits of the cultural superego upon the psyche of the individual. The following passage contrasts nature versus culture: "We who live amid the excitements of the city know nothing of the life of the mountain villagers. We are swept into the current of urban existence, until we forget the peaceful rhythms of simple country life, which smiles in the spring, toils in summer, reaps in autumn, rests in winter, imitating nature in all her cycles. We are wealthier than the villagers in silver or gold, but they are richer in spirit. What we sow we reap not; they reap what they sow. We are slaves of gain, and they the children of contentment. Our draught from the cup of life is mixed with bitterness and despair, fear weariness; but they drink the pure nectar of life's fulfillment. (*Th. M.,* p. 44).

[17] B.W., p. 15. When it comes to psychoanalizing the psychic of the rich, Gibran is a master. Accordingly, riches (1) grow from greed, (2) lead to miserliness, and (3) despair. His best essay on this subject is *Today and Yesterday.* The article speaks of a man who was poor "yesterday" but happy; "today" the same man has become rich, yet he is unhappy. Witness the differences in behaviors among the socio-economical classes: "Yesterday was I granted life and nature's beauty; today I am plundered of them: yesterday was I rich in my joy; today I have become poor in my riches. Yesterday I was with my flock as a merciful ruler among his subjects; today I stand before gold as a cringing slave before a tyrannous master. I knew not that riches would efface the very essence of my spirit, nor did I know that wealth would lead it to the dark caves of ignorance. And I reckoned not that what people call glory is naught except torment and the pit." (*T.S.,* pp. 39-40).

[18] Barbara Young, *This Man from Lebanon,* New York; Alfred A. Knopf, 1970, p. 128.

[19] *S.P.,* pp. 74-75. Yussif El-Fakri is the same person of whom we spoke early in this chapter. (Cf. above p. 89 sq.)

[20] *S.H.*, p. 24.

[21] *S.P.*, pp. 16-17.

[22] Antonio Caso, *La existencia como economía, como interés y como caridad*, 3rd ed., Mexico: Secretaría de Educación Pública, 1943, p. 43 (Translation by the author).

[23] *ibidem*, p. 102. (Translation by the author). Note that Gibran too considers art not as an economic activity but spiritual. "Art is a bird that soars freely in the sky or roams happily on the ground. No one can change its behavior. Art is a spirit that cannot be bought or sold." (*S.S.*, p. 91.)

[24] *ibidem*, p. 178. (Translation by the author).

[25] *ibidem*, p. 178. (Translation by the author).

[26] *M.S.*, p. 24.

[27] Al-Afghani, quoted in Muhammed al-Makhzumi, *Khatirat Jamal al-Din al-Afghani al Husaymi*, Beirut, 1931, p. 88; p. 218. (Translation by the author).

[28] Qasim Amin, *Tahrir al-Marah*, Cairo: Dar al maaref 1899, p. 154. (Translation by the author). It should be kept in mind that though the secularists identified themselves with European secularism, they never became, however, atheists nor doubted of the validity of Koranic Dogmas. In case of a conflict between religious truth and scientific truth, they would side rank with the *ulema* reformists.

[29] *Th.M.*, p. 28.

[30] *ibidem*, pp. 28-29.

[31] *ibidem*, p. 29.

[32] *ibidem*, p. 83.

[33] *ibidem*, p. 84.

[34] Barbara Young, *This Man from Lebanon*, New York; Alfred A. Knopf, 1970, p. 126.

[35] *S.H.*, pp. 71-73.

[36] *B.P.*, p. 274; pp. 276-278.
See also, Philip Hitti, *Lebanon in History,* New York: St. Martin's Press, 1957, p. 484.

[37] *S.H.*, pp. 92-93. *In the Dark Night* is another poem composed during the famine in Syria and Lebanon. (Cf. *Th.M.*, pp. 35-37).

[38] *S.H.*, p. 94. Gibran writes:

> ". . . And if my
> People had attacked the despots
> And oppressors and died as rebels
> I would have said, "Dying for
> Freedom is nobler than living in
> The shadow of weak submission, for
> He who embraces death with the sword
> Of Truth in his hand will eternalize
> With the Eternity of Truth, for Life
> Is weaker than Death and Death is
> Weaker than Truth." (*S.M.*, p. 94).

[39] The essay *The Fex and the Independence* is full or ironies. It denounces the narrow mindedness and obstinacy of the Orientals. The Orientals manifest paradoxical behaviors; on one hand, they critize the Occidentals; yet on the other hand, they keep on imitating the Europeans' life-style and using their products. (Cf. *S.S.*, pp. 73-75).

[40] The following is the way the rich should socially dialogue with the poor: "Take now, my brother, and return on the morrow with your companions and take you all of what is yours? (*T.S.*, p. 41). For a complete list of the reforms Gibran was seeking to introduce in the Middle-East, read the essay "Your Thought and Mine," in *S.S.*, pp. 109-114.

[41] *S.H.*, pp. 26-27. *See also* F. Nietzsche, *Genealogy of Morals* Transl, by F. Golffiing, (Garden City, New York: Doubleday, 1956), pp. 170-172.

[42] Barbara Young, *This Man From Lebanon*, New York: Alfred A. Knopf, 1970, p. 125.

[43] *Th.M.*, pp. 81-82.

[44] Franz Kafka, *The Trial*, New York: Vintage Books, p. 269.

[45] Franz Kafka, *Parables and Paradoxes*, New York: Schoken Books, 1961, p. 155.

[46] *ibidem*, p. 157.

[47] *S.R.*, pp. 36-37.

[48] *ibidem*, p. 36.

[49] ibidem, p. 56.

[50] *P.*, p. 43.

[51] *S.F.*, p. 49.

[52] *P.*, pp. 40-41.

[53] *W.*, p. 24.

[54] *FR.*, p. 28.

[55] Pascal, *Pensées*, Paris: Librairie Générale Française, 1962, p. 151, No. 329, (Translation by the author).

[56] *Th.M.*, pp. 103-104. Elsewhere Gibran writes: "He who vaunts his scorn of the sinful vaunts his disdain of all humanity." (*Th. M.*, p. 111). Note that this was the same thesis of Pascal. (*See* Pascal, *op. cit.*, ch. III).

[57] *M.S.*, pp. 34-35.

[58] *S.S., p.* 21. The italics are mine.

[59] *T.S.*, p. 35.

[60] Carl Jung, *The Undiscovered Self*, New Nork: A Mentor Book, 1958, p. 22. (Cf. *B.P.* p. 120).

[61] *T.S.*, p. 20.

[62] *T.L.*, p. 84.

[63] *T.S.*, p. 19.

[64] *ibidem*, p. 36.

[65] *S.R.*, p. 28.

[66] *T.S.*, p. 129.

[67] *S.H.*, p. 15; *B.W.*, pp. 95-96.

[68] Thomas Aquinas, *Summa Theologica*, P. I-II, p. 91, a.1.

[69] *S.S.*, p. 46.

[70] *T.L.*, p. 85.

[71] *P.R.*, pp. 47-48.

135

[72] *S.P.*, p. 14.

[73] Fortunately today the Catholic Church has mitigated her position toward marriages contracted in coercion. However, it is also a damn fact that only rich people get their marriage annulled, whereas few are the poors who are successful with this matter. My last remark is a rebuke against Fr. Andrew Dib Sherfan who seems to disregard the right comments of Gibran about the church and forced marriages. (Cf. Sherfan, *Kahlil Gibran: The Nature of Love,* New York: Philosophical Library, 1971, pp. 94-95).

[74] *S.P.*, p. 14.

[75] *V.M.*, pp. 41-42. *See also, P.,* pp. 44-46.

[76] *S.S.*, p. 53.

[77] *MM.*, p. 27.

[78] *ibidem*, p. 2.8

[79] *ibidem*, p. 28.

[80] *FR.*, p. 23.

[81] *ibidem*, p. 23.

[82] *ibidem*, p. 23.

[83] *ibidem*, p. 24.

[84] *S.H.*, p. 94.

[85] *W.*, p. 22.

[86] *ibidem*, p. 23.

[87] *ibidem*, p. 24.

[88] *ibidem*, p. 24.

[89] *ibidem*, p. 25.

[90] *ibidem*, p. 26 The italics are mine.

Chapter Six

LOVE THE QUINTESSENCE OF HUMAN EXISTENCE

A GREAT system of thought pivots around one basic fundamental notion. With this key notion, its author tries to explain existence and all the facets of life. In the mind of the author the fundamental idea becomes a threefold thesis: (1) a *metaphysical* description of existence; (2) an *ethical* categorical imperative for living morally; and (3) finally, a *psychological* counsel for developing a mature personality.

In Gibranian philosophy, *love* occupies the most important place. Already in the previous pages we show the relevancy of "love" in reference to both the mission of the poet, and for the establishment of an authentic society. Now, it remains to lay down the foundation of Gibran's theory-building, and construct his entire system of thought as it actually erects from the dynamics of love. Essentially, therefore his doctrine consists in this: the meaning of human existence is the conscious and progressive manifestation of that principle or source of everything, the manifestation of which in us is signified by love; thus love is the core of human life and the divine supreme law that should guide us and sustain natural law.

Nowadays, when international and national conflicts seem so easily to shatter our human relations, much is being spoken of love as the effective remedy for lessening the misunderstanding between nations, and individuals. However, because of the so many versions proposed by the myriad of the professional theologians, philosophers, psychiatrists, sociologists, magazine editors and literary minds—the true meaning of love is no longer apparent to us. Hence, the hope of this chapter is to reinstate and to reeducate us in genuine love. On this issue, Gibran is a Grand Master, and his interpretation deserves attention.

Basically Gibran distinguishes two forms of love, which correspond to the two regions of human existence, namely, the body and the mind. I personally denominate them by the familiar Greek names of *Eros* and *Agape*. For the sake of clarity, let me here mention that these two are not in Gibran's view contradictory; yet, he holds the possibility that Eros can be misused; only then one form of love will conflict with the other. Henceforth, for methodological reasons I divide this chapter in two sections: (1) Eros, and (2) Agape.

I. EROS

Critic of the Prevailing Misconceptions

Following the trend of thought of Gibran, I am not defining the concept Eros in a Freudian sense; broadly speaking, it signifies "sensuous love." Accordingly, the person derives his pleasure from bodily sensations, and sex is the prototype expression. However, concerning Eros, Gibran speaks of acceptable and perverted acts. A few words, will show the position of our author.

About the carnal love, I have the feeling that Gibran elaborated his theory because of his dissatisfaction with the previous philosophies of Eros. He cast his role as a judge of the prevailing two extreme schools that history has recorded, and while engaged in argumentation his position of "acceptable Eros" developed. These extremes teach either an extravagant "mortification" of the senses, or an extravagant "gratification" of the flesh. Yet, Gibran holds a midway position. His understanding of Eros involves an understanding of the correlated issues of "mind-body," "pleasure" and "pain." How? I believe the best way to grasp his position

138

is to draw respectively the differences between his ideas on Eros and the two historical approaches just stated.

1. Indeed, many ascetics of Platonic mysticism judge the sex-eros taboo, and despise the body which they consider to be the prison where the soul dwells enslaved by the physiological drives. One recalls for instance the famous words of Plato:

> Every seeker after wisdom knows that...
> his soul is a helpless prisoner, chained
> hand and foot in the body, compelled to
> view reality not directly but only through
> its prison bars, and wallowing in utter
> ignorance.[1]

Historically, Plato's mysticism appealed to the early fathers of the Church, who, fearing that their bodily-inclinations would drag them to seeking terrestrial happiness, "they shun all pleasures, lest they neglect the spirit or offend against it."[2] This was the period of the hermits, monks, and religious cloisters. Till today we find, however, the ascetics mortifying their senses, and flagellating their body, as still do some Christian monks, notably the Trappists. Yet Gibran's common sense of reality sees no evil in the biological functions of the body. After all, human existence is not a pure spirit like the angels, nor solely flesh as the animals. Man's being is psychosomatic. Furthermore, nothing that God has created is scandalous, not even sex; "God made our bodies temples for our souls."[3]

Moreover, Gibran who was well acquainted with Freud's psychoanalysis[4] and Jung's psychology, often times said that man could not successfully eliminate, suffocate or self-deny his bodily drives without becoming neurotic. He knew that an excessive rejection of a bodily desire would not nullify the wish but "repress it in the unconscious, until someday the desire would burst out at the surface, causing damages to the psyche of the individual. In *The Prophet* we read this psychoanalytic note:

139

Often times in denying yourself pleasure you
do but store the desire in the recesses of
your being.
Who knows but that which seems omitted today,
waits for tomorrow?
Even your body knows its heritage and its rightful
need and will not be deceived.
And your body is the harp of your soul.
And it is yours to bring forth sweet music from it
or confused sounds.[5]

The real problem with those who deem sex to be taboo, err in their hypothetical thinking that the body and mind are too separate entities. Gibran disagrees with such exaggerated spiritualism—which personally I attribute partly to our heritage of Manichaeism that believed in the co-eternality of the principles Good and Evil. Supposedly the body is the evil principle, and the spirit the good principle, one fighting against the other. Gibran lucidly points:

There is no struggle of soul and
body save in the minds of those
whose souls are asleep and whose
bodies are out of tune.[6]

Allow me at this point to interject a comment of mine. Despite that personally Gibran has not used the very same expressions of the existentialists about the meaning of the human body and its functions, we nevertheless get the impression that he conveyes their same basic ideas. That is, the relation man has to his body is not of a "possessive" kind nor of "having," but is a relation of "being." "I am my body" is a much better linguistic expression that does justice to Gibran's philosophy. However, it should be kept in mind that the statement "I am my body" should not be interpreted as if my existence equals solely my body, otherwise we would err in materialism that sees no other human

140

features beyond the bones, blood and physiological activities. To be faithful to Gibran's trend of thought, the expression "I am my body" merely signifies that my body is the embodiment of my self-consciousness, and conversely the self informs, permeates, and pervades the body, thus constituting a psychosomatic unity.

To repeat then against the dualistic philosophy, man by his metaphysical existence "is" a sexual being; and from the very biological fact that an individual is identified either as a male or a female, it is clear that sex is a reality diffused through all man's being and not to some part, though organically it is localized in some definite regions of the organism. Yet, as an energy, it pervades over the whole man. This is the meaning Gibran conveys when he says:

> Of Love, Understanding is necessary....
> To love I must understand—even understand
> with the *body,* too. When for instance I see
> a beautiful flower, my *body* understands its
> beauty, is drawn to it.[7]

And one day, when he was harassed by an impertinent inquisitive lady who kept on asking him, "But have you never been in love?",—Gibran unashamed answered:

> I will tell you a thing you may not know.
> The most highly sexed beings upon the planet
> are the creators, the poets, sculptors,
> painters, musician—and so it has been
> from the beginning. And among them sex is
> always beautiful, *and it is always shy.*[8]

Although now, Gibran affirms the bond between the physiological drives and intellectual activities, and justifies the innate biological need of sex, he nevertheless warns us against the perverted abuse of carnal-love. Here, he directs his critics against the "playboy" who practices the opposite exorbitances of the spiritualists. Also, he seems more bitter

141

against this extreme extravagance than he is toward the ascetic mystics.

2. Historically, the early Greek philosopher Aristippus of Cyrene (*ca.* 435-355 B.C.) was the first to advocate that the purpose of life consists in the complete gratifications of the bodily inclinations. His theory of hedonism held three principles which are still professed by the sex oriented minds: *One,* that happiness is identical to seeking pleasure and avoiding the least possible pain; *secondly,* that pleasure is quantitative and not qualitative; *thirdly,* that a man should never let go the opportunity of satisfying his biological urges, especially the enjoyment of sex, no matter what are the resulting consequences. Now, judged from the standpoint of Gibran's ethics, metaphysics and psychology, the Aristippus playboy's threefold principles are existentially erroneous.

Thus, concerning the *first principle,* Gibranism recognizes that pleasure is an essential part of life, but not to the point of confusing it with the goal happiness. Defintely it is God's desire that man searches for happiness.[9] Yet happiness is not synonymous to pleasure nor contradictory to suffering. Quite the contrary, happiness necessitates pain and pleasure.[10]

The Aristippus men "who seek pleasure as if it were all,"[11] as *The Prophet* surmises, are really hoping for a utopia. Because any attempt to find a psychological adjustment in the principle of tension-reduction which is their guiding motive for absolute pleasure, is doomed to failure and doomed rather to increasing the tension. This psychological statement of Gibran is shared by many humanistic counselors. Thus, the founder of the third Viennese School of Psychotherapy Viktor Frankl writes:

> I consider it a dangerous misconception of
> mental hygiene to assume that what man needs
> in the first place is . . . a tensionless state.
> What man actually needs is not a tensionless state
> but rather the striving and struggling for
> some goal worthy of him.[12]

Realistically speaking, then, man cannot evade the advent of pain in his life. And far from trying to minimize or to escape neurotically the striking of suffering, man should do better in accepting and finding the true meaning encompassed in suffering. Anxiety, failures, and frustrations are existential predicaments of human essence which when humbly accepted enrich one's life with genuine experiences. Joy and pain are complementary to each other. Hence, Gibran writes:

> I would not exchange the laughter of
> my heart for the fortunes of the
> multitudes; nor would I be content
> with converting my tears, invited by
> my agonized self, into calm. It is my
> fervent hope that my whole life on this
> earth will ever be tears and laughter.[13]

Furthermore, Gibran estimates that pleasure is only at best a by-product or a means-project, because itself it lacks the depth and the height of a concrete goal. In *The Prophet* we read:

> Pleasure is a freedom-song
> But it is not freedom....
> It is a depth calling unto a height,
> But it is not the deep nor the high.
> It is the caged taking wing,
> But it is not space-encompassed.

As for the *second principle* of the Aristippus man, Gibran provides us with countless lucid life examples that disprove its feasibility. Indeed, it would be imprudent on our part to jump on the first coming occasion for gratifying our sexual urges. Quality is far better than quantity. Actually, it is when sex becomes an end in-itself, and the sexual act is always practiced, that the greatest dissapointments in life occur. For instance, some psychological studies show that people who have had plenty of physical relations, end up by hardly feeling any climax in intercourse. We also know that the failure of many marriages stems from an original misintention that the conjoints had about love. They got married simply in order to experience sex, since outside of marriage their religion and superego forbade them to have intercourse. Gibran too in the story of *Madame Rose Hanie* recounts the disappointments of a man who having at first believed that his happiness lied in bodily enjoyments, later on abandoned in frustration such a goal, and dedicated himself like a miser to amassing wealth. Quality and moderation in sex are virtues of a healthy carnal-eros.

Finally, about the *third leitmotive* of the Aristippus which insists on unconditional sex, Gibran retorts that such principle yields a false picture of human existence. While the mortifiers of the flesh had a philosophy that defined the essence of man as *"res cogitans,"* i.e. a spiritual substance, the playboy's approach is *materialistic,* since he extols the body over the mind. In Gibran's opinion, whoever thinks that the meaning of life resides in the total enjoyment of his senses, regardless of the harm he might cause to his fellowman, has degraded human nature, become an animal, and not fulfilled his manhood. Our author pronounces terrible indictments, somehow similar to those of Soren Kierkegaard who in *The Banquet* describes pejoratively the behaviors of the *Don Juan.* Gibran calls the perverted sex-eros "the animal that is concealed in a human being."[15] If sex was all there is to man, then what difference would there be between the human and the beast? A dog is capable of having sexual intercourse! And animal species seek always to gratify their physiological needs; their existence is regulated by the biological law of homeostasis! Then what is there so unique to man?...

Above all Gibran rejects Aristippus' third principle of life, because unethically this principle allows the individual to place his interests over those of the other man. This is known as "egotistic hedonism." Yet, lust always infringes on the freedom of the other fellowman, and defames the Beauty present in the human body. "Beauty reveals herself to us....;

but we approach her in the name of Lust, snatch off her crown of purity, and pollute her garmet with our evil-doings."[16]

It is interesting to notice at this point, that Gibran blames the social nobility and the rich people for the recurrence of sexual perversions. He conjectures that among the wealthy persons, we find the great majority of Don Juans. A classic example of everyday sex vice is the story of Martha. One day a young nobility was trotting in the forests, and saw a beautiful girl gazing at the flowers and trees. He stopped and "in a manner no man had ever used to her before" chatted with Martha, who was very much imoressed by the wealth and kindness of the charming prince. The latter went so far as to promising to Martha to make her his wife. Unfortunately, after having taken advantage of the poor orphan, he let her down and departed. Martha pregnant became later a prostitute in the City of Lebanon, simply in order to provide housing and food to her child Fouad. Commenting on the story Gibran retorts:

> All this did he do, smiling, and
> behind soft words and loving gestures
> did he conceal his lust and animal desire.[17]

In connection to the foregoing I have found some texts where Gibran sounds a bit like the Platonists whom I discussed above. It is my personal conviction that Gibran wrote those lines not in contradiction to what he held at one time against the ascetic Platonist, but simply to counsel us contrary to the Aristippus man not to give way unrestrictedly to all the whims of the flesh; otherwise these erotic inclinations could run wild in our life, making us slave of our reinforced carnal habits. If this had to happen, we would twice hurt ourselves and hurt those whom we encounter as the story *Martha* shows. Thus, in his poem *Have Mercy, My Soul,* Gibran figures that a body grown strong in its desire is a prison for the spirit grown weak.

You, O soul, are rich in your wisdom;
this body is poor in its understanding.
You deal not with leniency
And it follows you not.
This, my soul, is the sum of wretchedness.[18]

And elsewhere he writes: "... my mind ... fled from the prison of matter to the realm of imagining, ..."[19]

I repeat, these passages do not make of Gibran a philosopher who severs the body from the mind; they merely remind us, contrary to the Aristippus philosophy, of Gibran's advice to keep control over our bodily desires, and to be moderate in our sexual life. Man should regard his sex-eros not as an end in-itself, but as a mode of expression for his disinterested love. At this moment Eros fuses into Agape, and becomes a version of genuine love. That is to say, sex is justified as soon as it becomes a vehicle of love-agape. It is vital to understand this point, for it is in this way only that Gibran sanctifies sex.

Speaking of Eros-Sex-Agape, let me add that I discovered in Gibran some prerequisite conditions that render the physical intercourse acceptable. These are "shyness,"[20] "honesty, reality,"[21] "honor and cleanness and decency,"[22] and above all, love for one another should be the motive for the sexual act. If one partner feels no real attachment for the other, then the act is prostitution. This is the logic Gibran develops about those marriages that have been contracted for other reasons that love-agape. In his opinion, the signing of marriage papers does not give permission to the conjoints to sleep together, if in the first place there was no love between them. Love is not a matter of legality of law. Nor is sexual love restricted to marriage situations. Gibran is permissive about premarital sex so long the two "care" for each others. Haskell reports:

He has no code about sex except honesty, reality. 'Should you say,' asked I, 'that if a man or woman loved seven and lived sexually with seven it was all right?' 'If the seven were all willing, yes,' said he.[23]

In conclusion, let us sum up the misconceptions of the disguised love. Love is not synonymous with sex, notwithstanding that sex when properly defined becomes a way of expressing the experience of that ultimate togetherness called love. Gibranism does not inhibit Eros, he simply subordinates it to Agape. Also, authentic love is not a love that "reckons" and "sorts out" for personal interests, such as financial purposes, social prestige.[24] On the contrary Gibran has all reasons to believe that a calculative love is a self-love that neurotically has never transcended the Freudian primary narcissistic stage of a masochist child.

Gibran's Sexual Life

Was Gibran sincere and consistent in his daily actions with what he preached philosophically to others about the sanctified sex?

Many biographers have discussed Gibran's sexual life. In my opinion most of what they wrote lacks biographical verifications. I consider some of their sayings either speculative or incomplete, because really they were acquainted with our author for only a short time. Therefore I see the justification to raise anew the theme "Gibran's sexual life."

The last book that Knopf published *The Love Letters of Kahlil Gibran and Mary Haskell, and Her Private Journal* (1972) brings new revelations to the scholars on Gibran. And although Miss Mary Haskell could not have recorded in her journal all the minute details of Gibran's private life, since she lived in Boston and he was in New York, still her biography contains the clue to our question.

In reading Haskell's diary and the correspondence the two sent to each other, I get the picture that Gibran was

147

definitely not an impotent sexual man. Rather like most of the great minds he seems to have believed that success in artistic and literary creativity, somehow demands the presence of a woman. And indeed, Gibran had rapports with many women. It is not possible for us biographers to estimate accurately how many women entered in his private life. Nevertheless, I count among them a French girl nicknamed Micheline who followed him to Paris in 1908 from Boston; the American biographer Barbara Young who remained with him from 1923 to 1931; an "older woman" in Paris who kept him in her home "because he had no money, because a woman was likelier than a man to supply money, and because such things weren't done without pay"[25]; and of course, his benefactress Miss Mary Haskell; and a host of female models who would pose nude during his painting.

Was then Gibran a sexual-minded? Not all! Haskell testifies that "Kahlil is not sexual-minded, but absorbed in bigger things." He was "physically shy,"[26] and sometimes ignorant about sex. In a letter he wrote to Haskell in 1917 in reply for the gifts and a book on sex that the latter had sent him, he confessed being naive about sexuality.

> Thank you for the sugar and the books. I shall consume both with much care! Somehow I have never been able to enjoy fully reading a book on sex. Perhaps I have not been curious enough, or perhaps I have been mentally timid. But I now want to know all things under the sun, and the moon, too. For all things are beautiful in themselves, and become more beautiful when known to man. . . .[27]

Instead of spending his sex-energy in intercourse, Haskell reaffirms that Gibran transformed the libidinal power into art-production.[28] All this comes to confirm what Freud said of artists, namely, they "sublimate" and "cathecte" their sexual warmth into creativity.[29] I find it interesting that

Gibran made statements in 1912 and 1914 similar to those of Freud concerning the sex-economy among the artists. Thus, he used to speak to Haskell: "And I too, have great warmth sexually. I think a great deal of sex power goes transformed into my work."[30]

Actually, his dedication to drawing and writing was the very reason why he refused to get married, notwithstanding that the idea of marrying Haskell haunted him from 1910 to 1912.[31]

> Discussing marriage one afternoon in the studio, after he had read the piece on *marriage* from *The Prophet*, one of the several guests said smilingly, 'Tell us, why have you never married?' Smiling also he replied 'Well...you see it is like this. If I had a wife, and if I were painting or making poems, I should simply forget her existence for days at a time. And you know well that no loving woman would put up with such a husband very long.'[32]

We are also told by Haskell that Gibran would sometimes abstain from physical intercourses, because he feared the possible "misfortune consequences"[33] of such a liaison, viz., "pregnancy" of the woman. Another reason for which he would keep his "sex emotion down"[34] was for sake of respect and love-agape he held towards the woman. "Love—the greater love—is extremely careful about intercourse and is bodily shy."[35]

I am not trying to prove with these quotations that Gibran always sublimated his sexual urges. Nor am I trying to convey to the reader the impression that Gibran had little sexual relations. Whoever peruses the private journal of Miss Haskell would rather see how intensely moved he was by the idea of sex.

> He had said, there are three centers in everybody —head, heart, sex. One or another or two of them

149

lead, in each person—not in the same equilibrium at different times perhaps in a given person. 'With me,' he said, 'head and heart led until a few years ago. And then sex'...[36]

Let us take, as an example, his rapport with Haskell. At no time has Haskell bluntly reported that she slept with Gibran. But she avowed that they kissed and freely touched each other.[37] She even one day undressed herself in his studio, and Gibran put his arms round her neck and kissed her on the breasts, as they stood.[38] Personally, I believe Gibran had a sexual relation with Haskell, as with many others who visited him frequently in his studio. Nevertheless, I also believe that he was not a sex maniac as some have pretended. From the very fact that we know he never hurt somebody, but was considerate of others, Gibran had sanctified sex in his life and converted it into Agape. A man acts as to what personality he is. The next section testifies that Gibran lived the precepts of Agape over and above the erotic impulses.

2. AGAPE

Originally, "Agape" was coined by the Greeks to describe the early Christians' "brotherly love" in connection with the Lord's Supper. With time the word came to signify the Evangelic-love in contrast to the Erotic-love or concupiscence. In Gibran, Agape stands for spiritual love, but not necessarily the Christian, although he is deeply influenced by Christ's sermons on Love. Gibranism extrapolates the philosophy of Agape illustrated in the New Testament, and makes it a natural, universal phenomenon pertaining to all creeds. Therefore, you don't need to be a Christian to practice Agape; such love is primarily a metaphysical datum and its directives apply unconditionally to any one who wants to live morally worthy, in as much as it is a psychological rule for developing a healthy personality.

To insure a clear exposition to the reader, I propose to elaborate step by step Gibran's phenomenology of Agape, and in the long run integrate the eclectic elements that our author develops in reference to love.

Love, The Essence of Existence

Every profound thinker has for a major concern the search for an answer to Shakespeare's question: "To be, or not to be," i.e. why is there being instead of non-being! In technical language we call metaphysics or ontology the discipline that searches for the meaning of existence. Up to the present day, the history of thought abounds with the many proposed metaphysics. Gibran too, discussed existence, yet his theory is not as abstract and theoretical as the philosophies of the scholar academicians. Gibranism is a people's philosophy, something quite different from a philosopher's philosophy. Nonetheless, his system makes much sense.

In his opinion, then, the true essence of existence is "love." In the essay *The Victors* we read the exclamation: love, "You are my very being."[39] Also, the novel *The Broken Wings,* calls love "the law of nature."[40] i.e. the *"raison d'être"* of existence. And in his poem *Song of Love,* he states that love is the very essence of nature, man, and the historical events. The world is guided by the principle of love. Love generates, produces, even sometimes destroys life, yet it always sustains the world in its eternity.

> . . . I smiled at Helena and she destroyed Tarwada;
> yet I crowned Cleopatra and peace dominated
> The Valley of the Nile.
> I am like the ages—building today and
> destroying tomorrow; . . .[41]

To understand why Gibran makes of love the ontological necessity of existence, we must recall that for him existence entails an act of "creation" and not of "fabrication" or "generation." His metaphysics is that of a believer in God. God creates existence. "The God separated a spirit from Himself and fashioned it into beauty."[42] Now, God creates out of an act of love. Furthermore, Gibran holds the same metaphysical idea of the scholastic philosophers, when he reasons that between the effects and the cause, there is a degree of proportionality in existence. Thus his logic maintains that if "God is love."[43]—because "The Infinite keeps naught save Love, for it is in its own likeness,"[44]—so will the products of God "be" made of love.

Gibran's philosophy of existence is *monistic,* in that he believes in the reality of the One principle that causes life. That source of everything is love. "...Everything bespeaks love."[45] Hence, Gibran answers to the Shakespearian interrogation: "If existence had not been better than non-being, there would have been no being."[46] The adverb "better" in this state of affairs stands synonymous to "love"; love, then, is the quintessence of existence, and "no thing shall prevail against it."[47] As for the second *"nous"* (in Greek, spirit) of the Manichaeians and Platonists, which is the Evil, Gibran disqualifies its autonomous reality. He assumes that if evil exists it is only present in man's actions, and it is never an independent principle, that governs the world as an equal to love.

At this stage, I remind the readers that our author is not the only thinker who philosophizes that love is the ontological core of existence. Our contemporary existentialists of the right wing, the theists, share Gibran's thesis. For instance, Kierkegaard, Marcel, Buber and Jaspers have concluded that the essence of being is love. They also teach, much like Gibran, that the self cannot genuinely encounter reality unless man assumes the existential attitude of love. In such attitude the individual does not differentiate what he is from what he finds in front of him. Because in the final analysis, the being of the individual man is not different from the other beings, since in the first place both the person and the rest of the universe have issued from the same source, namely, the Love of God. Nurturing such a metaphysical attitude one finds himself on the right path to discovering truth, and living in peace with the world. Gibran would ascribe to Marcel's statement *"esse"* is *"co-esse,"* to be is to be-with-the-rest-of-the-world. Gibran illustrates this metaphysical inseparateness in the following way:

> Everything in creation exists within you, and
> everything in you exists in creation. You are
> in borderless touch with the closest things,
> and, what is more, distance is not sufficient
> to separate you from things far away. All things
> from the lowest to the loftiest, from the smallest
> to the greatest, exist within you as equal things.[48]

Between the self and the rest of reality there is an intimate bond, which is explainable from the fact that the two come into being from an identical focus point: the love of God. Marcel too, considers love the best ontological attitude for communicating and entering into the sphere of existence:

> Love, insofar as distinct from desire or as
> opposed to desire, love treated as the subordination
> of the self to a superior reality, a reality at my
> deepest and more *truly me* than I am myself—love
> as the breaking of the tension between the self and
> the other, appears to me to be what one might call
> the *essential ontological* datum.[49]

If existence is fashioned of love, then what should man *do* in order to live up to the expectations of love? How does a man animated by Agape behave *morally* worthy? Which are the *criteria* and *norms* of genuine love? The following headings attempt to provide a sincere solution to these queries.

153

Love is Disinterestedness

One of the signs of Agape is that it doesn't "reckon" nor is "self-centered." Agape is vivified by the spirit of "giving" without calculation of receiving in return. Here, the self generously gives to others not with the pretence of what they need most for themselves, rather the self gives to the point of depriving itself of what it personally needs most. The kind of "giving" Gibran advocates is other than the material goods. Almustafa, the prophet, preaches that the giving of *oneself* is a far more superior type than the giving of possessions. "You give but little when you give of your possessions. It is when you give of yourself that you truly give."[50] To illustrate the deep meaning encompassed in the statement, I will cite the case of a lady whom I once heard responding to a call received from the Saint Vincent De Paul organization: Well, I really don't mind to help the unfortunates. I will send you every month a check, but please don't ask me to volunteer of my time for visiting the poor and the sick in the hospital. . . . In the prophet's opinion, this lady did not practice the noblest act of giving, because she refused to give of herself. It is easy to give of one's overabundant wealth, yet, the truly meritorious act is that of making oneself available to others.

> Generosity is not in giving me that which I need
> more than you do, but it is in giving me that
> which you need more than I do.[51]

True love, then, makes sacrifices for the happiness of the beloved. It is unselfish. Leibniz, the philosopher of the eighteenth century used to say: *Amare est gaudere felicitate alterius.* (To love is to seek the felicity of the beloved.) The novel *The Broken Wings,* provides us with an instance of this thinking of disinterestedness. In the chapter "The Sacrifice," we read that Gibran asked Selma, who knew that she had to marry the nephew of the bishop, to flee with him to another country despite a possible indictment from the prelate. But, Selma turned down the offer of Gibran on the ground that her beloved might someday be looked upon by the native villagers as an adulterer and a homebreaker. She was thinking in the interests of Gibran. notwithstanding that the proposal would have saved her from the fate of marrying a man she never loved. Witness how she expresses her unselfish feelings.

> Love only taught me to protect you even from
> myself. It is love, purified with fire, that
> stops me from following you to the farthest land.
> Love kills my desires so that you may live freely
> and virtuously. Limited love asks for possession
> of the beloved, but the unlimited asks only for
> itself.[52]

Love Knows No Time and No Space

To many minds, the adage "out of sight out of mind," seems to hold. Yet, retorts Gibran, should oblivion of the beloved result as a consequence of an abscence or a lack of physical encounter, then, it should be assumed that in the first place genuine love had not planted its deep roots in the hearts of the lovers. It is much safer to presume that their love was "romanticism." Paradoxically, the prophet teaches that spatial distance and the lapse of time increase love. By being far away from the beloved, the lover learns more to appreciate his partner, and ceases to take him or her for granted. "Love knows not its own depth until the hour of separation."[53]

In time of separation, love becomes a "longing" and a "hope" that inspires the anticipation of unification in the near future. When Almustafa, returned after twelve years to his homeland, a woman named Karima who assisted at the death of the prophet's mother, complained that he remained too long hidden from the people's face. But, the prophet Almustafa replied:

Twelve years? Said you twelve years, Karima?
I measured not my longing with the starry rod,
nor did I sound the depth there of. For love when
love is homesick exhausts time's measurements and
time's soundings.[54]

For a person to know if he is really in love, he should try
for a while the acid test of separation. Today many counselors
are beginning to recommend a trial separation for a couple
whose marriage is on the verge of crumbling. The idea is that
one sees best the situation when one is aloof. Love too, needs
distance. In a letter Gibran wrote in 1911 to Haskell, he
stated: "To understand the world one must be far, far away
from the world. . . . One must be at a little distance from
great things in order to see them well."[55]

The person who surges stronger during the moments of
separation, experiences that his love transcends the spatial
and temporal frontiers. And indeed, it is the mark of Agape
to be boundless. The prophet speaks wisely with the words:

Who among you does not feel that his power to love
is boundless? . . . And is not time even as love is,
undivided and spaceless?[56]

Love is Stronger Than Death

In connection with the idea that love is timeless and spaceless, Gibran develops his theory of love for the departed souls.
He maintains that death does not separate the lover from the
beloved. Death is not the end of a love affair. Love *per se*
involves a relation of communication, of intimacy, which can
never be destroyed, not even by death. Had love a life span,
then it would be futile and existence as such would be absurd
because there would be no guarantee for the value of the love-
deed. Forgetfulness is an indication of a love-desire, but not
of a love-deed. Gibran points out:

Verily the vastest distance is that which lies
between . . . that which is but a deed and that
which is a desire . . .
For in remembrance there are no distances;
and only in oblivion is there a gulf that
Neither your voice nor your eye can abridge.[57]

Here we are at the peak of Agape. In relation to the dead,
Agape assumes the attitudes of "hope," "faithfulness" and
complete "availability" towards the deceased. First *hope,* because such longing strengthens the will in time of despair and
sorrow. The lover convinces himself that the beloved has not
disappeared. The presence of the beloved accompanies the
lover everywhere. Hence, hope at this stage of love becomes
creative *fidelity.* Between the survivor and the dead arises a
relationship in which the self surpasses his awareness of a
solitary ego; he sees himself bound to the memories and the
resolutions he took while the beloved was alive. In other
words, the self experiences a deep *availability* of dedication
to the loved one. He remains faithful to the image of the
dead not only on Sunday or for a few hours every morning
but till the end of his life.

For Gibran love proves philosophically the *immortality of
the soul.* By the very fact that I still love my beloved even
after his death is not a hallucination nor a psychotic phase.
My love is a reality. My beloved probably waits for me some-
place, where we will unite again. Love outlives the biological
death. In the *Nymphs of the Valley* we are told that two
lovers met each other after two thousand years in the temple
of Astar, and finally realized their wish which was to be
together, a desire that was forbidden them by the priests.

Astarte bring back to this life the souls
of lovers who have gone to the infinite
before they have tasted of the delights
of love and the joys of youth. . . . We
shall meet again, Nathan, and together

157

drink of the morning dew from the cups
of the narcissus and rejoice in the sun
with the birds of the fields.[58]

All those who have believed in love, have emphasized the
role *God* plays in keeping the tie between the partners. Love
is stronger than death because love is a gift from God.[59] And
God himself is eternal. After vowing to each other faithfulness
and spiritual love, despite the fact that Selma was to be married legally to Mansour Bey, Gibran finds consolation in love
and retorts to Selma: "love, my beloved Selma, will stay with
me to the end of my life, and after death the hand of God will
unite us again."[60]

To understand Gibran on this point, we must be Gibran.
It is difficult for a scientific and technocratic mind to comprehend the meaning of that feeling. It is a personal experience
felt by the self. In Max Weber's and Nicolai Hartman's
words: neither intelligence nor the senses will ever make us
discover a real value. The simple definition of love will not
teach very much to him who has not loved. It is certain that
this value appears to us concretely insofar as we *live it,* and
sofar as we sense it penetrating our life of feeling, volition,
intellection, freedom, etc. . . ; in one word, we have to feel
its presence enveloping us entirely.

Yet, Gibran is not alone for proposing love as a proof for
the veridicality of immortality. The theistic existentialists have
advanced a similar argument. A character in one of Marcel's
plays says that to love is to affirm "Thou, at least, Thou shall
not die." Also, in a lecture titled *Death and Immortality,*
Marcel alluding to the death of his wife exclaimed: "You
cannot simply have disappeared; if I believed that I would
be a traitor."[61] I purposely quote from academic philosophers, in order to establish the relevancy of Gibran's simply
worded philosophy.

A closely related issue to the limitlessness of the feeling of love, is the meaning that love *per se* prescribes no national, cultural or political frontiers. Or to put it bluntly, love ought to be *universal*. Often times our author depicts love as an inexhaustible "power."[62] By this token he conveys that the human heart has the *natural capacity* to engulf the whole of humanity; Agape motivates man to enter in communion with the entire creation. "Who among you does not feel that his power to love is boundless?"[63] In Gibran's opinion, the cultural, religious and political values are largely responsible for the restrictions put on the power of love. For example, we know that politics indoctrinates the self to care for only those who are born in the same geographical milieu. Politics inculcates in the minds of its citizens attitudes of discrimination, segregation and prejudices towards the humans of other nations. Politics narrow the range of expansion of the love-energy. Actually, all the so-called extrinsic social values represent a hindrance to the growth of the spirit of humanism in the individual. That is why Gibran reacts harshly against the partition of the earth into government countries, and places humanism over patriotism.

> Humans are divided into different clans and tribes,
> and belong to countries and towns. But [for] . . .
> myself . . . the universe is my country and the human
> family is my tribe. . . .
> . . . If my people rose, stimulated by plunder and
> motivated by what they call "patriotic spirit" to
> murder, and invaded my neighbor's country, then
> upon the committing of any human atrocity I would
> hate my people and my country. . . .
> Humanity is the spirit of the Supreme Being on earth
> and that Supreme Being preaches love and good-will.[64]

159

Occasionally, Gibran maintained that love makes us develop a "universal consciousness,"[65] which is a sense of feeling meaningfully linked to humanity through the sacred ties of existence. Love at this moment becomes a categorical universal imperative that guides our conscience in her moral conducts. To illustrate the point, let me refer to another great philosopher Immanuel Kant, who somehow preceeded Gibran on this maxim. To Kant's contention, an action is morally worthy if one can will that it becomes a universal rule which all should imitate; otherwise it is wrong. That is, the acid test of the moral rightness of an action lies in whether one could allow that his action set an example which everyone should follow. If one cannot "will" this, then the conduct is evil. This is why lying is not morally justifiable under any circumstances; for we cannot will that lying becomes a universal practice which individuals ought to use.[66] Kant's ethical formulation repeats in different words Christ's golden rule that Gibran himself has adopted, namely, "Do unto others as you would have them do unto you." Of course, the only available standard we have to judge the pros and the cons of the deed, is the law of love. Love, therefore, originates in us a "universal consciousness," because its precepts command us at least to respect all humans regardless of their race, religion and socioeconomic class.

With this same trend of thought, Gibran adds that the practice of universal love develops in us what he calls "the Greater Self."[67] Accordingly, there are two "me's" in constant civil war against each other.[68] The small self is egotistic, and its scope of "human concern" is confined to parochialism; the greater self, on the other hand, is motivated by spiritual love, and aspires to a cosmic union with the universe. Humanists, visionaries, mystics and philanthropists have experienced the presence of "the larger and better self." Miss Haskell, in one of the entries in her private journals, provides us with a good description as to how the greater self of Gibran would behave and feel.

'Did you ever look upon the present through the eyes of the future?' said Kahlil at night. 'I have become familiar with the human mind today—in many parts of the world—its attitude toward things, its reactions, its tendencies, its modes of working and I know how it will look upon things a hundred years from now.' . . .

I have come to a sense of a larger I. . . . My Buddha, I call that larger, longer-living self; and now I pray to lend itself to the Larger's purpose. — . . .

There is, in Kahlil, a being longing simply to be allowed to love, to lavish itself, to speak its innermost, to be closer than inner souls can conceive—an unspeakable sensitiveness.[69]

Love, Hate, Forgiveness

How does Gibran reconcile the situation of enmity with the precept of universal love? I confess that I find Gibran's ethics of love quite realistic on the topic of "hate." He is not full of optimism like Leibniz, nor is he impressed by the pessimism of Hobbes. He knows that there exist sadistic men who enjoy hurting others. Still, he holds that Agape transcends the sclerosis of hate. *"Forgiveness," "tolerance"* and *"pity"* constitute the secret strength of a love harassed by hostilities. And rather than weakening the dynamics of love, the enmity of others is a beneficiary source for cleansing the heart, for renewing our humanism, and above all a blessed occasion for practising the universal love. If there were no outside negative interferences, then the course of love would be a matter of mechanical routine, a conditioned habit and a monotony. Fortunately, life gives us the opportunity to probe to ourselves our ability to love, even our opponents.

> It is only when you are pursued that you
> become swift.[70]

The truly good is he who is one with all
those who are deemed bad.[71]
Love which is not always springing is
always dying.[72]

The person "metamotivated" by *Agape*—to borrow a concept from A. Maslow's psychology—lucidly understands that
he simply cannot always succeed in having his neighbors
return his love. He has to live on his own with his enemies.
Towards his adversaries he assumes the attitudes of "forgiveness" and "kindness" which is "the shadow of God in man."[73]
Now, it is this "universal love," i.e. the sense of feelings
related unrestrictedly to the whole of Being, that binds the
individual to accept with *resignation* the sufferings, ridicules
and rejections that his enemies inflict upon him. After all,
love is not rosy, its ways "are hard and steep."[74] "For even as
love crowns you so shall he crucify you. Even as he is for
your growth so he is for your pruning."[75] Of course, Gibran
does not advise us to go after our enemies and seek that they
hurt us so that we keep on testing ourselves on the precepts of
love. This would be masochism rather than heroism.

What happens to "hate" in the metaphysics of Gibran?
Could hate be given a status of independent existence? The
metaphysics of hate is a crucial one. To grasp its place in
Gibran's system helps us explain two theses: (1) Why he
has insisted that love is all there is to existence, and that,
therefore, love by its very essence is absolute, timeless and
spaceless; and (2) why he thought of love as the sole existential attitude for meeting reality and gaining perfect knowledge of reality.[76]

To Gibran's contention, human existence, and all existences
could not have been fashioned by hate; only Love and Life
are identical.[77] Yet, the old Persian philosophers would have
us believe in the equal principles of Good and Evil. Gibran
discards the Evil principle, on the ground that Life is Harmony, Beauty, Truth. Had the Evil principle prevailed we
would have experienced confusion, contradiction and disorder

162

in the face of existence. Gibran goes even so far as to deny that there is any evil *per se* in human actions, or that man is capable of evil for evil. In other words, man cannot aim at evil as a end. Evil is never apprehended for, in and through itself. What is called evil, the individual perceives as a good, whose fulfillment it is believed will realize a desired goal. For example, a thief does not steal for the purpose of doing evil; rather he judges the act of robbing to be a desirable means for procuring himself good. The scholastic philosophers used to say that evil is a transformed good. Similarly Gibran maintains that evil is but a desire invested with the features of good.

> Of the good in you I can speak, but not of
> the evil.
> For what is evil but good tortured by its own
> hunger and thirst? . . .
> You are good in countless ways, and you are
> not evil when you are not good, you are only
> loitering and sluggard.[78]

Whenever Gibran speaks of hate, he does so from the psychological standpoint. I found three psychological statements concerning hate. (1) Hate is an *"emotion"* whose power is proportional to the energy of love. Chronologically, one must have loved first so that he may hate afterwards. Hence, hate is but love to hatred turned. Or also, as Mikhail Naimy, a close friend to our author, put it: "And what is Hate but love repressed, or Love withheld,"[79] Gibran illustrates the transformation of love into hate in the parable *The Love Song*. Once upon a time a poet composed a beautiful song on love and sent a copy to all his acquaintances, along to a lady he had just met. Some time later, a messenger came inviting the poet to visit the parents of the lady, in order to talk about the preparations for the "betrothal." But the poet replied: "My friend, it was but a song of love . . . sung . . . to every woman." Immediately the lady got aggressive, and exclaimed:

163

"From this day unto my coffin-day I shall hate all poets for your sake."[80]

(2) From another psychological viewpoint, only the weak personalities employ the technique of hate as a protective strategy in order to guard their self-esteem. Hate becomes a Freudian *mechanism of ego-defense* against circumventive discomforts and anxieties. This is common to personalities whose Agape has not become universal. They react violently towards the external obstructions with the shield of hate. Now, the students of Freud will remember that the use of defense mechanisms is an indication of neurosis. Gibran writes: "Often times I have hated in self-defense: but if I were strong I would not have used such a weapon."[81]

(3) Finally, Gibran dissuades us from practicing hate for mental health purposes. Hate destroys our mental hygiene; it weakens our faculties of thinking, feeling and volition; it raises up our blood tension, and in the long run may accelerate the moment of *death*. Note that Freud too attributed our biological death to the hyperaggressiveness withheld inwardly. In our context aggressiveness is identical to hate. Gibran in his turn equates hate with death. "Hate is a dead thing. Who of you would be a tomb."[82]

The conclusion we reach emphasizes that in love, forgiveness and kindness, the self preserves its health and self-actualizes its personality, because the self then learns to cope realistically with but not *escape* from the advent of frustrations and sorrows.

Love Gives Delicious Pain

Following what has been said in the preceeding section, it is clear that human history unfolds itself in situations of joy and sorrow. No man can be exempted from experiencing desolation. However, not everybody seems to accept with resignation this fate of human destiny. The pessimists advocate that because suffering is unavoidable then existence is *absurd* and God is our executioner. And many atheists have become unbelievers for failling to reconcile intellectually the recurrence of pain, either the physical, moral or psychological, with the idea of an Omnipotent, *Summum Bonum Deity.*[83] Yet in the opinion of Gibran, there is a way to justify human miseries. His argument is not scientific, but one of "common sense." Whoever adheres to it, I believe will find both the fulfillment of his humanism and eventually his faith in the Divine. Gibran's argument runs, therefore, as follows: rather than hindering the growth of self-identity, anxieties procure self-knowledge. The French poet Alfred de Musset once wrote: *"Nul ne se connait tant qu'il n'a point souffert."* Translated in Gibran's vernacular, Musset statement signifies that "perplexity is the beginning of knowledge."[84] Life would be quite dull, and the person a pantomime if there were no situations of tragedy to awaken us from the slumber of routine. The self gets more conscious, more involved when he faces afflictions. Similarly, concerning the positive life-events such as happiness, joy, contentment—the self could not *appreciate* them enough, if from time to time he were not tested by sufferings, pains and discomforts. "Who has not seen sorrow cannot see joy."[85] Hence, instead of complaining and blaming God, Gibran sees goodness even in the worst.

Actually, it is the spirit of Agape that counts for Gibran's attitude of resignation in front of vexations. Around 1903 when our author lost consecutively his mother, sister, and half-brother, he grew to visualize that pain and sufferings were necessary conditions that ought to be mixed with Agape, so that the foundations of the latter become unshakeable in the heart of the individual. A love that had to shed tears in order to prove its love is a true love. "Love that is cleansed by tears will remain eternally pure and beautiful."[86].

The adage says, there are no beautiful and scented roses without thorns. So too it goes for love. To love is to be willing to undergo self-sacrifices. And indeed, when you love, you assume the beloved's misfortunes, shortcomings and sorrows. The *responsibility* that accompanies love will sometimes cause you headaches. Verily, love is one with tears. Yet, they

are tears of "painful joy."[87] "The pain that accompanies love
. . . and responsibility also gives delight."[88] Once again, the
prophet Almustafa preaches:

> When love beckons you, follow him,
> Though his ways are hard and steep.
> And when his wings enfold you yield
> to him,
> Though the sword hidden among his
> pinions may wound you.
> And when he speaks to you believe in
> him,
> Though his voice may shatter your dreams
> as the north wind lays waste the garden.[89]

In brief, Gibran teaches that love is a *"molar behavior."*
He compares it to an atom with its sub-atomic particles.
"The chemist who can extract from his heart's elements compassion, respect, longing, patience, regret, surprise and forgiveness and compound them into one can create that atom which
is called LOVE."[90] And in *The Broken Wings* he states lucidly
that love is pervasive over the whole self. Also, he enumerates
the three states of presence of the beloved: in the mind, the
heart, and at nights in the dreams. "She [Selma] became a
supreme thought, a beautiful dream, and an overpowering
emotion living in my spirit."[91]

Love Develops Genuine Bonds of Intersubjectivity

The human being could not survive at all if he had to
depend on his own instincts and abilities alone. Biologically
and psychologically, the person needs the help of other minds
in order to grow healthy and self-realize his birth potentials.
In the words of our contemporary European philosophers,
man is a *relational being* by the very nature of his existence.
This simple truth was actually discovered and expressed more
than twenty centuries ago by the Stagirite, Aristotle, in his
famous dictum "Man is a social animal." Gibran too has

reiterated that man is a *communal* creature. No man is an island. Frankly, the self owes to others what he possesses and how he behaves existentially; "In truth . . . you owe all to all men."[92] The self can at no time and place divorce his existence from the presence of other minds; the self is somehow doomed (pardon me for the expression) to live his life always and everywhere, even during solitude, in relation to other selves.

> Your most radiant garment is of the other
> person's weaving;
> Your most savory meal is that which you eat
> at the other person's table;
> Your most comfortable bed is in the other
> person's house.
> Now tell me, how can you separate yourself
> from the other person?[93]

Being-together is a law of existence: for that, Gibran advises us to nurture good interpersonal relations instead of the negative social attitudes. In a healthy intersubjectivity the self gains everything, while in the opposite the self loses everything, including his psychological well-being, as we showed previously about "hate." Here, Gibran has in mind the principle of brotherhood and love as the solution for establishing authentic interpersonal contacts. Once more the prophet Almustafa teaches:

> We live upon one another according to
> the law, ancient and timeless. Let us
> live thus in loving-kindness. We seek one
> another in our aloneness, and we walk the
> road when we have no hearth to sit beside.
> My friends and my brothers, the wider road
> is your fellow-man.[94]

If we ruminate seriously on the last quotes, we should come in agreement with Gibran that at birth we are simply *"one-half"* of our self. The other half is outside of us and can be discovered just and only through the love-encounter with

167

the other. Gibran illustrates this point in the short tale *The Victors*. A poor fellah fell in love at the sight of a pretty girl. But he was not allowed to marry her because the girl belonged to a high social rank; she was the daughter of the Emir. While pensive in melancholy, the princess appeared to him and in a loving voice exclaimed: "You appeared in my dreams of sadness, and your image ended my loneliness. You are the compassion of my lost soul, and you are my *other half* from which I was torn when I came to this world."[95] The story ends saying that the two flee together to another village.

Gibran is not at all wrong when he maintains that true love develops one's personality. In practical life, there is no discovery of the self, no self-realization and no self-knowledge, until the individual consents to share life with another "self." And it is precisely the appeal of the other self which helps me to break loose from my self-centeredness, and liberate myself from myself. In my daily interpersonal dealings, the other's appeal reveals to me an entirely new, perhaps wholly unsuspected dimension of my being. In relation to him I find the answers to the Socratic question: Who am I? Am I a patient or impatient personality? Am I capable of faithfulness in marriage life? Have I been socially conditioned to hate Negroes, Jews, communists, etc?

The idea that human nature is a paradox, as many thinkers have stated, seems to hold true. Our topic at hand proves the veridicality of the paradox. Indeed, *on one hand*, we know that the individual man is a subject, a being who exists for himself, a presence to himself, a self-regulating being. Man is a selfhood. Yet, *on the other hand*, life shows that man is a selfhood, only in being fused with the non-I. This enigmatic aspect of human existence is put even in sharper relief by love. Love, as I pointed out previously in the section "love toward the dead," is the ready availability (*disponibilité* would say Marcel) of my being, its belonging to the subject which the other is. By giving and surrendering myself, it is manifested to me what my selfhood really is. Gibran conveys well this truth. "They say if one understands himself, he understands

168

all people. But I say to you, when one *loves people,* he learns something about *himself.*"[96]

From the preceding quotation it is clear that self-knowledge and self-realization (Who am I?) depends on the acceptance of the existence of others and not vice-versa. The other, as discovered through love and not the sense perceptions, is the prerequisite condition for establishing my self. As for adverse relationships such as hate, enmity, jealousy, etc., these seem often to hinder the maturity of self-identity. True self-knowledge comes only through amicable relationships. In the essay *The Philosophy of Logic,* Gibran ironically describes the case of a self-knowledge not acquired through love. One day Salem Effandi Daybiss, moved by the desire to find a personal answer to Socrates' dictum "Know thyself," went in front of a mirror and glanced at himself. But the only reflection he could see in the mirror was the shape of his body. And so he began to compare his nose to that of Voltaire and George Washington, his stature to that of Napoleon, his eyes to those of Paul the Apostle and Nietzsche, his neck to that of Mark Antony. At the end Salem Effandi resumed his thoughts shouting: "This is myself—this is my reality. I possess all the qualities of great men from the beginning of history to the present. A youth with such qualities is destined to great achievements."[97] Yet, as he came to decide the kind of achievement with which he should start, he found himself confused, not knowing "what great deed" he should begin with. And thus, he went to sleep "in his untidy clothes upon his filthy bed," as he always did. The lesson of the story concludes that Salem did not learn the real meaning of his existence; his self-knowledge narrowed down to knowledge of his physiognomy, because he sought to know himself through the use of the method of comparison and not through the love-encounter.

To sum up, Gibranism advocates that love, the "in-between," is the best human achievement for realizing our self-identity, in contrast to the inauthentic intersubjectivity professed by Jean-Paul Sartre and Simone de Beauvoir. The latter philosophers deny the ontological root of the need for interpersonal relationships. They assert that "the other person is my hell," "the other person is my downfall," "the other person kills my potentialities and robs me from my subjectivity." But Gibran rests content with the theistic existentialists that the individual establishes his selfhood in so far as he really believes "in the existence of others and allows this belief to influence his conduct."[98] For this very reason Gibran insists on calling the other my "half-self," and elsewhere my "other self."[99] "In truth the other person is your most sensitive self given another body."[100]

One day in his studio, Gibran told to Barbara Young: "We shall never understand one another until we reduce the language to seven words."[101] After a pause he asked Miss Young to guess which were these seven magic words. The latter was hesitant. Then Gibran slowly and almost breathlessly spoke. "These are my seven words: You, I, take, Good, love, beauty, Earth,"[102] And combining them together he made this poem:

> Love, take me.
> Take me, Beauty.
> Take me, Earth.
> I take you,
> Love, Earth, Beauty.
> I take
> God.[103]

Love Guarantees Freedom

An interpersonal relation that grows only on knowledge of the other person without love, such a relationship may eventually rob the other of his individuality and limit his *freedom*. In Jean-Paul Sartre's existential psychoanalytical words, such a meeting is grounded on *"the stare,"* whereby the person stared at becomes a being-for-the-sake-of-the-looker.[104] Gibran agrees with Sartre on this point. On July 8, 1914, Gibran confided to Haskell:

170

I have always held, with my *Madman* that those
who understand us (without love) enslave something
in us. It is not so with you. Your understanding of
me is the most peaceful freedom I have known.[105]

It is when love does not accompany the knowledge one
might have of another's personality, that the privacy of the
person is endangered, in that at any time his personality
weaknesses, intentions, projects, past life may be unveiled and
ridiculed. "Blackmail" is an instance of a knowledge lacking
the sense of Agape. Love then is the safeguard of freedom
and subjectivity. And vice-versa, to Gibran's contention, there
could be no real freedom unless love animates human relationships. *The Broken Wings* emphasizes: "Love is the only freedom in the world because it so elevates the spirit that the laws
of humanity and the phenomena of nature do not alter its
course."[106] And in the *Spirits Rebellious,* Madame Rose Hanie
recognizes that "the spiritual law of Love and Affection" gave
her the courage to abandon the life of adultery she was leading with her husband Rashid Bey Naam, an old man who
married her with her parents' consent but not her's.

I was a sinner in the eyes of God and myself
when I ate his bread and offered him my body
—in reward for his generosity. Now I am pure and
clean because the law of Love has freed man and
made me honorable and faithful.[107]

Yet, paradoxically as it seems, the freedom engendered
through love is not a freedom of absolutism that would
preserve the individual from any stringent forces nor of liber-
tinage, in that he could do anything he pleases, rather it is a
freedom that imposes limitations on the instinct, impulses and
the self-interests. It prescribes norms and conditions for conducts. Freedom is not easy; it is hard; it is a heavy "burden"
for it weighs on the individual's sense of *responsibility*. A man
who has attained a high level of freedom knows that he has

171

to weigh consciously and conscientiously his acts before the execution of the decisions. For he knows that his decisions will have tremendous repercussions on his environs and those whom he loves.

Definitely, it is Agape that enchains and handcuffs freedom; love implies responsibility, or as *The Prophet* puts it, love signifies "to care"[108] for the beloved. "The truly free man"— writes Gibran—"is he who bears the load of the bond slave patiently."[109] Elsewhere, we find once more the concepts "slave," "love" and "freedom" interconnected:

> You are free before the sun of the day
> and free before the stars of the night; . . .
> . . . You are even free when you close your
> eyes upon all there is.
> But you are a slave to him whom you love
> because you love him,
> And a slave to him who loves you because
> he loves you.[110]

Nevertheless, the servitude caused by love and responsibility is a "pleasant" one, and therefore should not be confused with the kind of slavery imposed by political despots or the blind coercions of the environment. The difference between the love-slavery and coercive-slavery consists in that the latter is imposed by an outside-will while in the former case the self seems to be his own conditioner.[111] The lover choses of his own a matrix of obligations and duties which he promises to be faithful to. And whenever he transgresses one of his principles, he feels remorse and blames himself for having failed to cope with the ideal conduct he had obligated himself with. In this respect, Gibran says that love alleviates the yoke of freedom and responsibility. He even sees love giving more freedom than limiting the self. "And thus your freedom when it loses its fetters becomes itself the fetter of a greater freedom."[112] At this point, however, it should be kept in mind that Gibran is not advocating an absolute freedom of doing; quite the con-

172

trary, he knows that man in extremely limited in his physical actions; the only type of freedom he accepts is in thinking. In the region of thinking, man's privacy is safeguarded from the intrusion of any outside coercion. "You may chain my hands and shackle my feet; you may even throw me into a dark prison, but you shall not enslave my thinking because it is free."[113] And precisely, it is in the thinking of the lover that the beloved occupies his existential place. The essential of love is not to fulfill materially all the wishes of the beloved, but to let him know that the lover wishes intentionally (i.e. in his thinking) that the beloved's desires be someday realized. So as it seems, love does increase the freedom of the two partners to the point of letting each one establish his own *subjectivity* and develop his own *personality,* the following section explains what I mean.

Love And The Plea of Uniqueness

The law of creation proclaims that there was never in the *past* as there is not *now* and there will never be in the *future* two identical human existences. Each one of us is an unrepeatable historical event in the history of thought and is called upon to fulfill his idiosyncrasies.

Gibran has no scientific proofs to substantiate his firm belief in the uniqueness of man. Yet, his observation is accurate; today the humanistic biologists, psychologists and biochemists have established scientifically the truth of human uniqueness. The greatness of Gibran consists in having formulated poetically, philosophically and mystically many truths that science had to discover through painful investigations. In his vocabulary the words "lonely," "loneliness" or "solitary" are meant to express the predicament of "idiosyncrasy." Thus, one of the favorite themes the disciple Almuhtada liked to preach to the people after the death of his Master, was the issue that life-loneliness is a metaphysical consequence of our individuality.

173

Your spirit's life, my brother, is encompassed
by loneliness, and were it not for that loneliness
and solitude, you would not be *You,* nor would I be
I. Were it not for this loneliness and solitude, I
would come to believe on hearing your voice that it
was my voice speaking; or seeing your face, that it
was myself looking into a mirror.[114]

Oftentimes Gibran contended that the world would be too
small if there just existed two identical human beings. "If
there were two men alike, the world would not be big enough
to contain them."[115] The reader who is acquainted with existentialism, should remember that this school is precisely called
such because its adherents speculate from the standpoint of
the individual. The person is not a Platonic universal idea,
nor a Hegelian logical species, but a concrete, unique reality
whose life's meaning is caught in the whirls of the historical
moments he happens to participate to. In my opinion, Gibran
is a fullfledged existentialist, despite that he never used the
label nor knew about its founder.[116] Future historians of
Arabic philosophy should keep in mind my estimation, lest
they commit a grotesque error of historiography. And now in
order to sustain my belief about Gibran's existentialism I
will quote freely from some leading Western existentialist the
passages that emphasize the uniqueness of man. Thus Soren
Kierkegaard, the father of existentialism, often stated: "My
listeners, do you at present live in such a way that you are
yourself clearly and eternally conscious of being an individual."[117] The Spanish José Ortega y Gasset also wrote:
"There is no abstract living. Life means the inexorable necessity of realizing the design for an existence which each one of
us is. . . . We are indelibly that single programmatic personage
who must be realized."[118] Along the same line, Martin Buber
also held: "Every person born into this world represents
something new, something that never existed before, something
original and unique. It is the duty of every person to know . . .
that there has never been anyone like him in the world, for

if there had been someone like him, there would have been no need for him to be in the world. Every single man is a new thing in the world and is called upon to fulfill his particularity in this world."[119]

Although now Gibran insisted emphatically at the manner of the European existentialists that man should develop his idiosyncrasies, he warned us, however, that the conditions in which modern society lived constituted a real threat to the growth of the individual. Most particularly he denounced the spirits of "conformism" and "totalitarianism" as detrimental social patterns that yield groups of "crowd" and impersonal statistical entities. It is interesting to note at this stage that Gibran considered all his heroes to be *"Madmen."* They were mad not because of some mental derangement or psychosomatic illness but because they all refused to identify themselves with and behave like the rest of the crowd. So in the eyes of the big bulk, they were abnormal and mad since they departed away from the norms of traditions, customs and the "mass." In *The Wanderer* we are told that a youth wilfully escaped from the presence of his parents and teachers and came to live in a madhouse. When asked why, the youth candidly replied: my father wanted me to be a reproduction of himself; while my mother wished that I follow the path of my grandfather; still on the other hand my sister always reminded me of the perfect example of her husband; in his turn my brother thought that I should be like him, a fine athlete. As for my teachers, they were all determined to have me a reflection of their own personalities. "Therefore I came to this place. I find it more sane here. At least, I can be myself."[120]

The plea for uniqueness is in constant danger; our political ideologies, educational systems, religious institutions, social laws, family environments, yes, even our friendly relationships, tend all of them to rob us of our subjectivity, suffocate our freedom to realize a self-identity. The only way to remedy such a situation is to lead the life of *Agape*. For genuine love is disinterested, not despotic, not egoistic, and does not

175

interfere in the other person's freedom of "to-be", "to-do" and "to-belong." Quite the contrary, authentic love establishes interpersonal relationships which guarantee freedom of subjectivity. Here Gibran illustrates with some examples how love works in the intimate relationships of marriage, parenthood and friendship.

(1) In the case of marriage he asks that none of the two spouses attempt to copy the personality of the other. The statements that describe marriage as the union of two bodies with one soul, or two souls in one body, are statements of fantasies, romanticism and not of realistic love. Actually, it is when the partners in love begin to imagine that they should each become the other, that failure of this realization causes psychological exasperation and eventually the divorce. The success of a good marriage lies in the practice of mutual respect and in the ability to help each other to actualize his idiosyncrasies. I remember Shakespeare once said: "Variety makes beauty." And now let us hear the prophet on the subject of matrimony:

> Love one another, but make not a bond
> of love:
> Let it rather be a moving sea between
> the shores of your souls.
> Fill each other's cup but drink not from
> one cup. . . .
> Sing and dance together and be joyous,
> but let each one of you be alone,
> Even as the strings of a lute are alone
> though they quiver with the same music.
> . . .
> And stand together yet not too near
> together:
> For the pillars of the temple stand apart,
> And the oak tree and the cypress grow
> not in each other's shadow.[121]

(2) Many parents believe, with good intentions, that they have a legal and an ethical right to make their children conform to their ways of thinking and doing. But, this is the very reason of parent-child *gap*. In present day psychoanalysis it is acknowledged that *extreme possessiveness* and *overprotection* on the part of the parents will cause the child either to develop a weak and neurotic personality,[122] or to revolt and abandon his parents' mansion. Hence, Gibran here too exhorts the parents to express their love in self-sacrifice, and not to be oppressive.

> You may give them your love but not
> your thoughts.
> For they have their own thoughts.
> You may house their bodies but not
> their souls.
> For their souls dwell in the house of to-
> morrow, which you cannot visit, not even
> in your dreams.
> You may strive to be like them, but seek
> not to make them like you.
> For life goes not backward nor tarries
> with yesterday. . . .[123]

(3) Finally, on friendship, Gibranism seems to repeat the Holy Book which says: "When you have found a friend, you have found an inexhaustible treasure." A true friend is one to whom you may go when you are sad, in joy or in need, knowing that you will be accepted and comforted without preconditions to repay him back.

> Your friend is your needs answered.
> He is your field which you sow with love
> and reap with thanksgiving.
> . . . you come to him with your hunger,
> and you seek him for peace.
> And let there be no purpose in friendship
> save the deepening of the spirit.

177

CONCLUSION

Gibranism is a Metaphysics of Love. It is in itself the expression of the spiritual meaning of being. It is a mystical attitude oriented toward the value of being. Furthermore, Gibranism teaches that though the love-experience is expressed in countless ways, the characteristics of genuine love remain identical in all the interpersonal relationships. "Beloved, the fires of Love descend from heaven in many shapes and forms, but their impress on the world is one."[124]

Also, it is understood for Gibran that love is not generated after long courtship and repeated dates. Love is not something that you have to fall in love with. Love is an internal spiritual condition that permeates our whole being.

> It is wrong to think that love comes from
> long companionship and persevering courtship.
> Love is the offspring of spiritual affinity and
> unless that affinity is created in a moment, it
> will not be created in years or even generations.[125]

Finally, the dialogue between the lover and the beloved needs not to be expressed in "words." Once Gibran said to Miss Barbara Young: "Silence is one of the mysteries of love."[126] In *The Broken Wings* too we find the dialogue of silence animating the conversation of the lovers.

> We were both silent, each waiting for the
> other to speak, but speech is not the only
> means of understanding between two souls.
> It is not the syllables that come from the
> lips and tongues that bring hearts together.
>
> There is something greater and purer than
> what the mouth utters.
> Silence illuminates our souls, whispers
> to our hearts, and brings them together.[127]

FOOTNOTES

1 Plato, *Phaedo*, 82e.
2 *P.* p. 71.
3 *S.S.*, p. 54.
4 *B.P.*, p. 278.
5 *P.*, p. 72.
6 *S.F.*, p. 26.
7 *B.P.*, p. 113. (The italics are mine).
8 Barbara Young, *This man From Lebanon*, New York: Alfred A. Knopf, 1970, p. 129.
9 *S.R.*, p. 23. I remind the reader that Gibran has never spoken of Aristippus. I am solely responsible for introducing Aristippus' philosophy. I am doing so, simply in order to clarify Gibran's position in respect to the playboy who seems to recapitulate Aristippus' *Weltanschauung.*
10 *B.P.*, p. 67.
11 *P.*, p. 70.
12 Victor Frankl, *Man's Search For Meaning*, Washington Square Press, 1963, p. 166.
13 *W.G.*, p. 74.
14 *P.*, p. 70.
15 *N.V.*, p. 20.
16 *W.C.*, p. 48.
17 *N.V.*, p. 21.
18 *T.S.*, p. 44.
19 *ibidem*, p. 51.
20 Barbara Young, *This Man From Lebanon*, New York: Alfred A. Knopf, 1970, p. 129.
21 *B.P.*, p. 113.
22 *ibidem*, p. 69. On the other hand, the sexual attitudes of the Casanova are exhibitionism, hypocrisy, fake, dishonorable, unesthetic and indecent.
23 *ibidem*, p. 113.
24 *S.R.*, pp. 17-20.
25 *B.P.*, pp. 136-137.
26 *ibidem*, p. 113.
27 *ibidem*, p. 292.
28 *ibidem*, p. 113.
29 Sigmund Freud, *On Creativity And The Unconscious*, New York: Harper & Row Publishers.
30 *B.P.*, p. 113 and p. 169. It is clear from these passages that Gibran must have read something of or about Freud. Also, the Reader should

179

remember that Freud came to America in 1909 at the invitation of Professor Stanley Hall, President of Clark University, Worcester, Mass.

[31] *ibidem*, p. 22; p. 24; p. 29; p. 72.

[32] Barbara Young, *This Man From Lebanon*, p. 129; *see also B.P.*, p. 70.

[33] *B.P.*, p. 223.

[35] *ibidem*, p. 224.

[36] *ibidem*, p. 194.

[37] *ibidem*, p. 185.

[38] *ibidem*, p. 220.

[39] *T.L.*, p. 56.

[40] *B.W.*, p. 43.

[41] *T.L.*, p. 59.

[42] *ibidem*, p. 15.

[43] *T.S.*, p. 24.

[44] *ibidem*, p. 32.

[45] *T.L.*, p. 55.

[46] *S.S.*, p. 32.

[47] *T.S.*, p. 32.

[48] *S.S.*, p. 48.

[49] Gabriel Marcel, *Being and Having*, New York: Harper & Row, Publishers, 1965, p. 167 (The italics are mine).

[50] *P.*, p. 19.

[51] *S.F.*, p. 34.

[52] *B.W.*, p. 106.

[53] *P.*, p. 8.

[54] *G.P.*, p. 8.

[55] *B.P.*, p. 49.

[56] *P.*, pp. 62-63.

[57] *G.P.*, p. 22.

[58] *N.V.*, p. 31 sq.

[59] "Love is a precious treasure, it is God's gift to sensitive and great spirits." (*B.W.*, pp. 104-105).

[60] *B.W.*, p. 64.

[61] Gabriel Marcel, *Searchings*, New York: Newman Press, 1967, p. 64. *See also, Presence and Immortality*, Pittsburgh, Pa.: Duquesne University Press, 1967.

[62] *S.R.*, p. 11.

[63] *P.*, p. 62.

[64] *T.L.*, pp. 81-82.

[65] *B.P.*, p. 335.

[66] *Kant Selections*, ed. by T.M. Greene, New York: Scribner's, 1929, p. 302.

[67] *FR.*, p. 30 sq.

[68] *B.P.*, p. 118.

[69] *ibidem*, pp. 102-103.

[70] *S.F.*, p. 39.

[71] *ibidem*, p. 44.

[72] *ibidem*, p. 76.

[73] *S.F.*, p. 14.

[74] *P.*, p. 11.

[75] *ibidem*, p. 11.

[76] In a letter to Haskell he wrote: "Yes, beloved Mary, we know without knowing that we know, and we unconsciously live according to something in our depth which our surfaces do not understand. The real thing in us is in the presence of all that is real outside of us," namely, love, (*B.P.*, p. 291).

[77] *S.S.*, p. 32.

[78] *P.*, pp. 64-66.

[79] Mikhail Naimy, *The Book of Mirdad,* London: Stuart & Watkins, 1962, p. 62.

[80] *W.*, p. 9.

[81] *S.F.*, p. 41.

[82] *ibidem*, p. 47.

[83] M.J. Cotereau, secretary of the Federation of French Free-thinkers, avowed during the course of a discussion on secular versus religious morality held in Brussels in February 1960: "I do not believe in God because if he existed, he would be Evil. I had rather deny him than make him responsible for evil."

[84] *T.S.*, p. 33.

[85] *ibidem*, p. 33.

[86] *B.W.*, p. 32.

[87] *B.P.*, p. 67.

[88] *S.S.*, p. 36.

[89] *P.*, p. 11.

[90] *S.S.*, pp. 36-37.

[91] *B.W.*, p. 42.

[92] *S.F.*, p. 66.

[93] *ibidem*, p. 30.

[94] *G.P.*, p. 30.

[95] *T.L.*, p. 58 (The italics are mine). In contrast, S. Kierkegaard ridicules the expression of "half" in love. "In considering a person, one naturally supposes him to be an entity, and so one does believe till it becomes apparent that, under the obsession of love, he is but half which runs about looking for its complement. . . . In fact, the more one thinks about the matter the more ridiculous it seems." *(Selections from the Writings of Kierkegaard,* transl. by Lee M. Hollander, Garden City, New York: Doubleday & Co., Inc., 1960, p. 65). But on the other hand Plato in his *Symposium* develops an allegory of love in which the yearning between the two sexes is explained in terms of an original union which was split in two by the power of the Gods. As a result of this division the two sexes arouse; ever since they have been seeking one another as complementary halves. (Plato, *Symposium,* 189d-191d).

[96] *S.S.*, p. 37. (The italics are mine).

[97] *ibidem*, p. 66.

[98] Gabriel Marcel, *Homo Viator,* New York: Harper & Row, Publishers, 1962, p. 22. Similarly, Karl Jaspers, another existentialist, writes: "The

individual cannot become human by himself. Self-being is only real in communication with another self-being." ("On My Philosophy," Felix Kaufmann, transl., in *Existentialism: From Dostoyevsky to Sartre,* Walter Kaufmann, ed., Cleveland: Meridian Books, 1956, p. 145). Martin Buber too shares the same idea: "There is no *I* taken in itself, but only the *I* of the primary word *I-Thou* and the *I* of the primary word *I - it.*" *(I and Thou,* New York: Charles Scribner's Sons, 1958, p. 4).

99 *T.L.,* p. 74.

100 *S.F.,* p. 46.

101 *ibidem,* p. 30.

102 Barbara Young, *This Man From Lebanon,* New York: Alfred A. Knopf, 1970, p. 91.

103 *ibidem,* p. 92.

104 Jean-Paul Sartre, *Being and Nothingness,* transl. by Hazel E. Barnes, New York: Philosophical Library, Inc., 1956, Part III, Ch. IV.

105 *B.P.,* p. 198. (The words within the brakets are mine).

106 *B.W.,* p. 25.

107 *S.R.,* p. 16.

108 *P.,* 47.

109 *S.F.,* p. 50.

110 *ibidem,* p. 32; *See also PR.,* p. 55.

111 *P.,* p. 49.

112 *ibidem,* p. 49.

113 *W.G.,* p. 29.

114 *V.M.,* pp. 39-40.

115 *S.S.,* p. 5.

116 Actually, Kierkegaard never used the label existentialism, though historians consider him to be the father of this movement of thought. The Italian philosophers Nicola Abbagnano, Luigi Pareyson, Annibale Pastore, were first to popularize the new "ism" for "existentz."

117 Soren Kierkegaard, *Purity of the Heart,* New York: Harper & Row, Publishers, 1956, p. 184.

118 José Ortega Y Gasset, "Pidiendo un Goethe desde dentro", in *Obras Completas De José Ortega Y Gasset,* Madrid: Revista De Occidente, S.A., 1966, Vol. IV, p. 400. (Translation by the Author).

119 Martin Buber, *Hasidism and Modern Man,* New York: Horizon Press, Inc., 1958, p. 139.

120 *W.,* pp. 42-43, (The italics are mine).

121 *P.,* pp. 15-16.

122 Anna Freud, "The Role of Bodily Illness in the Mental Life of Children," *Psychoanalytic Study of the Child,* Vol. 7. New York: International University Press, 1952, p. 78.

123 *P.,* p. 17.

124 *V.M.,* p. 97.

125 *B.W.,* p. 42 sq.

126 Barbara Young, *This Man From Lebanon,* New York: Alfred A. Knopf, 1970, p. 130.

127 *B.W.,* p.38.

CHAPTER SEVEN

GIBRAN'S PHILOSOPHY OF RELIGION

ONE OF THE strong appeals of Gibranian philosophy felt by his readers, in the in-depth emphasis it puts on spirituality. Gibran is called a *Prophet* by his followers, because in this technocratic twentieth century his teachings still play the same effective social role in educating the minds in spirituality, as did the earlier prophets during their times. His prophetic message can be described as (a) an impassioned utterance; (b) poetical; (c) intensely preoccupied with God and moral issues; (d) forcefully compulsive to declaring the will of God, even sometimes with a tone of anger against the crudulity of the hypocrites.

Essentially, Gibranism holds that the goal of social life and the aim of personal life should consist in the perfect realization of the spirit of Agape which definitely culminates in the triumphant realization of the Kingdom of God both on earth and in the heart of the individual. In such a project, the practice of religion attests to a psycho-spiritual manifestation of the presence of God. However, as we know religion has not always been interpreted by the establishment of organized creeds, as a *natural* inclination of the soul toward his Creator. And here is where we find our author rebelling against the institutionalized beliefs, while on the other hand stressing the indispensability of religious faith in human existence.

In order to bring out the real position of our author on the issue of religion and God, I propose to divide this crucial chapter in three parts: (1) Critics of Organized Religion; (2) Nature of Authentic Religion; (3) Some Comments on *Jesus The Son of Man.*

183

I. CRITICS OF ORGANIZED RELIGION

Any knowledgeable person in the history of thought knows that institutionalized creeds have often times been attacked by great religious men themselves. In the eyes of the latter it was observed that organized religions were at the bottom the cause of moral degeneration, social injustices, political corruption and the decrease of faith. Thus, instead of promoting peace, love and understanding among people and among nations, often each institutionalized religion, with the help of its specific codes, rigid ritualistic ceremonies and guilt oriented consciences, would install in the heart of its own faithful the sentiment of hate, prejudice and bigotry toward the faithful of other Churches.

Without delving into the past, let me at least mention a few well known God-lovers who denounced the evils of organized religions on the ground that they perpetuate the spirit of "Machiavelianism," the unscrupulous scheme of practicing duplicity in statecraft and religion. For example, Leo Tolstoy blamed the State Church for the violence found in the world: "If only the men of our world were freed from this lie—from the perversion of Christian doctrine by Church faith and from the vindication and even the exaltation of the State which is advanced on the basis of faith, but which is incompatible with Christianity and is based on violence—then of itself there would be eliminated from the souls of all men, Christian and non-Christian, the chief obstacle to the religious recognition of the supreme law of love that tolerates no exceptions or violence."[1] S. Kierkegaard too was bitter against his own Protestant Church: "That religious conditions are wretched, and that people in respect of their religion are in a wretched condition, nothing is more certain."[2]

These very same feelings are also shared by Kahlil Gibran who revolted everytime that "truth," "human freedom," and "the will of God" were in danger. When alive he was called by his countrymen "heretic," and was excommunicated in 1904 from his Maronite Church precisely for having declared war against the organized religions. Actually, in all his controversial essays on religion his polemic centers around the "clergy" (Khouri). He holds the priests responsible for the many social and individual miseries encountered today in the world. *Khalil the Heretic* is in my opinion the best essay that expresses explicitly the real position of Gibran toward "ecclesiastical religion." A deep analysis of it will outline Gibran's main arguments.

The story is about an adolescent who entered the monastery in order to prepare himself for priesthood, yet after a brief period the youth was expelled by his superiors as unfitted for clerical life. The motive we are told for passing such a judgment is that Khalil dared one morning to preach to the monks about the true meaning of religion, while criticizing them also for fooling the poor with their pharisaic teachings. The essay calls Khalil a *reformer*. Why a reformer? I found four reasons in the article for which Khalil, the protagonist of Gibran, was anticlerical: simony, despotism, Machiavelianism, and treacherousness. Now, these reasons are not fairytales nor incidental but historically true, for they portray the role the clergymen played in Lebanon at the time of Gibran. A few words will explain the intent of these four epithets.

Simony

Historically the term simony is taken from Simon Magnus, the magician of Samaria who begged the Apostles to impart upon him the power of conferring the gifts of the Holy Ghost in exchange for a big sum of money (Acts 8.18-24). Essentially then simony is the buying or selling of the spiritual or something spiritual for a temporal or material price. The practice of simony spread calamitously over Europe, especially from the 9th to 11th centuries. Not only the lower clergy and convents committed this sacrilege but even among the high officials of the Catholic Curia the traffic of exchange between the material and spiritual was common. Thus the Pope Gregory VI (1045-1046) was accused of simony. Supposedly, during these periods, you could buy a piece of land in Heaven, or bargain your way out of penances by buying indulgences that would shorten your stay in purgatory.[3]

Well, for one Khalil condemned the clergy for doing the sin of simony. Twice he tells us that the priests of Deir Kizhaya in Northern Lebanon, used to trade their prayers for money; and that they would punish those who refused to buy financially their blessings. "What teachings allow the clergymen to sell their prayers for pieces of gold and silver"?[4] Elsewhere we read: "he (the pastor) sells his prayers, and he who does not buy is an infidel, excommunicated from Paradise."[5]

Despotism

On other occasions, Khalil reports that the monks were despots and tyrannical; that they would revert to physical violence, if crossed in words by a secular man, with the pretext of the in-the-name-of-God.[6] They also oppressed the poor villagers and voluntarily kept them in utter ignorance of the Scriptural knowledge and knowledge of nature. In the essay *John the Madman,* Gibran goes so far in describing his hero John as being persecuted by the priests because the latter caught John reading the Gospel, the forbidden Book. "The priests objected to the reading of the Good Book, and . . . warned the simple-hearted people against its use, and threatened them with excommunication from the church if discovered possessing it."[7]

The idea that Gibran is here trying to bring to light is that the messengers of God did not want their fellahins to be educated so that they remain in power and therefore instill fear among the simple minded people. Ignorance is the strongest weapon in the hands of despots for ruling over their slaves.[8]

186

Yet, contends Gibran, there could be no happiness and no true understanding of religion unless ignorance "be removed."[9] After all, "God does not like to be worshipped by an ignorant man who imitates someone else."[10]

Machiavellianism

Again historically the word "Machiavellian" is derived from Niccolò Machiavelli (1469-1527), the famous Florentine stateman, author of *The Prince,* who argued that every means is legitimate to secure the desired end, which was considered to be always political; he even conceived that politics could use religion and morality as *instrumentum regni,* i.e., instruments.

Now, in Gibran's opinion, the established Churches are nothing else than institutions hungry for power, either political, economical, or in social prestige. They employ the pretense of religion to reinforce their will and wishes among the faithful. Throughout both writings, *Khalil the Heretic* and *John the Madman,* we see the church officials occupying themselves with politics, exerting political pressures on the Sultan governors of the regions, investing themselves with governmental privileges, and amassing tremendous wealth.

To really appreciate the value of Gibran's critics, it is worthy to trace the history of the then Lebanese clergy. As you recall, Lebanon was ruled by the Ottoman Empire which had embraced the Islamic faith. On the other hand, the members of the Maronite Church were for the great majority poor farmers. In order that Christianity became important in the Porte's politics it was necessary for her to become feudal. The Christian seculars themselves participated in making their Church feudal by gifting lands and properties to the clergy. However, as the Church grew in her possessions, she became extremely greedy, always demanding more from her faithful who were employed to cultivate the lands and had to pay her sometimes exorbitant taxes. It was the strong economy of the Church that won her the political power of the Turkish Sultans. Often a Turkish governor had to yield to the will of the priests, if indeed he wanted to remain in power. And unfortunately there were times when the fathers would dictate to the Ottoman representatives the political decisions to be taken, though they proved to be detrimental to individual villagers. Thus, in the story of Khalil it is Father Elias who suggested to Sheik Abbas to punish Khalil for absolutely no real offense.

The political corruption of the Church is even more apparent in the short essay *John the Madman,* where we are told that John was twice the target of the priests. During the first time he was imprisoned because his oxen had devastated the plantations of the convent and consequently was forced by the priests to repay the damage, following which, however, John called the clergymen mercenaries, hypocrites and irreligious. As for the second time, John's father was asked by the Governor who wanted to please the pastors, to disseminate the rumor that his son was "mad." This happened after that one day John, in the square of the town Bsherri, stretching his hands towards the sky invoked Jesus to come to restore religion that the prelates had dishonored.

Now both Khalil and John were ridiculed by the Reverends for having discovered the true teaching of Christ, revolted against the unorthodox teachings of the priests, and used direct quotation from the New Testament to intimidate the clergy's behavior. Gibran tells us explicitly that Khalil and John were persecuted for their knowledge of the Scriptures. Also the two personages appear as reformers. Their reform, however, is not the advocation of a new creed; it is merely a return to the primary source of Christian belief, namely the Gospel. Like Martin Luther, therefore, Gibran heralds the Holy Book as the true teaching of Christ. The Jesus of Khalil and John is the God of love, forgiveness, kindness, and compassion, and detached from every political favouritism.

Finally, Gibran reacts with indignation toward organized religion because it falsifies the true meaning of the Scriptures, and spreads errors. In his opinion these Scriptural mistakes stem from the twin ignorances: the literal uneducation of the clergy itself,[11] and its ignorant interpretation of the literal sense of the Holy Texts. In regard to the last argument, Gibran makes his point through the parable *The Blessed City*.

A youth was once told of the existence of a "blessed city" where inhabitants lived happily according to the Scriptures. Moved by curiosity, adventure and a desire to lead a perfect life in a perfect environment, the young man went searching for this city. After forty days he discovered a town where each person had but one eye and one hand. Approaching some people he asked them to indicate to him the way to the "blessed city." Their answers were that this was it. Amazed by the physical appearance of the individuals, he further inquired what had happened to them. In reply they took him to the temple and showed him "a heap of hands and eyes." Still astonished the youth exclaimed: "Alas! what conqueror has committed this cruelty upon you? . . . And one of the elders stood forth and said, 'this doing is of ourselves. God has made us conquerors over the evil that was in us.'" Then all pointing to an inscription engraved over the altar, the youth read the famous passage where it is written: If an eye has offended thee, cast it away, for it is better to enter the Eden with one eye than to be damned in the Gehenna. And if a hand has committed sin, cut it off, for it is better to be admitted in Heaven with one hand instead of going to Hell on the account of the evildoing of this hand.

The youth more astonished than before, turned toward the crowd and cried: Is there any one among you who possesses two eyes or two hands? And they replied: none among the grown, except the infants who can't yet read nor understand the Scripture. Upon listening to these words, our visitor nodded

189

his head with disappointment and straightway left that "blessed city."

The parable terminates with irony, sarcasm and a moral lesson all of which are encompassed in the final words of the youth: "When we had come out of the temple, I straightway left that Blessed City; for I was not too young, and I could read the scripture."[12]

Intrinsic vs. Extrinsic Religion

We would be wrong to suspect for one moment that Gibran's anticlericalism was an expression of irreligiosity. Actually, to put it bluntly, Gibran was a deeply religious person. He simply objected to the manner of the "use" of religion by the State Church; he observed that religion put in the hands of the clergy-agency becomes something to "use" but not to "live." This is what we call "extrinsic religion"; in such a context faith surfaces at the outskirts of good intentions, but never implants profound roots in the soul. The logic of extrinsic religion is always utilitarian in orientation. Also, religion gets to be practiced not as an end in itself, but as a motive that serves other motives, e.g. need for security, political power, ambition for social prestige, or pecuniary greed. On the other hand, continues Gibran's critics, the extrinsic religion of the organized church promotes racial and ethnic bigotry, religious prejudice, and leads its faithful to discrimination, segregation and denials of other's rights. Extrinsic religion commits all these wrong-doings under the standard of the will of God, love of God and teachings of Christ. For example, till not long ago, the Catholic Church in which Gibran was baptized, professed that there was no salvation and redemption of mortal sin outside of its own faith.[13]

No wonder that Gibran wrote: "The truly religious man does not embrace a religion; and he who embraces one has no religion."[14] If a person affiliates with a particular church, and shares its morality and legality, then frankly, conjectures Gibran, this person has not discovered the "intrinsic" nature of religion. For religion is not a book of codes or a lawyer's manual; nor is God a privilege entrusted only to the clergy.

In my opinion, Gibran is harsh on established religion because he sees a similarity between society as an institution built on fabricated laws and the church, another social institution resting on man-made laws promulgated by a self-appointed hierarchy of clergymen. Essentially, a sectarian church exists so long as it prescribes laws of conduct that differ markedly from those of other organized creeds. And a believer is Protestant, Catholic, Jewish, Orthodox or Muslim, if, and only if, he claims to follow the precepts of his own church, which most of the time, by the way, conflict with the precepts of other churches. God here ceases to be a Deity and the Creator of humanity; rather he gets reduced to a puppet or a glamorous object for which each partisan religion fights the other sects in order to be the first to claim possession. History attests to this fact; remember, for instance, the Holy war of the early Muhammedans *(jihad)* or the Catholics' *Inquisition* period, or the Jews' exasperating Hope of the coming of *Christ conqueror* of the lands in the world, etc. . . .

Gibran, like all great mystics, was intensely religious and therefore had no preference for any "formulated" religion. He believed in the "communion of spirits"[15] and in "Oecumenism" that makes all men "brothers before the face of heaven."[16]

Your thought advocates Judaism, Brahmanism, Buddhism, Christianity, and Islam.

In my thoughts there is only one universal religion whose varied paths are but the fingers of the loving hand of the Supreme Being.[17]

This "one universal religion" is what we call *intrinsic religion.* Accordingly, the person motivated by the interiorized

191

total creed of his faith, intends more on serving religion than on making it serve his interests. In this respect religion is nothing else than a natural *élan* of the soul, a gift given to all human mortals; it has no political, no ethnic, no acquired, no formal baptismal origin. Its manifestation is in the practice of Agape, the only real divine law. Of course Gibran knows that it is possible for the individual man to suffocate this intrinsic spiritual impulse of loving everything created. Nevertheless, the point that he is bringing to light stresses that religion and the presence of God are immanent, and therefore, they ought to be searched from within the soul. "God has placed *in each soul* an apostle to lead us upon the illumined path. Yet, many seek life from *without,* unaware that it is *within* them."[18]

Under the following heading, let us ponder in a detailed manner on the issue of intrinsic religion.

2. NATURE OF AUTHENTIC RELIGION

"Homo Est Naturaliter Animal Religiosum"

Since its birth, mankind has shown an attachment for the "sacral." Driven by superstitions and educated in mythology, the primitive clans already exercised ritual ceremonies. Pre-animism, Totemism, Fetishism, Idolatry and many more were the early forms of worship. With the progress of tools and the expansion of the group, however, our ancestors' polytheism decreased in number. Then slowly with the advent of the positive sciences, agnosticism and atheism have become fashionable forms of beliefs.

This brief introduction raises the question of whether man "is" by his very being a "religious" creature? Gibran answers positively. And on the same line of thought, Gibran maintains that religion has no cultural origin, only the "manner" of worshipping is cultural. Actually, to be faithful to Gibran's hermeneutics of religion, I should rather state that if there

192

The sidewalk passing by Gibran's tomb.

The doorway to the tomb of Kahlil Gibran.

Kahlil Gibran's Tomb.

The study of Kahlil Gibran, as preserved in the Museum dedicated to him in Bsherri, Lebanon.
Photo: CNT/MAGNIN

The bedroom of Kahlil Gibran, in the Gibran Museum located in the town of his birth, Bsharri.

are various prescribed liturgical ceremonies practiced around the world, this is possible because in the first place religion is a *metaphysical* dimension of human reality, and consequently there is a primordial "manner" of worshipping, natural to the soul. Praying, bowing, repenting are natural impulses. It is only when churches established Canon laws and enforced rigid commands for the "manner" of worshipping, that the alienation between "religion" and "practice" occurred. Now organized religions put heavy emphasis on "practice"; repentence for instance is no longer a natural inclination of the soul asking forgiveness from the Compassionate God, but an asking of forgiveness from an institution for having transgressed an invented prohibition. Here Gibran replies: "Inhibitions and religious prohibitions do more harm than anarchy"[19]—for as we know, they ride the psyche with guilt complexes, thus causing neuroses.

Religion therefore, is eternally inscribed in the very core of human existence and is not the privilege of some institution. In a letter he sent to a friend, Gibran wrote about *John the Madman:* "I found that earlier writers, in attacking the tyranny of some of the clergy, attacked the practice of religion. They were wrong because religion is *a belief natural to man."*[20]

It is interesting for us who are dissecting Gibran's thoughts and cross examining him in the light of history, to find that many great philosophers have similarly held that "man is a religious animal." For example, St. Augustine's cry conveys the same idea as Gibran's: "Thou hast made us for Thyself, and our heart will not find rest until it rest in Thee."[21] St. Thomas Aquinas too made of religion a natural desire in man: "Man has a natural inclination to know the truth about God."[22] The contemporary existential theologian philosopher, Paul Tillich, shares also the same thesis: "When we say that religion is an aspect of the human spirit, we are saying that if we look at the human spirit from a special point of view, it presents itself to us as religious. . . . You cannot reject religion with ultimate seriousness, because ultimate seriousness, or the state of being ultimately concerned, is itself religion."[23]

Amazingly, even the atheists and agnostics of today are beginning to claim that they too are *religious,* though their object of worshipping is different from the theists. For instance, Jean-Paul Sartre, the leading atheist existentialist avows in his autobiography that he is religious while the Christian believers are irreligious. "An atheist was a . . . fanatic encumbered with taboos who refused the right to kneel in church, . . . who took upon himself to prove the truth of his doctrine by the purity of his morals, . . . a God-obsessed crank . . . ; in short, a gentleman who had religious convictions. The believer had none."[24] In the USA the atheist philopher, Ernest Nagel, maintains that "atheism is not necessarily an irreligious concept. . . . The denial of theism is logically compatible with a religious outlook upon life. . . . Atheism is not to be identified with sheer unbelief."[25]

In conclusion, there seems to be a common consent between Gibran, the theist philosophers, and the atheists, that religion arises from the basic structure of human nature. However, lest I confuse my readers, let me add that for our author in contrast to the atheist, religion is not merely a natural inclination, or a matter of forming convictions, or having faith, but above all religion elevates the soul towards a beatifying union with *God* as the *Creator of the universe.* In the following section I will show that Gibran never ascribed to Nietzsche's theology of the death of God which has, nevertheless, become the leitmotive of contemporary atheism.

Is There Such A Thing As An Absolute God?

Among modern speculative theories of religion, we find three major schools of thought that argue our issue with different presuppositions. *For one,* the atheists profess to be religious, citizens of good moral standards and anti-theist. Their religious faith, however, is *anthropocentic* and *humanistic.* As for God, they teach that this is a fiction of our subconscious wishing protection from the crushing superior

194

forces of nature. In other words, God is a projection of the self or father image authority, or if one prefers, "man is fundamentally desire to be God." It is interesting to know at this stage that all the leading atheists, Nietzsche, Marx, Freud, Sartre, have notwithstanding recognized that the religious belief in God must have helped civilization at one time to get rid of the many superstitions inherited from the primates. But now, they say science can take care of man's needs. Faith in and love of man alone constitute their religion. Echoing Nietzsche's cry of the death of God[26], Sartre, to give an example, writes:

> God is dead. Let us not understand by
> that he does not exist or even that he
> no longer exists. He is dead.
> He spoke to us and is silent. We no longer
> have anything but his cadaver. Perhaps he
> slipped out of the world, somewhere else,
> like the soul of a dead man. Perhaps he was
> only a dream...God is dead.[27]

From the point of view of literature I was fascinated to find some of Gibran's essays that favour an anthropocentric religion. As a literary piece, only, *The Grave Digger* has much ressemblance to Nietzsche's *Zarathustra* in style, form and content of ideas. The article ridicules the belief in the supernatural on the basis that "Man has worshipped his own self since the beginning calling that self by appropriate titles, until now, when he employs the word 'God' to mean that same self."[28]

As I said, such an essay should not confuse our understanding of the real position of Gibran. We should rather study such essays from the standpoint of the value of comparative literature, but never with the assumption that the ideas herein are those of Gibran, the philosopher. Because, actually, Gibran has publicly rejected Nietzsche's pessimistic philosophy. His religion is theocentric.

His [Nietzsche] form [style] always was soothing
to me. But I thought his philosophy
was terrible and all wrong. I was a worshipper
of beauty... [of God].[29]

At the opposite of atheism, many theist intellectuals ad-
vance the theory that it is possible to prove God's existence
by means of philosophical thinking. This *second* school makes
of religion something rationalized and discovered logically.
The history of philosophy abounds with many logical pro-
posals: Augustine, Anselm, Aquinas, Descartes, Leibniz, etc.

The *third* approach to religion denies that God's existence
could be proved rationally; yet nevertheless, its partisans claim
to be theocentric for reasons other than the logical investigations. Gibran, Kierkegaard, William James, Marcel, Buber
represent this school.

Against the atheists Gibran and the others of this movement, spurn Nietzsche's theology of the death-of-God on the
ground that the soul has a natural "hunger for that which
is beyond itself," and because "the soul seeks God as heat
seeks height, or water seeks the sea. The power to seek and
the desire to seek [God] are the inherent properties of the
soul."[30]

But also against the theist logicians, Gibran and the tenets
of the third school of religion resent making of God a game
for the gifted mathematical-type-thinking minds, or an idea
that fits a compartment of our finite intellect. In Gibran's
opinion, it is easier for the human mind to talk *to* God but
not *about* Him, for "we cannot understand the nature of God
because we are not God."[31] The human intellect is limited,
imperfect, and consequently impotent to comprehend God
directly, the Infinite and the most Perfect. Often times Gibran
confined to Miss Haskell: "It is not because I don't want to,
but because I just can't talk about God."[32]

I have the feeling that somehow, Gibran abhorred any type
of intellectual explanation of God, because he was afraid to

196

commit the sin of intellectual pride so common among the antitheists and some Christian philosophers. Yet, on the other hand, his refusal for a philosophical proof of God on the ground of the finitude of our reasoning ability, reminds us of Kant who asserted that human understanding was so constituted in itself that it lost itself in contradictions when it ventures to reason from any factual data or any necessary features of experience, to conclusions about things in themselves and the existence or the nature of God. However, if we compare closely Kant's reasons to Gibran's, a sharp line of demarcation is seen to separate the two. Kant's position was a matter of skepticism that he inherited from the empiricist David Hume and which expressed itself as a mental doubt towards anything metaphysical. Gibran on the other side, does not completely eliminate the possibility of knowing God through sense-experience. He calls the data of "the sense-experience" the "visible expressions of God."[33] The world attests to God's presence, as the effects to their Cause.

Nevertheless, this understanding of God through creation, is not a philosophical understanding *"about"* God, but is a natural inclination which psychologically motivates our mind and body "to" speak religiously "to" God in the practice of prayer, repentance, bowing. As He is in Himself, God is incomprehensible; yet he can be known in the bond of mutual relationship. Here Martin Buber agrees with Gibran that religion is theocentric, and not founded on a noetical act. "It is not necessary to know something about God in order really to believe in Him: many true believers know how to talk *to* God but not *about* Him."[34]

Faith

Gibran's religious worship of God is a matter of "faith." In that respect he is very close to Kierkegaard and the existentialists of the right wing. Faith for both Gibran and Kierkegaard is not the object of a scientific investigation. Hence, the two distinguish between "faith" and "knowledge." The latter represents the state of affairs that are liable of being either empirically or logically demonstrated; faith, however, is a spiritual disposition to accepting propositions which are *not* known, are extremely *unreasonable,* but which are believed to be *true.* Witness how Gibran and Kierkegaard are very much alike on the topic of religious faith. Kierkegaard writes:

> Suppose a man who wishes to acquire faith; let the comedy begin. He wishes to have faith, but he wishes also to safeguard himself by means of an objective inquiry. . . . What happens? . . . Now he is ready to believe, . . . and he ventures to claim for himself that he does not believe as shoemakers and tailors and simple folk believe, but only after long deliberation. Now he is ready to believe [i.e. to accept on faith]; and so now it has become precisely impossible to believe it. . . . For the absurd is the object of faith, and the only object that can be believed.[35]

In this passage Kierkegaard explicitly affirms that faith is the "absurd," a "paradox," and, startles the mind of the philosophers and scientists. By the way even St. Paul in his Epistle to the Corinthians acknowledged the fact that it was an insult to man's intelligence and foolishness to accept something on faith.[36]

Well, Gibran feels the same way towards man's faith in God. For sake of precision, let us quote and paraphrase our author's basic conception of faith. I have personally numbered the words which I propose to expound.

> Faith is (1) an oasis (2) in the heart (3) which will never be reached by the caravan of thinking.[37]

(1) This citation makes clear that faith like the oasis defies the physical and mental eyes of man. Like the oasis

it is not something which you could lay your hands upon, or detect through a microscope or telescope; to the scientific world it is a hallucination, a fiction. Yet to the hallucinator himself, the hallucination is something real, and he believes in it. As J. Dewey used to say "illusions are illusions, but the occurrence of illusions is not an illusion, but a genuine reality." Faith from the standpoint of systematic thinking is the *absurd;* as from the standpoint of the individual affected by it, faith is real and like the oasis it points to a lack, a craving that the soul has for it. Translated in Gibran's technical terminology, this lack signifies that the soul has an "inherent desire to reach God", and which is indeed apprehended as a "hunger."[38]

(2) Here the use of the term "heart" stands opposite to "thinking." Henceforth the oasis or faith is directly related to and real for the heart alone. All this amounts to saying that faith in God can only be attained when the individual consents with resignation not to attempt to reduce the Supreme Being to an object that the mind could dissect into its properties and elements.

Like most of the contemporary humanistic philosophers, Gibran draws a sharp dichotomy between *"la logique du coeur"* and *"la logique de la raison."* In his opinion, the "heart" has better and more efficient ways of grasping truth than the slow pace and the indicisiveness of discursive reasoning. Note that William James, a fellow contemporary —(of whom Gibran, I believe, must have heard of)—has with the same vigor defended the thesis that faith makes sense to a soul animated only by "passions" and scarcely interested in proving scientifically its worth.[39]

In some other entries of his works, Gibran details the motives for confining faith to the region of the heart. He writes: "Faith is a knowledge within the heart, beyond the reach of proof."[40] Hereby, he acknowledges that faith is not a blind, mechanical or habitual ignorance. Quite the contrary, faith in itself is a source of knowledge which is unknown to scientific thinking. Such knowledge is of God, immortality, human destiny, human origin, etc.... Man's passions or feelings perceive the truth of these facts without the believer suffering from any hang ups. "Faith perceives Truth sooner than Experience [i.e., scientific experiments] can."[41] Actually, it would be a weakness on the part of faith if it had to "explain" or "prove" its truth; because to desire just for an instance, that faith probed its premises, this would be an indication of incredulity, the mental attitude which is incompatible to faith. Hence, Gibran states: "the necessity for explanation is a sign of weakness,"[42] and "the truth that needs proof is only half true."[43] After all, the purpose of faith is to stir the will-to-believe of the person. Also the essence of faith is to remain incomprehensible to logic and science.[44]

(3) Finally, we should bear in mind that for Gibran faith is superior to science. And though "the caravan of thinking" may ridicule faith as an impossibility (oasis), so in its turn faith defies thinking as incapable of comprehending it. Again, if thinking treats faith as a pathological syndrome, ironically so to speak, faith in its turn treats thinking as "impotent" epistemologically to pierce the realm of the "beyond-the reach-of proof" (i.e., faith).

From what preceeded, it is clear now why Gibran never provided us with a philosophical argument on behalf of the nature and the existence of God. He never raised the Middle-Age methodological questionings of *"An sit?"* (is-there a God?) and *"Quid sit?"* (What is the essence of God?). He was primarily concerned with stressing the double relations: the importance of God for the man in faith, and, the relation of God to man. Hence, we come to our next section.

Immanence of God

How does man relate to God? How should man express his faith towards God? Where should man search for God? These questions are crucial in Gibran's *Weltanschauung*. We may sum up their answers in one affirmation: God, faith, and religion are *"intrinsic"* to man. The error of organized religions consists in having extrapolated and alienated God from man, confined God to the priests, and restricted the visit of man to the Divine in the Church on Sunday, the Mosque on Friday, the Synagogue on Saturday. But, Gibran replies: "The Church is within us. You yourself are your priests."[45]

Gibran's theory of the immanence of God establishes three implications.

(1) Such a belief assists the individual's *CONSCIENCE* to become *PERSONALISTIC*. The individual is motivated to search out God in his own unique way, for the interior presence of the Supreme Being appears differently to different persons. Also, it affirms that none of the formulated creeds possesses the whole truth about God. On the contrary, as the Hindu Wisdom teaches: "Truth is one but men call it by many names. So too Gibran professes his ecumenism by saying: "God made Truth with many doors to welcome every believer who knocks on them."[46] Furthermore, the idea of immanence makes of the human body the genuine and primordial tabernacle that hosts the Creator.[47] Accordingly man should seek God in himself, in his neighbours or in nature. God's presence is felt everywhere and not in one fixed geographical sanctuary. Moreover, in order that the person expresses his faith towards God, he simply needs to love, respect and care for others. In the authentic human relation of I-Thou, the individual "I" successfully encounters, sees and addresses God clothed under the shape of the human "Thou."

Let us speaks no more now of God the Father.
Let us speak rather of the gods, your neighbours,
and of your brothers, ...
Again I bid you to speak not so freely of God,

201

who is your All, but speak rather and understand one another, neighbour unto neighbour,
a god unto a God.[48]

(2) Another implication of this Divine immanency entails
that *MAN* is *GODLIKE*. As the last quotation explicates, however, we should bear in mind that when
Gibran concedes "we are God,"[49] he is not all all repeating Nietzsche's view that the human is the maker
of everything and beyond whom there is no superior
Reality. To put it in simple terminology, Gibran enter-
tains the thought that because God indwells in us, we
in our turn are rendered divine. Actually, Gibran is not
the first to hold the Godliness of man. It is a common
belief among the mystics of the Orient (the Sufis, Naimy,
Rihani, Iqbal, the Hasidists) to regard man as a "microtheos." Gibran and the Middle-Eastern mystics demonstrate the "microgod" of man through the spiritual
assumption that between God-nature-man there is an
indispensable interrelation of "mutual emergence." In
philosophical language, we call this emergence: "evolution." Accordingly, existence is not made up of static
atoms or chunks of matter. Life is dynamic, and always
in the making. Referring to Darwin's theory of Evolution, Gibran finds it incomplete; for the author of the
Origin of Species, limited his perception to organic life;
spoke of evolution in terms of "accidental" variations;
never succeeded in answering the question why evolution
has so far followed the course which it has in fact taken;
and above all omitted God from the process.[50] Yet, in
the vision of our author, the evolution that started aeons
ago, must have involved the dialectical movement of
God-nature-man.

At this point, let me express an apparent difficulty
I am encountering in interpreting and paralleling with
history, the obscure passages where Gibran delves with
the topic of evolution. As I read his private metaphys-

ical journal of January 6, 1916 to March 1, 1916, and April 18, 1920, I get the impression at first sight that Gibran is leaning towards a "disguised materialism"; in a way similar to the theories of DeVries, Lamark and Spencer, who speculated that matter was at the beginning animated by an internal powerful energy that erupted into cosmic development. Thus, for example, Gibran states that "Reality is Transmutation of Matter: Everything is matter,"[51] and "God is not the creator of man. God is not the creator of the earth. God is not the ruler of man nor of earth."[52] But on a second thought, I figure that it would be a historical mistake on our part if we had to read the literal sense of such statements, without an attempt to disclose the mysticism or allegory or metaphor of the whole text. If these articles were to be submitted to a microscopic analysis through the spectacles of history, I believe that a much clearer understanding of Gibran's position could be reached, and which would prove that our author was a firm theocentric thinker. Let us try to shed some light on these texts.

Gibran's theory of evolution maintains that God is *Desire*[53] and as Desire He evolved into earth and man. Ever since then, "desire" has become the creative force that "changes all things. It is the law of all matter and all life."[54] Now, this emergence of the universe was caused by "love," which is the never extinguishing energy, but, always increasing impetus. God desired that "man and earth . . . become like Him";[55] He desired that man and earth share His happiness. And to see that He becomes the gravitational center, He installed in man's soul and the world an innate "hunger" to rise to and seek Him. Gibran writes: "God is growing through His desire, and man and earth, and all there is upon the earth rise toward God by the power of desire."[56] Note that Gibran does not equate God with man and earth. He considers the world and human beings as *"a"*

203

part of God,[57] thereby implying that the Supreme Being is greater in divine perfection than the created.

Speaking of the concept creation, Gibran believes in it and often refers to it;[58] yet, occasionally he prefers to interchange the use of this concept for a more biological, scientific and philosophical notion, namely, "evolution," or "emergence." Hence when he contests: "God is not the creator of man. God is not the creator of the earth"[59]—this double negation is less indicative of a skepticism than a linguistic matter of choice of words. Why does Gibran refuse to employ the term "creation"? What could this word convey symbolically to make our author exchange it for the label "evolution"? The answer is the following: the notion "creation" *could* suggest functionally the same meaning as "production," i.e., the producer once he manufactures his product, stands *outside* his artifact, and *transcends* his invention both in the sense of being a non-provider and exhibiting a dissimilarity in existence.[60]

But this in the opinion of Gibran is wrong. Because the creatures are not made of a different stuff than their Creator; nor is creation a random calculation, or a performance on an outside pre-existing reality, nor an extrinsic act performed at one time in the past and now alienated from the Creator. Again, the Creator is not seen by Gibran as an Aristotelian Prime Mover unrelated and unconcerned with His creation. Quite the contrary, creation is still outgoing today in the world; and between the Creator and His creature there is a great resemblance in type of existence. No estrangeness between God and His work! God reveals himself in matter-nature and in man; He indwells in every part of the Cosmos; *on one side* He emerges as "walking in the cloud, outstretching His arms in the lightning and descending in rain.... [And] smiling in flowers, then rising and waving His hands in trees";[61] *on the other side,* He evolves as a "microtheos" in human spirits.

In her private journal of April 18, 1920, Miss Haskell reports that Gibran once told her: "Some believe God made the world. To me it seems more likely that God has grown from the world because he is the furthest form of Life. Of course the possibility of God was present before God himself."[62] If such statements are taken in their literal sense, then the reader might conclude Gibran was a materialist. But, if they are understood allegorically, and read very carefully in conjunction with the statements: God is Desire, and desire-love is the inherent mighty power and mighty law that changes all matter and all life—then a threefold conclusion follows:

(i) the world is not something made after the manner in which an industrialist makes soaps, but as Gibran says, the world has "emerged" from the growing desire which God had to process "the earth to become like Him, and a part of Him."[63] (ii) The world did not exist physically before God; rather the converse is true. The divinity of the flower, clouds, rain, trees, etc., evolved because God was present as possibility before these divine objects evolved in fact. In other words, Gibran suggests that in a primordial state God-nature-man constituted a single nebula. In the evolution process, however, God separated himself from the world and the upshot was a process of separation analogous to the theory of Empedocles in which under the influence of Love the four elements became separated. That God grows from the world, means to Gibran that God receives the perfection of the world unto himself and preserves it; He takes the world up into himself and re-enacts the perfection of the world. And *vice-versa* when Gibran claims that the world emerges from God, he means that God supplies the potential for the Becoming of the world. (iii) Finally, nature is not merely composed of chunks of atomic matter, for "all matter—affirms Gibran—seeks a form." This seeking is the result

205

of the law of desire. The form is the "meaning" or "the signification" of the being of matter. Each object means something specific, stands for a concrete purpose distinct from that of other things. An apple tree, for instance, means what it is because such is the form "appleness" which characterizes it in its being of matter. In simple words, there is a *mysticism of reality,* an interior spiritual aspect in each matter; it is God inhabiting matter, but who is not identified with it.[64]

To keep on this subject, it is apparent in the writings of Gibran that the Divine emergence and the Divine immanence is best perceived in the birth of the human form. Accordingly, the human spirit evolves twice as divine, if I may say so. How? Why? Man, answers Gibran, is both a *"microtheos"* and a *"microcosm."* And in each of these states of existence, man exudes his godliness.

It is worthwhile to recall that the vision Gibran holds of the world, man and God, resembles very much Blake's *apocalyptic vision.* Blake outlined the correspondence between the material and the spiritual; Gibran likewise describes the unity of existence, as a coming together of polarities. Specifically in the genesis of man we see manifestly the phenomenon of unity in multiplicity *(e pluribus unum),* and that of multiplicity in unity *(unitas multiplex).*

To understand this point, let us first expound on the *"microgod"* of man. Under the influence of the Bible, Gibran portrays the birth of man as an emergence from God through a process of separation: "And the God of gods separated a Spirit from Himself and created"[65] man. Elsewhere in his metaphysical journal, he depicts this process of separation as a Hegelian process of conceptual clarification through which God undergoes, in order to emerge at the end as the maker of human consciousness which begins to seek, and becomes fully aware of Him.

Thus, Gibran recounts:

> When I sleep something in me keeps awake to
> follow it and to receive more from it and
> through it. My very eyes seem to retain that
> slowly developing picture of the birth of God.
> I see him rising like the mist from the seas and
> the mountains and plains. Half-born, half-con-
> scious. He rose. He himself did not know him-
> self *fully* then. Millions of years passed before
> he moved with His own will, and sought more
> of Himself with his own power and through His
> own desire. And man came. He sought man
> even as man and the soul of man were seeking
> Him. Man sought him first without conscious-
> ness and without knowledge. Then man sought
> Him with consciousness but without knowl-
> edge..[66]

Now it was Gibran's understanding that human consciousness was the last to develop in the chain of the
Divine evolution.[67] For this very reason, he entertained
the thought that the unity of human existence embodied
the greatest multiplicity. In his words, "we are more
than we think. We are more than we know."[68] What
he really means is that man besides being fashioned in
the image of God, also represents in his being the to-
tality of created nature. He is a *"microcosm,"* a whole
universe though in miniature. The article *The Spirit*
describes the genesis of man after the manner of the
philosophers Empedocles and Hippocrates, who believed
that the person as a microcosm reflected in his own
make-up the four elements—fire, water, air, earth—of
nature as microcosm. Gibran writes:

> And the God took *Fire* from Wrath's furnace,
> and a *Wind* from the desert of Ignorance,

and Sand from the *seashore* of Selfishness,
and *Earth* from beneath the feet of the ages,
and He created man.[69]

Comparatively speaking, Aristotle's rational psychology and the Scholastics' metaphysics hold a similar view. Their axiom says: *anima humana est quodammodo omnia*[70], i.e., the human soul reflects in itself everything that exists. This thesis Gibran explains in the following way:

Everything in creation exists within you,
and everything in you exists in creation.
You are in bordeless touch with the closest
things, and, what is more, distance is not
sufficient to separate you from things far
away. All things from the lowest to the loftiest,
from the smallest to the greatest, exist within
you as equal things.[71]

The culminative idea that Gibran reaches—as he philosophizes about the immanence of God in man, about the issue "microtheos," and about the composition of man the "microcosm" as made of everything in the world—maintains that human existence is the intersecting point between two infinites, two ends, two extremities, viz, the infinity of the Supreme Being (Microtheos), the infinity of the Cosmos (Macrocosm). This apocalyptic vision of Gibran which goes beyond the sense perception, is the very reason why, a while ago I called man twice divine; the person possesses the divinity of nature plus he possesses another form of divinity which is not granted to the world-matter, namely, a spirit which is directly as God's idea, as the image of God. "We ourselves are the infinitely small [in comparison to the Macrotheos and the Macrocosm] and the infinitely great [in comparison to the macrocosm because of our spirituality]; and we are the path between the two."[72]

208

(3) At last but not the least, Gibran includes in his philosophy of the "Immanence of God," the mystery of
the Divine *OMNIPRESENCE*. The attribute signifies
that God is everywhere present: in the leaf, in the river,
in the sun, in the atom, in myself, and in my neighbours.[73] The whole creation attests to the living presence
of God the Creator. This is one of the reasons why
Gibran rejected the teaching of theological rationalism
as propounded by the established religions, and instead
professed his belief in the natural and non-dogmatic
religion.

However, speaking of God's presence in man and in
nature, Gibran draws a line of demarcation between the
divinity of the person and the divinity of matter. God
is not present within both of us in an identical manner,
and this for a twofold reason. *First,* man is an axiolog-
ical, an evaluatory, category; yet matter has no ethical
life. And furthermore, the existential purpose of man
in this world is to find genuine happiness. Here Gibran
reminds us of the dual attitude Christianity has assumed
towards the person. For example, on the one hand, the
neo-Platonist fathers of the Church seemed to demean
man in recognizing him as corrupted, sinful, called to
humility and blind obedience. And this Gibran finds un-
forgiveable on the part of the priests. But on the other
hand, Gibran acknowledges that the Christianity of the
Gospel exalts man, recognizing him as the image and
the likeness of God. Thus, one of Gibran's heroes
exclaims:

> Vain are the beliefs and teachings that make
> man miserable, and false is the goodness that
> leads him into sorrow and despair, for it is
> man's purpose to be happy on this earth and
> lead the way to felicity and preach its gospel
> wherever he goes. . . . We came not into this
> life by exile, but we came as innocent creatures

of God, to worship the holy and eternal spirit and seek the hidden secrets within ourselves from the beauty of life. This is the truth which I have learned from the teaching of the Nazarene.[74]

And another of his heroes proclaims:

God does not want me to lead a miserable life, for He placed in the depth of my heart a desire for happiness; His glory rests in the happiness of my heart.[75]

Secondly, the divinity of man differs from that of matter, on the basis of the mystery of *immortality* which characterizes man alone, while the divinity of matter is fugacious and temporary.

I propose to return to the topic of immortality immediately after having explained this coming section.

Transcendence of God and God's Relation to Man

We should beware not to infer from the preceding section of "Immanence" the conclusion that Gibran commited the heresy of *pantheism,* which is a philosophical and theological doctrine that God is everything and everything is God. It is true that Gibran delved into the dialectic God-nature-man in such a manner that his theory seems to remind us of Hegel (1770-1831), the famous post-Kantian philosopher whose dialectic of the Spirit precisely terminated in pantheism. Hegel believed that there was only one Reality which he called the Absolute Spirit, a synonym for God. He also explained that the Absolute Spirit underwent a never ending cycle through the stages of thesis, antithesis, and synthesis. At the thesis stage, the Spirit did not know fully Himself. For this, He would alienate and exteriorize Himself in many forms and shapes; and in this antithesis stage, Hegel saw the creation of man and nature, he considered each individual person and every atom to be nothing else but historical moments in the evolution of God Himself. Finally, Hegel conjectured that in the synthesis stage, the Absolute Spirit would know Himself as to what He "is" and could "do." But because the Absolute Being is infinite, Hegel induced that once the Spirit reached the synthesis period, He would revert-back to the thesis level and repeat indefinitely the cycle.[76] All in all Hegel did not make the distinction between the Creator and His creatures. He taught that creation was the very presence and existence of the Creator. God, he thought, was pure immanence.

Now, the process philosophy that Gibran advocates, and which I have outlined in the previous pages, hardly professes the Hegelian pantheism. As a matter of fact, our author strongly believed in the transcendence of God, and the autonomy of man, and the individuality of the world. For him, *"desire"* is the law of creation in as much as it is the law that keeps God-man-nature interdependent, but not in the sense of identical. Together God, man and nature form a perfect *union* in existence, though one is not the other. The inherent property of the soul is "the desire to seek" God; nature too moves upward towards God; in his turn the Divine receives unto Himself both the perfections of man and the perfections of the world and preserves them. All this amounts to saying that Gibran conceives of man as a co-creator with God. The perfection of the world was not *ab initio* formally accomplished; rather, God wanted that man contributes to the perfection of the world.

Philosophically speaking, the metaphysical system of Gibran is not pantheistic but *panentheistic*. Accordingly, the godly in the world must be brought through man's action to ever greater and purer perfection. The human being has a role in creation which enables him to be a co-worker with the Divine in the perfection of the world. Hence, the emphasis of Gibranism is on the actual realization of the life of faith—

211

the inward experience of the presence of God and the actualization of that presence in all our conducts. In this sense Gibran's process philosopher has great similarities with Bergson,[77] Mikhail Naimy his friend the Lebanese philosopher,[78] Ameen Rihani his compatriot a Sufi,[79] the Russian existentialist Berdiaev[80] and even with Teilhard de Chardin, the remarkable Jesuit Scientist.[81] To prove my point about the significance of Gibran's vision concerning God's immanence and transcendence, let me compare it with the theory of Teilhard de Chardin (1881-1955). In his posthumous book *The Phenomenon of Man,* Teilhard pictures creation as a continuous upward process toward ever higher and better things; today we are at the stage of the "noosphere," at which human consciousness has appeared. Optimistically, Teilhard saw the whole movement of revolution tending toward an ultimate stage, the "omega" (God), which will be the climax of the development of the "noosphere." Furthermore, Teilhard considered that although infinite and transcendent is the "omega," God will still remain in immanent continuity with the ongoing process of nature, and man.

Similarly, Gibran describes the transcendence of God by saying that the seeking of man and of nature is an upward seeking toward the Supreme Being. Now this power of seeking and desiring does not vanish, for instance, when the soul reaches God; quite the contrary, the soul retains its individuality, in that in God, it keeps on seeking more of itself *ad infinitum*; because it then becomes conscious of being *in* God the absolute, the infinite who cannot be encompassed all together by a "finite" being. Gibran writes:

> The soul never loses its inherent properties when it reaches God. Salt does not lose its saltness in the sea; its properties are inherent and eternal. The soul will retain consciousness, the hunger for more of itself and the desire for that which is beyond itself.
> The soul will retain those properties through all eternity, and like other elements in nature it will

remain absolute. The absolute seeks more absoluteness, more crystallization.[82]

Therefore as a transcendent Being, God relates to man,
however, not after the manner a master relates to his slaves;
but, as man is in need of God, God is also in search of
man. Here Gibran reiterates what the contemporary Christian
philosophers and the right wing of existentialism have taught
about God's relation to man, namely, the human is not a
means for God, and he was not created for the Glory of God.
Otherwise, we would imply that God is imperfect and lacks
something which only man could supply Him. Actually such
a doctrine demeans both man and God; for any doctrine that
demeans man, demeans God as well; since the person is a
divine-human being.

The best way to describe the relation of God to man, is
to acknowledge first that each is a *per se* existence, yet
mutually interrelated and in search of each other.

> When the soul reaches God it will be
> conscious that it is in God, and that
> it is seeking more of itself in being in
> God, and that God too is growing and
> seeking and crystallizing.[83]

To be precise, Gibran always portrayed God with the
features and the personality of a sensitive *woman*. Why? in
his opinion, as it was for Kierkegaard, the female sex is
far from being inferior to man, she is rather more perfect.[84]
Also the qualities of compassion, providence and love suit
better the female than the masculine gender. Consequently,
speaking of God's relation to man, Gibran understands that
relation to be qualitatively similar to that of a woman, and
specially of a *"mother."*

> Most religions speak of God in the masculine
> gender. To me He is as much a Mother as He is a

213

Father. He is both the father and mother in one;
and Woman is the God-Mother. The God-Father
may be reached through the mind or the imagination
But the God-Mother can be reached through the
heart only—through love.[85]

As we see, Gibran defends the transcendence of God with
the argument that the Super Being establishes living relations
with the humans through the bond of LOVE. Incidentally
for this very reason Gibran undertook to rewrite the New
Testament with his book *Jesus The Son of Man*. Supposedly
one of the motives for which Jesus descended upon the earth
was to change the images of His Father as depicted in the
Old Testament. The God of Moses was a god of vengeance,
punishment; while the God of Jesus is "a God too vast to be
unlike the soul of any man, too knowing to punish, too loving
to remember the sins of His creatures."[86]

Also, within the context of God's love for man, Gibran
outlines a theology of *eschatology*. It runs as follows: God is
absolute kindness, love, forgiveness. What man calls *evil*, is
something which he personally denominates but not God;—
"God does not work evil."[87] And when man begins to fear the
devil, this dreadful experience frightens his heart and mind
as a result of lack of confidence and trust in God—"Fear
of the devil is one way of doubting God."[88] Furthermore, what
we know of the reality of *hell*, is not a matter-of-fact, as if
there existed a physical fire in another world; our personal
fear of hell constitutes hell itself, and our damnation is a self-
blame which occurs in moments of despair and at the time we
refuse to accept the absolution from God's bounty.—"The
fear of hell is hell itself, and the longing of paradise is paradise
itself."[89]

The foregoing sections on immortality, reincarnation, and
death, represent further developments of Gibran's doctrine
of eschatology.

Gibran strongly believes in the immortality of the soul. Yet he does not offer us a philosophical or a logical syllogism to support his argument; his belief is a simple matter of conviction on the grounds of *faith* which teaches him that the eternal divinity of man will never perish. And he does not care whether or not the astute scientific minds agree with his personal faith. Thus, he would tell Miss Haskell: "I'm probably one of the surest of people, and stubborn when I'm sure. If all the other inhabitants of the earth, for instance, believed that the individual soul perished with death it would move me not an atom to agree with them, because I know my soul won't perish."[90] Incidentally this attitude in thinking has become a universal fashion among the humanists and the existential philosophers; nowadays, the humanists hold that there are many human events that lie beyond man's ability to comprehend them either logically or scientifically. One of those metaphysical mysteries is the phenomenon of death and immortality.

Gibran consents to the fact that the physical appearance of man upon this earth is not everlasting. Death strikes man in his innermost personality. However, this death can only be biological, never spiritual. The phenomenon of biological death is the result of a physical clash between the organic elements of man and the chemical elements in nature. Nature is an enormous mass of forces which easily crush the smallness of man and destroy him. In *The Voice of the Master,* Almuhtad instructs the people that the earth with its geological cataclysms and cosmic eruptions overpowers the forces of man; and besides damaging to whatever man erects on the face of the earth as castles, towers, temples—nature also wrecks man in his biological make-up.[91]

Almuhtad's sermon on "Of the Divinity of Man," reflects the influence that Gibran bore from the French philosopher B. Pascal who once stated: "Man is but a reed, weakest in nature, but a reed which thinks. It needs not that the whole

215

Universe should arm to crush him. A vapour, a drop of water is enough to kill him. But were the Universe to crush him, man would still be more noble than that which has slain him, because he knows that he dies and that the Universe has the better of him. The Universe knows nothing of this."[92]

In a like style and content Gibran demonstrates the greatness of man over nature through the fact that the person remains godly even after he dies.

> But man in his Divinity I saw standing like
> a giant in the midst of Wrath and Destruction,
> mocking the anger of the earth and the raging
> of the elements.

> Like a pillar of light Man stood amidst the ruins
> of Babylon, Nineveh, Palmyra and Pompei, and as
> he stood he sang the song of Immortality:

> > Let the Earth take
> > That which is hers,
> > For I, Man, have no ending.[93]

His convictions concerning the immortality of the soul explain why he never looked at the phenomenon of death from a pessimistic angle. On the contrary he exalts the coming of death, "and entitle(s) it with Sweet names, and praise(s) it with Loving words, secretly and to the Throngs of taunting listeners."[94] This attitude makes Gibran an Epicurist. Because for Gibran and Epicurus life and death are but one and the same thing. Epicurus teaches: "You should accustom yourself to believing that death means nothing to us, since . . . living well and dying well are one and the same thing."[95] Note the similarity with Gibran: "For life and death are one, even as the river and the sea are one."[96]

It is possible to compare Gibran's eschatalogy to Epicurus's philosophy of death as long as the reader remembers that there is still a difference between the two. Actually, Epicurus

216

A display of books and drawings of Gibran, in the Gibran Museum in Bsherri, Lebanon.
Photo: CNT/MAGNIN

Situated on the road to the Cedars (of Lebanon), is Bsherri, the home village of Kahlil Gibran.
Photo: CNT/NASSIF

A view of Bsherri, Kahlil Gibran's home village in Lebanon.
Photo: CNT/MAGNIN

A Memorial to the Martyrs of Lebanon, in Beirut.
Photo: CNT/VAROUJAN

implores us not to dread the idea of death in order to avoid the pains that such reminiscence could cause in our being. Now Gibran does not advocate such an extreme hedonism, although his philosophy leaves room for a certain type of hedonism. Speaking in the strict sense of history, Gibran's exposition on death is meta-religious and preceeds the existentialists' conception. For example, Gibran and Heidegger conceive death as the culminative stage of perfection in human existence. Man is being unto death *(Sein zum Tode)*. To die means to fulfill the purpose of human reality. For to be human *(Dasein)* implies to be born, to suffer, love, work, feel guilts, *and die*. Death is an existential situation which no human mortal can escape; it is the very last predicament of man. Furthermore, Gibran, like the Christian existentialist, looks at death as the deliverance of the spirit from the body-matter. Death gives freedom to the spirit.

> For what is it to die but to stand naked
> in wind and to melt into the sun?
> And what is it to cease breathing, but to
> free the breath from its restless tides, that
> it may rise and expand and seek God unen-
> cumbered?"[97]

Reincarnation

From the preceding lines, it becomes obvious that Gibran's philosophy of religion is anti-Nietzschean; as we know the hero of Nietzsche, Zarathustra, denied the immortality of the soul:

> "By my honor, friend—answered Zarathustra—
> all that of which you speak does not exist: there is
> no devil and no hell. Your soul will be dead even
> before your body: fear nothing further."[98]

217

Gibran left innumerable texts which proclaim the everlasting existence of man. The real difficulty, however, that I experience, with these articles in the issue of the rebirth of the soul, which is included in his theory of eschatology. As I wrote in Chapter Three, Gibran got acquainted with the doctrine of the transmigration of the soul through his reading of the Middle Age Islamic philosophers, who were influenced on one hand directly by Indian Religion, and on the other hand by Neo-Platonism.[99] According to both doctrines, the Veda and Platonism, the soul after death, undergoes a continual process of rebirth and purification until it is completely purified, and then returns to its god. Now how far has the theory of Nirvana and the transmigration of the soul influenced the thinking of Gibran? *For one,* there is plenty of evidence that shows that our author believed in the return of the soul to the life on earth. For example, in *The Poet From Baalbek,* Gibran conveys his belief in reincarnation in the following words:

> And the Emir inquired, saying: "Tell us,
> oh sage, . . . will my spirit become
> incarnated in a body of a great King's
> son, and will the poet's soul transmigrate
> into the body of another genius? . . .
> And the sage answered the Emir, saying,
> *"Whatever the soul longs for, will be*
> *attained by the spirit.* Remember, oh
> great Prince, that the sacred Law
> which restores the sublimity of Spring
> after the passing of Winter will reinstate
> you a prince and him a genius poet."[100]

Similar words are also found in *The Prophet:*

> Fare you well, people of Orphalese.
> This day has ended. . . .
> Forget not that I shall come back to you
> dust and foam for another body.

218

A little while, and my longing shall gather
A little while, a moment of rest upon the
wind, and another woman shall bear me.[101]

Again in *The Garden of the Prophet* we read the same
prophecy about the return of Almustafa:

O Mist, my sister, my sister Mist,
I am one with you now.
No longer am I a self.
The walls have fallen,
And the chains have broken;
I rise to you, a mist,
And together we shall float upon the sea
    until life's second day,
When dawn shall lay you, dewdrops in
    a garden,
And me a babe upon the breast of a
    woman.[102]

Should we conclude from all these passages that Gibran
was a direct follower of Buddhism, or even of Platonism?
Contrary to the error of Miss Barbara Young, his biograper,
it seems to me that Gibran has accepted the doctrine of
"rebirth," and has definitely used the technical expression of
"reincarnation" in order to convey his convictions in the
transmigration of the soul.[103] Yet, as I think deeper on the
meaning that Gibran ascribes to the concept of "rebirth"
and compare his theory with that of Buddhism and Platonism,
I notice some differences between them. For instance, unlike
the Veda philosophers Gibran does not hold the theories of
purification and Nirvana—"To me, he states, all reality is
movement. Repose is the harmony of motion. But Nirvana is
motionless."[104] But also, unlike Plato, he does not suggest
that the status of living of the reborn soul depends on the
ethical conducts that the soul had practiced during her
previous life on earth.[105] In all simplicity, Gibran maintained

219

that a soul will always come back and will retake the same social status of action in order to continue from there where she left during her last death. And now if you ask him why should the soul come back?—His answer is that *"Love,"* either the positive one or the negative one, is the very motive that keeps the continuity of the cycle of life to go endlessly. However, it appears that Gibran excluded the souls contaminated by the spirit of indifference, from being reborn anew. His biographer, Barbara Young, reports:

> It was his profound certainty that
> the life that is the human spirit
> has lived and shall live timelessly,
> that the bonds of love, devotion and
> friendship shall bring together these
> endlessly reborn beings, and that
> animosity, evil communications, and
> hatred have the same effect of reassembling
> groups of entities from one cycle to
> another. Indifference acts as a separating
> influence. Those souls who neither love
> nor hate but remain entirely self-contained
> as regards one another, meet but once
> in the pattern of ages.[106]

Let us comment in brief on the above quote.

To Gibran's contention what we call hate is nothing else but "love turned into hate." Therefore, it is really love that accounts for reincarnation, since even hate is a former love changed into negative, with the exact same quantitative and qualitative aspect of positive love. As by "indifference," we understand those souls who are "useless" because they have no inclination for the either/or conducts. Consequently, why should they come back, when they have accomplished nothing in their previous life that deserves to be continued, nor have they undone something that now necessitates to be done for the best? It is clear to Gibran's logic that if creation is the work of love, then life on earth should pivot around the axis of love; and hence, there is a need in the world for those souls, who have practiced authentic love, that they return; in as much as another chance in a future life, should be granted to those souls who have practiced inauthentic love in order that in their new rebirth they retransform their negative destructive love into positive constructive power. These were Gibran's beliefs—"this was his faith—changeless as day and night, and as forthright."[107]

3. SOME COMMENTS ON *JESUS THE SON OF MAN*

Gibran was a great admirer of Jesus and His philosophy of life. In most of his religious essays, Gibran describes his heroes as strong believers in the teachings of Christ. Thus, in *Khalil the Heretic* and *John the Madman* we find the protagonists of the story holding in their hand the New Testament at the time they were caught by their enemies, the clergy *(Khouri)*. As Miss Barbara Young has well testified, Gibran perfected his conception of Jesus in the evening of November 12, 1926, when, following a moving mystical vision, he wrote down the very first words of what later had to become his monumental book *Jesus the Son of Man*.[108]

It is my firm conviction that Gibran undertook to recompose the history of Jesus in order to complement the one-sidedness that has prevailed among the scholar theologians concerning the nature of Christ. While the Church has put too much emphasis on the *divine* aspect of Christ, the primary motive of Gibran has rather consisted in portraying the *human* nature of Christ. All this concurs with what I said in the previous pages, namely, that Gibran has humanized religion and has given it human characteristics which radiate the immanence of God in man. Also, to put it bluntly, Gibran has stressed the human features of the personality of Christ, precisely in order to remind us that religion and God are not some kind

221

of a privilege restricted to the rich or the clergy. Actually, as Gibran saw it, the mission of Jesus never consisted in establishing an organized institution with rules, codes, sanctions, and a hierarchy of minds. Furthermore, Jesus never meant to erect a specific geographical location where God his Father would and should be physically present.

> Jesus came not from the heart of the circle
> of Light to destroy the homes and build
> upon their ruins the convents and monasteries.
> He did not persuade the strong man to become
> a monk or a priest. . . . Jesus was not sent
> here to teach the people to build magnificent
> churches and temples amidst the cold wretched
> huts and dismal hovels.
> . . . He came to make the human heart a temple,
> and the soul an altar, and the mind a priest.[109]

The beauty of the book *Jesus the Son of Man* lies in the lavishly poetic phraseology and in the creative imagination that Gibran expresses through the thoughts and deeds of Jesus. As I compare Gibran's Jesus to the work of the four evangelists, it follows that there are some truth and some discrepancies in the writing of Gibran. The discrepancies stem from the fact that many of the personages that Gibran included in the dyadic relation of Christ, are simply fictitious persons who never existed. For example, the men Georgus of Beirut, Barca the merchant of Tyre, Sarkis called the madman, and many more, are the creation of Gibran. Yet, it is my personal opinion that the exegesis, the thinking, and the deeds of his Jesus correspond to the personality of the evangelists' Jesus. As a matter of fact Gibran describes the Nazarene as possessed with *ambivalent* emotions: kindness towards the sinners, and simultaneously raging against the merchants in the temple.[110] Gibran stressed the antinomies of emotions for the simple reason that his conception of Jesus as a man was closely similar to the nature of the man in the street. That is,

222

it is human to have emotions of kinship, compassion, along with the opposite emotions, rage, rebellion, revolt. Gibran goes even so far as outlining the physical beauty of Jesus, and shows how such a body beauty moved the heart of the female listeners.[111]

Now does Gibran commit the old theological heresy of the Jacobites Monophysites, or of the Nestorians? It is hard to give a clear cut theological answer. I know that he believed in the divinity of Jesus, who came on this earth in order to redeem mankind from its downfall original sin—"Have mercy, O Jesus, on these multitudes joined together as one by Thy name on the day of the resurrection. Have compassion on their weakness."[112] Yet, on the other hand, it is apparent that he overemphasized the human nature of Jesus to the point of giving the impression that he denied the divinity of Christ. Passages as the following ones are misleading:

> Once every hundred years Jesus of Nazareth
> meets Jesus of the Christian in a garden among
> the hills of Lebanon. And they talk long; and each
> time Jesus of Nazareth goes away saying to Jesus
> of the Christian, "My friend, I fear we shall never,
> never agree."[113]

And elsewhere he states

> There are three miracles of our Brother
> Jesus not yet recorded in the Book:
> the first that He was a man like you and me;
> the second that He had a sense of humor;
> and the third that He knew He was a conqueror
> though conquered.[114]

Also his *Jesus the Son of Man* put the accent on the expression "He was a man."[115]

Now, it is my personal conclusion that Gibran did not so much reject the divinity of Christ in as much as he intended

223

to replace the old conception of Jesus who stands above the human, with a more humanly accessible image of the Nazarene. He assumed that in delving in depth into the human aspect of our Saviour he could (1) motivate man to follow the examplar path of Jesus—another son of man—and (2) could inspire man to develop his greater self the divine, after the manner Jesus has realized His godly greater self.

Jesus the Son of Man has its charm, and it can be read by anybody including the unbeliever, without that the latter feels any imposition to embrace the faith of Christianity. Of course the book does not seek a legal confirmation on the part of the Church for its authenticity, although Gibran has repeatedly confessed that he saw and talked to Jesus himself on a number of occasions.[116] I highly recommend it to the reader. Finally, in the words of its reviewer, Mr. P. W. Wilson,

> ... In the endeavor to explain or at
> least to suggest the significance of
> Jesus in the universe, Mr. Gibran has
> to resort to imagery, which evidently,
> is an endeavor by means of line and
> shadow to express the inexpressible.
> Like William Blake himself, he is
> striving to define the unseen in the
> forms which are visible to the eyes.[117]

FOOTNOTES

1 Leo Tolstoy, "The Law of Violence and the Law of Love," in *A History of Russian Philosophy*, ed. by Kline, New York: Columbia University Press, Vol. II, 1967, pp. 225 sq.

2 S. Kierkegaard, *Selections from the Writings of Kierkegaard*, transl. by Lee Hollander, Garden City, New York: Doubleday and Co., Inc., 1960, p. 226.

3 Cf. "Simony" in *New Catholic Encyclopedia*, New York: McGraw Hill Book Co., 1967, vol. 13.

4 *S.R.*, p. 97.

5 *ibidem*, p. 101.

6 *ibidem*, p. 70 sq.

7 *S.H.*, p. 74.

8 *S.R.*, p. 87.

9 *ibidem*, p. 81.

10 *ibidem*, p. 80.

11 "In the opinion of the head priest, a man cannot become a monk unless he is blind and ignorant, senseless and dumb." (*S.R.*, p. 59).

12 *MM*, pp. 42-44.

13 Barbara Young, *This Man From Lebanon*, New York: A. Knopf, 1970, p. 41. See also, *W.*, p. 15.

14 *S.S.*, p. 46.

15 *T.S.*, p. 136 sq.

16 *S.R.*, p. 93. Elsewhere he writes: "If we were to do away with the various religions, we would find ourselves united and enjoying one great faith and religion, abounding in brotherhood." (*W.G.*, p. 63).

17 *S.S.*, p. 112.

18 *S.S.*, p. 49. (The italics are mine).

19 *ibidem*, p. 41.

20 *M.S.*, p. 57. (The italics are mine).

21 St. Augustine, *Confessions*, BK I, C. 1.

22 St. Thomas Aquinas, *Summa Theologica*, I - II, p. 94. a.2.

23 Paul Tillich, *Theology of Culture*, New York: Oxford University Press, 1959, pp. 5-9.

24 J.P. Sartre, *The Words*, Greenwich, Conn.: Fawcett World Library, 1966, p. 62.

25 From *Basic Beliefs: The Religious Philosophies of Mankind*, ed. by J.E. Fairchild, (New York: Sheridan House, Inc., 1959), p. 167. In Europe it is becoming fashionable to title books as *La Foi d'un Paien*

(transl. "The Faith of a Pagan", Jean-Claude Barreau, Paris: Editions du Seuil, 1967); also, Francis Jeansen, a follower of Sartre, published recently a book, *La Foi d'un Incroyant* (transl. "The Faith of an Unbeliever," Paris: Editions du Seuil, 1963). All this confirms what Gibran stated about religion as "a natural belief to man."

26 F. Nietzsche, *Zarathustra*, "Prologue."

27 J.-P. Sartre, *Situations I,* Paris, 1947, p. 153.

28 *S.H.,* p. 109.

29 *B.P.,* p. 83.

30 *ibidem,* p. 267.

31 *ibidem,* p. 264.

32 *ibidem,* p. 121.

33 *ibidem,* p. 264.

34 Martin Buber, *Eclipse of God,* New York: Harper and Row, Publishers, 1965, p. 28. Note the similarity between Buber and Gibran when both parallel the expressions "talk to God" and "about God."

35 S. Kierkegaard, "Concluding Unscientific Postscript," in *A Kierkegaard Anthology,* ed. by Robert Bretall (Princeton: Princeton University Press, 1947), pp. 220-221.

36 St. Paul, *I Corinthians,* Ch. 1, V. 17-23.

37 *S.F.,* p. 71

38 *B.P.,* p. 267.

39 W. James, *The Will to Believe and Other Essays in Popular Philosophy,* New York: Longmans, Green and Co., Ltd., 1896, pp. 1 - 30.

40 *S.S.,* p. 27.

41 *ibidem,* p. 41.

42 *ibidem,* p. 27.

43 *ibidem,* p. 18.

44 *ibidem,* p. 32.

45 B. Young, *This Man From Lebanon,* Alfred A. Knopf, 1970, p. 38.

46 *S.S.,* p. 13.

47 *S.H.,* p. 18.

48 *G.P.,* pp. 39-40.

49 *ibidem,* p. 41.

50 *B.P.,* p. 265.

51 *ibidem,* p. 265.

52 *ibidem,* p. 266.

53 *ibidem,* p. 266.

54 *ibidem,* p. 266.

55 *ibidem,* p. 266.

56 *ibidem,* p. 266.

57 *ibidem,* p. 266.

58 *T.S.,* pp. 21-22.

59 *B.P.,* p. 266.

60 I am sure Gibran would not argue with the scholastic philosophers about the difference in meaning between the concepts "creation" and "production." Yet his decision for giving up the word creation is less a matter of philosophical dispute, in as much as for poetical, mystical and practical

reasons. Not everybody can understand the abstract philosophical definition of creation as found in the scholastic's metaphysics.

61 *P.,* p. 79.

62 *B.P.,* p. 329.

63 *ibidem,* p. 266.

64 *G.P.,* p. 41, also see *P.,* p. 79.

65 *T.S.,* p. 21.

66 *B.P.,* p. 266.

67 *ibidem,* p. 267.

68 *ibidem,* p. 268.

69 *T.S.,* p. 21 sq. (The italics are mine).

70 Aristotle, *De Anima.*

71 *S.S.,* p. 48.

72 *W.,* pp. 80 - 81.

73 *P.,* pp. 78 - 79; *G.P.,* p. 41.

74 *S.R.,* p. 64.

75 *ibidem,* pp. 22 - 23.

76 Hegel, "Logic," in *The Philosophy of Hegel,* ed. by Carl J. Friedrich, New York: The Modern Library, 1954, pp. 203 - 217.

77 Henri Bergson, *Creative Evolution,* New York: Henry Holt, 1911.

78 Mikhail Naimy, *The Book of Mirdad,* London: Stuart and Watkins, 1962, Ch. 34.

79 Ameen Rihani, *The Path of Vision,* Beirut: The Rihani House, 1970.

80 Nicolai Berdjaev, *Solitude and Society,* transl. by G. Reavey, London: Geoffrey Bles, 1947.

81 Teilhard de Chardin, *Phenomenon of Man,* New York: Harper and Row Publishers, 1965.

82 *B.P.,* p. 267.

83 *ibidem,* p. 267. See also, *M.M.,* pp. 9 - 10.

84 Note the similarity between Kierkegaard and Gibran on the issue woman: "it is my joy that, far from being less perfect than man, the female sex is, on the contrary, the more perfect," (S. Kierkegaard, *Selections From the Writings of Kierkegaard,* transl. by Lee Hollander, Garden City, N.Y.: Doubleday, Co., 1960, p. 103). Gibran likewise writes: "Women are better than man. They are kinder, more sensitive, more stable, and have a finer sense about much of life." (*B.P.,* p. 286.

85 *W.G.,* p. 30.

86 *J.S.M.,* p. 32.

87 *V.M.,* p. 56.

88 *S.S.,* p. 23.

89 *ibidem,* p. 8.

90 *B.P.,* p. 342.

91 *V.M.,* pp. 49 - 52.

92 Blaise Pascal, *Pensee,* Paris: Librairie Generale Francaise, 1962, p. 130, No. 264. (Translation by the author). Note the fact that Gibran too used the word "reed" in connection to death and immortality. (*P.R.,* p. 71).

93 *V.M.,* p. 51 - 52.

94 *S.H.,* p. 136.

[95] Epicurus, *The Philosophy of Epicurus*, ed. by G.K. Stirodach, Evanston: Ill.: North-wesetrn University Press, 1963, p. 180.

[96] *P.*, p. 80.

[97] *P.*, p. 89. Also in a letter to Haskell, May 16, 1916, he writes: "No, Mary, death does not change us. It only frees that which is real in us —our consciousness—and the *social* memories that lie in our consciousness. . . . Human consciousness is the print of the infinite past. The infinite future will make it ripe but it will never change its properties." (*B.P.*, p. 274).

[98] F. Nietzsche, "Zarathustra," in *The Portable Nietzsche*, ed. by W. Kaufman, New York: The Viking Press, 1968, p. 132.

[99] M. Fakhry, *A History of Islamic Philosophy*, Columbia University Press, 1970, p. 47.

[100] *Th.M.*, pp. 5 - 6.

[101] *P.*, pp. 94 - 95.

[102] *G.P.*, pp. 66 - 67. See also, *B.P.*, p. 427.

[103] Miss Young erroneously tells us that Gibran "never used the word" reincarnation. Yet, I found the word written in some of his articles. (See for instance *Th.M.*, pp. 1 - 8. Compare with B. Young, *This Man From Lebanon*, New York: A Knopf, 1970, p. 84).

[104] *B.P.*, p. 335.

[105] Plato, *Phaedo*, 80e - 81 d. In Plato's opinion, only the philosopher never returns back to this life; yet, a soul which returns will receive a certain shape of a body which corresponds to the type of acts she performed during her previous existence on earth.

[106] B. Young, *This Man From Lebanon*, New York: A. Knopf, 1970, p. 94.

[107] *ibidem*, p. 94.

[108] *ibidem*, p. 99.

[109] *S.H.*, p. 103.

[110] *J.S.M.*, p. 89.

[111] *J.S.M.* p. 12 - 15.

[112] *N.V.*, p. 74.

[113] *S.F.*, p. 77.

[114] *S.F.*, p. 84.

[115] *J.S.M.*, p. 107.

[116] *B.P.*, pp. 167 - 168. *Also* in Barbara Young, *This Man From Lebanon*, New York: A. Knopf, 1970, pp. 99 - 111.

[117] P.W. Wilson in "Jesus Was the Supreme Poet," *The New York Times Book Review*, Sunday, December 23, 1928, reproduced in *Kahlil Gibran. Essays and Introductions*, eds. S.B. Bushrin and J.M. Munro, (Beirut: The Rihani House, 1970) p. 165.

CHAPTER EIGHT

EVALUATION OF GIBRANISM

I N THE foregoing writing I have tried in many ways to bring to light the essential of Gibran's philosophy. It is time now to come to a *subjective* critic of the foremost fundamental themes that characterize Gibranian trend of thought. To be concise yet precise, I propose to present in a systematic way my negative reaction, and my positive evaluation of our author's *Weltanschauung*.

1. *Weaknesses in Gibran*

As I ponder on the history of philosophy, I find that no serious thinker has ever come too close to the perfection of truth. Not only man is finite in his existence, but also limited in his knowledge. It is human to err. To come to the point, I have personally experienced dissatisfactions with the ways Gibran has treated some philosophical problems. In my eyes, his system commits three logical fallacies and one methodological mistake. These are: the fallacies of overgeneralization; oversimplification and incompleteness, and the methodological lack of systematization in his presentation. A few words will explain what I mean.

The fallacy of *overgeneralization,* or as the manuals of logic call it *"secundum quid,"* is the most predominant error in his system. The fallacy consists in drawing absolute conclusions from the occurrence of a few particular instances. This attitude in thinking we find in Gibran. For example,

229

he tends to be harsh against the social laws, the institutionalized marriage, and the established religion, on the basis that he has personally witnessed in a limited number of situations, the injustice, corruption and immorality that man-made laws, traditional marriage and the clergy have unfortunately sometimes exhibited. Again, his conception of the rich as evil and degenerate, leaves no room for someone to be virtuous and rich at the same time. Now, this either-or type of logic is incorrect, because it offends against the great variety of human situations.

To make myself clear, let us expound on his fallacy of *oversimplification* which is closely tied up with the above sophistry. Gibran commits this error in the fields of legal philosophy and theodicy. About the former, Gibran with almost no background in law, dares to condemn all man-made laws, as if some of these were not actually logically derived, directly or indirectly, from the natural laws. And yet, in the opinion of the professional ethicists, many of the man-made laws are norms of moral conduct established on the natural or divine laws; and their purpose is to safeguard the practice of the two other laws. This idea Gibran has missed. But also concerning the fact of the formulated creed, Gibran is oversimplifying the matter. He is shortsighted for having failed to see that the social agency of the clergy is something that God himself has instituted for communal ends. It is rightly said that if God had sent his angels as his priests, instead of chosing his messengers among the weak human mortals, we would have then complained that the preaching of the angels surpasses our human finiteness. I think that Gibran expects more than the human priests can accomplish. He forgets that priests are human, and therefore, liable to mistakes.

As for the third fallacy, *incompleteness,* his system raises so many pertinent questions: natural laws, reincarnation, marriage, etc.—and yet falls short in answering them in full details. For example, he was not in favor of legal marriage and yet he never solved the perplexing questions of divorce, of who is to take care of children, of alimony, of polygamy, etc.

230

Finally, in terms of *methodology,* his system lacks coherence, systematization, and logical procedure. Being too poetical and spontaneous, his ideas are dispersed, here and there, in many unrelated books or articles. This accounts—in my opinion— for his being widely read but little understood by his own followers.

3. *Relevancy of Gibranism*

All throughout the manuscript I have tried many times and in many ways to praise Gibran, and relate his concepts to our everyday existential situations. Lest I repeat myself here, I would like to state briefly a few of the merits of his thinking.

Despite the fact that Gibran never thought nor wrote in the manner of an Aristotelian philosopher, and never dreamed to create a new *"ISM"* it is still my belief that the system he developed deserves the title of philosophical. Actually, the term philosopher is too difficult to define, because it is not a reality that can be touched by our senses, rather it is a state of mind and emotion experienced in relation to life. I would call a mind a philosopher if he manifests the desire to pursue some fundamental questions which concern human reality. Now, Gibran fits this definition of mine, for he has pondered on the predicament of human existence. For a too long time, Gibran was not accepted as a genuine thinker who should occupy a chapter in the history of either Arabic or Western philosophy. This prejudice on the part of the academicians is the result of their ignorance in the wide spectrum of philosophy in as much as it is due to their little knowledge of Gibran. My whole purpose for delving into *comparative* philosophy, was to locate the exact place where Gibran's philosophy squares with traditional schools. My conclusions lead me to assertain that Gibran is an *existentialist* of equal caliber as some of the right wing of existentialism. Gibran is closer to Kierkegaard, Marcel, Buber, Berdjaev, Ortega y Gasset,

Unamuno—than he is to Heidegger, Sartre, Merleau-Ponty, Simone de Beauvoir...

Though an Arabian existentialist, he stresses the idea of "perspectivism" which emphasizes the individual point of view. That is to saying, his philosophy does not entangle with abstract thinking, but centers around concrete existential moments of life. His heroes live the anxieties and sublimations of the historical, economical, and geographical situations that comprise their actions. This confirms the fact that his literature is *engagée*—committed. He does not write poetries and prose poems simply for literary and artistic reasons, but also, his literature is his style for conveying his philosophical ideas.

As for his being unsystematic, as I critized a while ago, well, it is a trade-mark of many right wing existentialists —Kierkegaard, Marcel, Buber, Berdjaev—to write impulsively, and purposely without a methodology. Their motive is the following: priority should be given to emotions, in counter-reaction against the rigid rationalism of Descarte and the stereotyped idealism of Hegel.

Speaking of existentialism, we should bear in mind that this contemporary "ism," which is more of a label than an actual philosophical ideology, allows that its tenets diverge from one another. What are then the essential features of Gibran's existentialism? For one, Gibran is unique for combining Hindu, Middle-Eastern and Western ideas. Also, one of his advantages is that he relates intimately with his American readers and points directly to the pressing issues which confront U.S.A., such as ecology, environmentalism, spiritual revival in Jesus (remember the movement "Jesus Super Star"). Another trait of his philosophy is simplicity, freshness and humanism. Finally, his existentialism is mystical, as it is the case with most of the right wing. Gibran is a mystic because he explores the spiritual aspect of reality. Nothing is purely material. Molecules, things, events, deeds encompass a "meaning"; they stand for "something," a "purpose."

These and other points which I outlined in the chapters, form the bulk of Gibran-*ism*. I was happy to read that Professor St. Elmo Nauman has recently included our author in his scholarly history of American philosophy as a contemporary influential figure. *(Dictionary of American Philosophy,* Philosophical Library, 1973). At last, let me quote the definition, that Mr. Claude Bragdon, gave for Gibranism:

> The character and depth of his influence upon the entire Arabic world may be inferred from the fact that it gave rise to a new word, *Gibranism.* Just what this word means English readers will have no difficulty in divining: mystical vision, metrical beauty, a simple and fresh approach to the 'problem' of life . . . extraordinary dramatic power, deep erudition, lightning like intuition, lyrical life, metrical mastery, and Beauty which permeates the entire pattern in everything he touches.

(quoted in Barbara Young, p. 37)

SELECTED BIBLIOGRAPHY

Gibran, Kahlil.—*Sand and Foam,* New York: Alfred A. Knopf, 1969.
    The Prophet, New York: Alfred A. Knopf, 1970.
    The Wanderer, New York: Alfred A. Knopf, 1971.
    The Garden of the Prophet, New York: A. Knopf, 1969.
    The Forerunner, New York: Alfred A. Knopf, 1970.
    Nymphs of the Valley, New York: Alfred A. Knopf, 1969.
    The Earth Gods, New York: Alfred A. Knopf, 1969.
    The Madman, New York: Alfred A. Knopf, 1945.
    Twenty Drawings, New York: Alfred A. Knopf, 1919.
    Jesus The Son of Man, New York: Alfred A. Knopf, 1970.
Beloved Prophet.—The Love Letters of Kahlil Gibran and Mary Haskell.
    ed. by Virginia Hilu, New York: Alfred A. Knopf, 1972.
Gibran, Kahlil.—*The Wisdom of Gibran,* ed. by Joseph Sheban, New
    York: Philosophical Library, 1966.
    The Procession, transl. by George Kheirallah, New York: Philosophical
    Library, 1958.
    Mirrors of the Soul, transl. by Joseph Sheban, New York: Philosophi-
    cal Library, 1965.
    Spirits Rebellious, transl. by A. Rizcallah Ferris, New York: Philo-
    sophical Library, 1965.
    Spirits Rebellious, transl. by A. Rizcallah Ferris, New York: Philo-
    sophical Library, 1947.
    Tears and Laughter, ed. by Martin Wolf, New York: Philosophical
    Library, 1949.
    Thoughts and Meditations, transl. by A. R. Ferris, New York: Bantam
    Books, 1968.
    A Tear and A Smile, transl. by H. M. Nahmad, New York: Bantam
    Books, 1969.
    Spiritual Sayings, transl. and ed. by A. R. Ferris, New York: Bantam
    books, 1970.
    The Voice of the Master, transl. by A. R. Ferris, New York: Bantam
    Books, 1967.
    The Broken Wings, transl. by A. R. Ferris, New York: Bantam Books,
    1968.
    A Self Portrait, transl. by A. R. Ferris, New York: Bantam Books,
    1970.
    Secrets of the Heart, transl. by A. R. Ferris, New York: Signet Books,

WORKS ON GIBRAN

Otto, Annie Salem.—*The Parables of Kahlil Gibran,* New York: The Citadel Press, 1967.

Young, Barbara.—*This Man From Lebanon,* New York: Alfred A. Knopf, 1970.

Sherfan, Andrew Dib.—*Kahlil Gibran: The Nature of Love,* New York: Philosophical Library, 1971.

Naimy, Mikhail.—*Kahlil Gibran: A Biography,* New York: The Philosophical Library, 1950.

Challita, Mansour.—*Luttes et triomphe de Gibran,* Beirut.

Bushrui, Suheil, ed.—*An Introduction to Kahlil Gibran,* Beirut.

Hamdeh, Bushrui, Munro and Smith, eds.—*A Poet and His Country: Gibran's Lebanon,* Beirut.

Bushrin, S., and Munro, J.—*Kahlil Gibran: Essays and Introductions,* Beirut, 1970.

Bragdon, C. F.—*"Modern Prophet from Lebanon," Merely Players.* New York: Alfred A. Knopf, 1929.

Knopf, Alfred.—*"News Release,"* letter dated November 21, 1961.

Lecerft, Jean.—"Djabran Khalil Djabran et les origines de la prose poetique moderne." *Orient* No. 3 (1957), pp. 7-14.

Ross, Martha Jean.—"The Writings of Kahlil Gibran," Unpublished Master Thesis, The University of Texas, Austin, 1948.

Russell, G. W.—"Kahlil Gibran," *Living Torch.* New York: Macmillan Co., 1938.

Al Houeyyek, Youssef.—*Zoukriati ma' Joubran.* Written by Edvique Juraydini Shaybub. Beirut: Dar el Ahad.

Jaber, Jamil.—*May wa Joubran,* Beirut: Dar el Jamal, 1950.

Jaber, Jamil.—*Joubran, Siratuhu, Arabuhu, Falsafatuhu wa Rasmuhu,* Beirut: The Rihani House, 1958.

Massoud, Habib.—*Joubran, Hayyan wa Mayyitan,* Beirut: The Rihani House 1966.

Saiegh, Tawfic.—*Adhwa' Jadidah Ala Joubran,* Beirut: Dar al Sharquiah, 1966.

Naimy, Mikhail.—*Al Majmou' at al Kamilat Li Mouallafat Joubran Kahlil Joubran,* Beirut: Dar Sader and Dar Beirut, 1959.

Ghougassian, Joseph.—"The Art of Kahlil Gibran," *Ararat,* 1972, Vol. XIII, No. 1-2.

(Concerning the other books consulted, refer to my footnotes.)

INDEX

238